UNITED MIND

UNITED MIND

RETHINKING HOW WE LEAD OUR LIVES, WORK TOGETHER, AND CHANGE OUR WORLD

AMITA SHUKLA

Vitamita House
Bethesda, Maryland, USA

Published by Vitamita House, a division of Vitamita LLC, Bethesda, Maryland, USA.

www.vitamita.com

The Vitamita House and Vitamita names and logos are trademarks of Vitamita LLC.

If you would like to contact the author, schedule a speaking engagement, or obtain information about discounts for bulk purchases, please e-mail: contact@vitamita.com.

First Edition: January 2022

Library of Congress Control Number: 2021923663
ISBN (Paperback): 978-0-9909068-3-4
ISBN (eBook): 978-0-9909068-4-1

Printed in the United States of America

With deep gratitude to every mind whose paths crossed mine,
this is dedicated to all beings who dare to venture within.

Table of Contents

Author's Note

Dear Reader:

We are about to embark on a journey into one of the most mysterious and awe-inspiring spaces in the universe. Like any great adventure, this promises to transform its traveler. The mind that opened this page will not be the same as the one that turns the last.

Before we begin, here are a few words to help orient you. The stories on these pages are inspired by real ones yet written in fiction form. All identifying details have been changed. Though this blurs the line between fact and fiction, that is ultimately inconsequential since their deeper truths transcend both, as we shall see.

This work emerged from more than a decade of primary and secondary research across diverse disciplines. It further evolved through intuitive insights whose origins are part of the mystery we explore here. Hence, while some references are included, it is impossible to cite all sources. You may wonder then, *how do I know what is true?*

For that, I offer this: Do not accept anything you read here—or anywhere, for that matter—at face value. Question and probe it with your own mind. Experiment and play with it to see how it holds true for you. Your own experience will be your best guide.

Trust that you will know, and that this will make more sense as your journey here unfolds.

Venturing into the human mind to unlock its mysteries is a timeless quest—an eternal dance between science and art, the material and ethereal, and the seen and sensed. As we study our tangible outer world, science's discoveries rewrite our textbooks. As we explore our intangible inner realm, our heart's truths rewrite our life stories.

Where this journey will lead you, and where that then takes you, we cannot yet foretell. Be open to all that you encounter. Bring curiosity and wonder. Let go of what you think you know. Hold gently what you learn about yourself, others, and the world. Keep what serves you, release the rest. At each step, let your wisdom be your guide, trusting it knows more than you realize, far beyond the limits of your wildest imagination.

Warmly,
Amita

PART I

Introduction

The Prince and the Sage

Once upon a time, some say millennia ago, there lived a young, carefree Prince in an idyllic kingdom nestled in the plains of a lush, fertile land. His parents, the King and Queen, surrounded him with all the comforts of palace life and gave him an unparalleled education to make him a great king someday.

Yet as the Prince approached the sunset of his teenage years, the weather patterns shifted in his mind. Gray clouds descended on his former cheerful self. Tempests of darkness appeared unannounced, storming the lightness in his heart. The palace's courtiers helplessly watched despondency creep over him, like a stubborn vine on the delicate branches of his pure, innocent youth.

Who am I? What is the purpose of my life? Why do I have all this while others suffer beyond these walls? As such questions swirled through the Prince's mind, he moved through the palace's daily routines with feigned interest, losing all passion for their pleasures.

As the seasons turned, the Prince's mood cast its shadow across the pastoral land. Mundane Sunday afternoon chatter in village squares became tinged with quiet despair. Tense family dinners and hushed town halls echoed the anxiety of a kingdom on edge.

The King and Queen spent many sleepless nights discussing the future of their son—and his future kingdom. The Chief Courtier, who supervised the Prince's education, invited scholars from lands near and far in attempts to change the Prince's mind—with no visible effects on him. Finally, the King and Queen decided to summon a humble Sage from the nearby hills to counsel their son. This wise man, as the legend went, had long ago mastered the secret of life.

When the Prince received news of one more teacher on his way, he rolled his eyes. Here he was, forced to make yet another appearance before the royal court. Tired of feigning even the slightest interest, he resolved, this time, he would not put on a show.

The next day, sullen and downcast, the Prince shuffled into court without so much as acknowledging the Sage. The courtiers gasped. *Such disrespect*, they mumbled aghast. The Sage looked at the Prince and smiled, for what seemed like an eternity, until the Prince glanced up to meet his eyes.

In the deep calm of the Sage's face, the Prince sensed something melt within. He relaxed the clench in his fist and lowered his guard. For the first time, the Prince felt this gentle soul might understand rather than reprimand him. He slowly took a seat.

For the next ten days, from sunrise to sunset, the Sage appeared before the royal court to share precious pearls of wisdom on life. To every question posed by the restless Prince, the Sage responded with boundless patience and compassion. Illuminating insights sparkled from his words. Through tales of kings and queens who ruled before, parables of ancient spirits and old souls, and stories of warriors and saints, he unfolded the deepest essence of a good life.

With the Sage's caring guidance, the Prince entered dark, hidden spaces and long-locked rooms in his mind and heart. In confusing thoughts and feelings that he had feared before, the Prince found new meaning and significance. Through such patient inner exploration, the Prince shattered limiting beliefs, transcended stubborn mental traps, and rewrote stale stories.

With time, the Prince experienced rising crests of unwavering contentment and serenity. Darkness dissolved and clarity dawned. Calm descended on his being. Wisdom displaced fear, and trust replaced doubt. The responsibility of leading his kingdom, which had felt like an overwhelming burden before, now filled the Prince with lightness and joy. He went on to become a beloved king who led with compassion, humility, and grace, gaining the respect of friends and foes far and wide and inspiring generations since.

The questions the Prince faced—on the secret to a good life, the meaning and purpose of our work, the eternal battles between dark and light (in our minds and in the world), and the solutions to humanity's struggles—are the same ones we each confront today.

If the Prince lived in our times, we might have said the Sage tapped into principles from neuroplasticity, psychotherapy, positive psychology, and performance coaching, as well as, practices such as visualization, affirmations, and mindfulness. If neuroscientists could scan the Prince's brain in a functional magnetic resonance imaging (fMRI) machine, they might have studied the activity of his neurons and mapped their network topology.

But even our most advanced tools would be limited in decoding the Prince's deepest transformation. In the millennia since the Sage held court, we have made astounding leaps in studying the human mind. Yet we can still not predict the birth of an idea, see the spark of an epiphany, or pinpoint the origins of wisdom.

Even today, the best "tool" we have to know our mind is the one the Sage revealed to the Prince. Its essence is simple yet profound. Through experiential mastery of his mind, the Sage guided the Prince to discover the power of knowing his own.

Inspired by the Sage's wise questions and intuitive insights, the Prince became a calm witness to the content of his mind—its thoughts and feelings and their deeper tendencies and stories. Ultimately, the Prince gained a power even the world's mightiest kingdoms could not conquer or possess—he became the king of his own mind.

Our mind is the most powerful force we encounter in our lifetime. When our thoughts are like those of the restless Prince, we easily get confused or overwhelmed. We experience inner struggles or get in our own way. We forget the beauty all around us, or fail to see solutions that rest in plain sight. Or, like the Prince, despite having all our needs met, we still sense an inner void.

The same mind, when like that of the serene Sage, guides us to experience deep contentment and joy. We discover life's beauty, wonders, and wise teachings everywhere. Regardless of what we own in the world, we feel as if we carry boundless treasures in our heart.

No wonder then, as the cliché aptly states, our mind is both our worst enemy and best friend. Or, as philosophers and poets through time have said in myriad ways, our mind "can make a heaven of hell, a hell of heaven."[1]

But it does not have to be this way. In the lifelong waltz between fear and hope, failure and progress, and confusion and clarity, we are the ones who choose with whom we dance from moment to moment. And as sages through the ages remind us, whether we realize it or not, we always have a choice.

Most of us use our mind in limited ways and assume that is as good as it gets. Or we come to believe that our mind's tendencies are beyond our control. Yet our mind harbors incredible potential to change itself. When we unlock this power, we transform how we lead our lives, interact with each other, and solve challenges in our lives and in the world.

Yet while many eagerly embark on trips to explore new places, whether in distant lands or their own backyards, few as enthusiastically venture into their inner terrain. Once we go within, we discover that the inward journey's (in)sights are at least as spectacular as earth's grandest wonders. For this adventure—one of humanity's most ancient and universal quests—leads us to the essence of our being. It takes us home in our hearts.

But, even when we decide to journey inward, we may wonder, *where do we start?* None of us are born with a user's manual for our mind. Travel companies don't offer package tours for inner space. Schools and workplaces don't provide required curricula for navigating the mind. So, how do we learn to unlock our mind's talents, transcend its traps, and make it our best friend for life? That, my dear fellow travelers, is the journey we now begin.

CHAPTER 1

The State of Our Minds

Since our earliest ancestors first learned to think beyond the next hunt, our mind has both astounded and baffled us. At best, it has led us to touch the moon, to decode the building blocks of life, and to share ideas that unite us. At worst, it has driven us to invent bombs that can annihilate us, to incite violence and wars, and to build walls and harbor stories that divide us.

Hence, although our outer world has advanced from cave walls to computer screens, progress in our inner one remains open to debate. In one of the ultimate ironies of evolution, some of our most sophisticated inventions harbor the capacity to amplify some of our worst primal tendencies.

Take the mobile devices that have become permanent residents in most human pockets. On the one hand, they let us reach across the globe, connect with distant family and friends, and access the world's knowledge at our fingertips. On the other, they isolate us in information bubbles, enable the rapid spread of false news, and fuel anxiety and depression. Often, they reinforce impulsive and addictive tendencies by design, through hidden algorithms that are reshaping our minds in ways we barely understand.

When we are unaware of how our mind works, we tend to obey its ways, blind to their sway over us. This leads us to squander human potential at mind-boggling scales. For instance, despite knowing what is good for us, we may still not do it. Or, despite knowing what is bad for us, we may still pursue it. We dream of a better future yet let yesterday hijack tomorrow. We have ideas to change the world yet fall on our fears. We yield to false beliefs, irrational doubts, and fictitious stories—about ourselves, each other, and the world. We wear lenses tinted by our mind and, oblivious to their presence, assume we see an untainted reality. Along the way, countless hopes, dreams, and ideas meet their destinies in dust.

THE FUTURE OF THE MIND

Today, learning to unlock our mind's potential is more urgent than ever. In eras past, basic cognitive skills gave us a survival edge. We tamed fire and sowed crops. We crushed plants into balms and built cranes stronger than the elephants that hauled marble to the Taj Mahal. Determined to outdo birds and fish, we learned to fly the skies and swim the seas. Along the way, we crashed and drowned. But we never gave up, rarely faulted our creations, and stayed ever focused on improving them.

As our digital age inventions surpass the abilities of our bodies *and* our minds, we face unprecedented threats. As computers emit and transmit more data than we can ingest, let alone digest, they are displacing ever more human skills. Decades ago, taxi drivers memorized city maps to master their trade. Today, navigation software can outperform humans with exquisite precision, guided by real-time traffic data. And automobiles themselves are becoming increasingly autonomous.

All this raises urgent, existential questions on the essence of our existence: As machines reshape and replace us, what will be the role of humans? As our skills become obsolete, how do we navigate change? As algorithms sway us, how do we build on what unites rather than divides us? As we face massive global challenges, how do we solve them to uplift us all, rather than to benefit some at the cost of others? In short, how do we use our intelligence more wisely to not just survive but thrive together in the future?

The answers to these questions are not leisurely musings, as ancient philosophers might have pondered over campfire or wine. They represent the greatest challenges of our times and matter as much to an entrepreneur in Silicon Valley or Bangalore as to an executive in London or Tokyo. They are as relevant to a factory line worker in America's heartland as to a farmer in rural Africa or a rancher in Australia. For, what's at stake is not just the future of one community or nation, but that of an entire planet—ours.

Today, invisible foes such as viruses, both biological and digital, can travel our world at breakneck speed and bring us to our knees. Climate crises, such as fires, droughts, and floods, are devastating livelihoods around the globe. While some may dream of jetting off to Mars, or burrowing into bunkers belowground, our collective future depends on all of us fighting for each other's and our planet's survival as if our life depends on it—because it does.

To create a sustainable future that serves us all, we must each keep humanity—and our shared humanity—top of mind. For, while our inventions can dazzle with performance, they cannot give us meaning. They can code, compute, and link, but cannot comfort, care, and love. That which we ultimately seek, in search of which we often create them, our inventions themselves cannot give us.

Also, a traditional education focused on "hard" skills in narrow domains no longer ensures a lifelong career. Rather, we each need to master "soft" skills, such as creativity, resilience, and compassion, to guide how we use any hard skills we learn.

Thus, as we chase the cutting edge, we must also nurture the enduring edge we each already have—in our mind. Hence, as we advance through the age of artificial intelligence, this is a book about our timeless natural kind.

THE MAKING OF A MIND

When the Sage first appeared before the royal court, his opening words captivated the Prince: "This despair you feel, questioning the world and your role in it, is a natural response of an awakening mind. Seeing so much suffering in the world, how can a caring being not feel worried or overwhelmed?"

The Prince exhaled with an eternity-spanning sigh of relief. Deep tranquility engulfed his being. For the first time, he felt someone understood his torment.

"We will explore wisdom to transform fear and doubt into courageous action," the Sage continued. "Life is much simpler than it may feel to you right now. Inner calm and contentment are our basic nature. Trust that your mind is okay, more so than minds numb to the suffering of their fellow beings."

The Chief Courtier gulped in shame. For months, he had lectured the Prince with opposing words in attempts to "fix" his thoughts.

Later that evening, as the Prince strolled through the palace's fragrant gardens, amidst lush fountains and rolling hills, he revisited the Sage's words: "From our first breath to our last, we come to know our mind through our thoughts. Without thinking, our mind thinks it ceases to exist. What we assume as our reality—both outer and inner—is all created by our mind."

The Prince thought back to the scholars who visited the court before the Sage. Many brought carts full of scrolls that they cited in attempts to change the Prince's mind. But while the Prince's body sat in court, his mind wandered afar, disengaged. The Sage, in contrast, sensed the essence of the Prince's turmoil and asked him questions to guide him to his heart's truths. The Prince hung on to the Sage's every word. He now grasped the essence of the Sage's wisdom. *My state of mind truly shapes how I face everything.* He wondered, *how do we come to be this way?*

❦   ❦   ❦

From birth, we depend on other members of our species to feed, clean, and nurture us. As we learn to walk and talk, their language, habits, and customs are imprinted on us. We explore the world with curiosity and wonder, weaving what we experience into stories we remember. As we grow older, schooling and professional training layer on specialized knowledge and skills. And throughout life, we engage in conversations and banter to affirm—or adapt—the beliefs, ideas, and ideals that define us. This is how a mind is made.

Rarely, do we reflect on how we became who we are and how that guides our lives and our views on the world. Most of us venture inward either inspired by a longing to know ourselves better or, more likely, catapulted by a life-changing crisis that leaves us no choice but to face our deepest selves. As we enter our inner space, the journey itself begins to transform how we view everything.

For instance, we realize how the greatest threats to our survival rest in neither nature's nor humanity's creations but in a mind out of step with its heart. When such an inner divide seeps into the world, it can lead to conflict, violence, and even war. This is how most of history's darkest chapters were written.

Each time, we survive such chapters led by minds who remind us of our shared humanity. They selflessly serve their fellow beings with kindness and compassion. As they shine their light onto the world, they reunite us—with our own hearts—and with each other. They inspire us to live our days filled with peace, joy, and love.

Both—the dark and light—reside in every mind. Which we let lead is, in each moment, ours to decide.

THE INTENTION OF THIS BOOK

As the Sage concluded his stay at the royal court, he visited the King and Queen in their private chamber to bid them farewell.

"The gift you have given us is priceless," the Queen said, greeting him. "This is a small token of our appreciation, though it falls far short of our gratitude." A pair of courtiers appeared carrying a large chest filled with gold and jewels. The Sage smiled. The King felt relieved at his pleasure.

Then the Sage spoke, "I appreciate your gift but have no use for it in the hills. Nature provides generously for my needs and takes no payment in return. Instead, this is what I ask of you: I am a mere messenger of wisdom that reverberates through the forests, flows with the rivers, and strums the songs of birds. Take its essence to heart, live by it, and share it with every being you meet. This way, minds thousands of years from now can find the same light in its truths. By sharing such treasures, we are each enriched with boundless inner wealth."

Then the Sage shared another secret with the King and Queen: the deeper meaning behind his visit. Both listened enthralled and sensed vast new portals open up to them. Humbled, they accepted the Sage's request. And that is how we meet here today. As for the secret, well, that is for the pages to come.

Our journey from hereon will be guided by a simple concept to help us decode and master our mind: At the simplest level, most of our thoughts emerge in three basic states of mind that guide our doing, thinking, and being. When we don't know how these states run our mind, it can feel like a space divided against itself and lead to the countless challenges that consume our attention, rob our peace of mind, and make our mind feel like a foe. When these states unite in harmony, we attain inner peace, are empowered to unlock our mind's potential, and feel like it is our best friend.

Whether you are a curious explorer of your mind, a wanderer seeking clarity on the next chapter of your life, a leader guiding a team, a trailblazer charting a new path, an artist expressing truths, or a soul searching for them, knowing your mind transforms how you walk each step of your way.

With a united mind, we experience less worry and stress and more resilience and well-being. We become more open-minded, authentic, and creative. We release the limiting beliefs and stories that masquerade as our reality. We rediscover the joy of play and the power of wisdom. We connect to our sense of meaning and purpose. We gain the profound freedom that rests in leading our mind rather than feeling led by it. We sense a connection with everything around us and lead this life, in this world, in these times, in a whole new light, with a lightness previously unimaginable.

❧   ❧   ❧

The Table of Contents at the start of this book provides a detailed road map for the rest of your journey here. Before we explore the three states of mind in Part II, the next chapter briefly describes how the ideas in these pages emerged. Through the years, many readers and audiences have asked, which I get. Before embarking on any great adventure, we want to know our travel guide.

CHAPTER 2

A Journey into the Mind

Sometimes, we travel the world only to discover that what we were looking for was with us all along. We think our outer world defines our journey while it is really our inner one that guides it. I stumbled upon this truth at a young age but grasped its wisdom only decades later.

I was born in Kiel, Germany to parents from India who moved there for their graduate studies. When I was nine, we moved to Finland for a year and then to India for three before settling in the United States, just as I turned 14. English was the fifth language I learned. In Germany, I felt like a native yet looked like a foreigner. In India, I looked like a native yet felt like an outsider. In Finland, there was no ambiguity.

In each new home, in meeting strangers and making new friends, I searched for what we shared. Even when we spoke different languages or wore diverse skins, I sensed how gestures and feelings often transcended words. We laughed, cried, and felt joy and pain in the same ways within. Even without words, we connected through our hearts.

In college, this quest to know our shared humanity evolved into a passion to help nurture health and well-being. I studied biochemistry, with an eye toward medicine. Yet, while poring over science texts at the library late into the night, I often marveled at simple innovations that had transformed human health. This shifted my focus to finding and nurturing new ideas that could improve the well-being of people around the world.

A few years after college, I joined a venture capital firm. There, for close to nine years, I searched for, and invested in, cutting-edge health innovations developed by the world's leading clinicians and scientists. Each year, we evaluated hundreds of promising ideas, resulting in less than a handful of investments. The startups that survived this rigorous process received access to all the money, resources, and expertise they needed to succeed.

As the years passed, I was intrigued to see more companies meet failure than success. Curiously, more startups failed due to setbacks in the teams that led them than due to failures in the ideas that had led to their creation in the first place.[2] *How can this be?* I wondered. *These are the world's best and brightest minds. If they can't get it right, what are we getting wrong?*

With time, alongside evaluating innovations, I started to closely study the minds behind them. Soon, I felt as if a parallel universe unfolded, revealing fascinating insights.

INSIGHTS BEYOND SCIENCE

Investing in innovation relies on a fine balance between analyzing highly technical knowledge and making intuitive decisions in the face of limited data. I was fascinated by how different kinds of minds straddled this edge.

Among investors, I noticed how some would get engrossed in tangible data or minutiae, while others focused on the long-term big picture. Some would look for low-risk, incremental advances, while others confidently placed bold bets that held the potential to transform healthcare.

Among innovators, in the face of challenges, some sustained a child-like curiosity to find solutions, while others became easily overwhelmed or paralyzed by their complexity and magnitude.

Among scientists, whose work is built on objectivity, I noticed how their ways of thinking could introduce subjective variables.

For instance, in evaluating a new discovery, some might laud it as a notable breakthrough, while others would dismiss it with equally compelling rigor. When their perspectives were challenged, some sustained an open mind while others defended or dug deeper into their positions.

Among industry consultants and experts, some conscientiously avoided all conflicts of interest (real and perceived), while others convinced themselves they were immune to (un)conscious biases, viewing them as a malady that afflicted others.

And among startup founders and teams, in the face of setbacks, some persevered with courage and confidence to creatively fail their way to success. Others seemed easily defeated by factors they saw as being beyond their control.

Through such patterns and insights, I began to discern why, sometimes, even all the money and expertise in the world fail to solve a challenge. And how some who start from scratch, such as upstarts toppling titans, immigrants building a new life, or trailblazers charting a new path, can attain remarkable success.

I realized that, whether through life's experiences or conscious practice, some minds had learned to think differently. The edge these minds held was not visible on resumes or framed on walls, yet its power was profound and its impact even greater.

Such minds faced both ups and downs with equal calm. They stayed humble and grounded before both failure *and* success. They had clarity on their intentions and stayed steadfastly true to them. These minds knew their own worst fears and foibles and sought to transcend them. Ultimately, they strove to serve a cause greater than themselves, whether by aspiring to better a single life or to help heal the whole planet.

I began to wonder, *what is the deeper secret of such minds? How can others learn to think like them?* And, *how, in our hunt for ever better tools, had we come to neglect mastery of our most powerful one—our own mind?*

With time, I realized that our life unfolds through an invisible dance between the seen and unseen. When we focus our attention on what we can see, that guides how we come to know the world.

This is the realm of tangible science and data. Yet, as we dive deeper into the seen, we inevitably confront the unseen.

This is where many explorations end because our tools for looking at the world offer no way to perceive the intangible. For example, while medicine can map biochemical pathways, healing itself remains largely a mystery. Or, while physicists can write equations on the laws of the universe, the movements of quantum particles stump even our most elegant mathematics.

Once we experience the realm of the unseen, we realize how it guides everything we see. We do not grasp this through sensory inputs or intellectual knowledge but through an inner knowing, which some call intuition or insight. I realized that in facing challenges, whether in our lives or in the world, we often focus on their tangible aspects while neglecting their deeper, holistic whole.

Here is a metaphor to explore this. Imagine a faucet has been left on in a plugged kitchen sink.[3] As water overflows, the home's residents see it flow across the floor and frantically search for mops. They may even debate which mop is best until they realize what matters more than any mop—finding and turning off the faucet.

While most of us might not act this way in a flooding kitchen, in many other domains of life we expend substantial resources, energy, and time on spilled water. We get focused on designing new mops, studying their science, teaching the art of mopping, and rewarding its mastery.

When we face a crisis, mop-like, quick-fix solutions are often critical to help us survive. Once a disease has spread, whether in a person or as a global pandemic, "mops" such as treatments and hospital beds help save lives. But when a disease first starts, simple acts can turn off its faucet and help prevent or reduce its spread.

As such insights infused my mind, my job of sifting through new treatments for diseases began to feel limited and limiting, like looking for new mops. For, we long not just to avoid symptoms and pain but to feel well in our whole being. Ignoring this truth became not just inconvenient or uncomfortable—it was impossible. I had seen the faucet and could not keep mopping.

FINDING THE EDGE

After close to a decade in the trenches of innovation, I embarked on a full-time exploration of holistic health. Soon, all roads kept leading me to the "faucet" of well-being—the human mind. Yet, as I pored through neuroscience research, talked to experts, and attended scientific conferences, I faced a new challenge.

We likely have more disciplines to examine the human mind than any other dimension of our existence. Neuroscience studies its physical aspects, psychiatry its biochemical reactions, and psychology its behavioral effects. Philosophy explores our mind's moral impact, sociology its societal influence, and spirituality its deeper meaning.

Yet no one discipline offered a truly holistic perspective on the mind. Most could not even agree on a unified definition of it. When a field lacked tools to study certain aspects of the mind, it tended to dismiss their significance, a notion once eloquently expressed by quantum physicist Werner Heisenberg: "What we observe is not nature in itself, but nature exposed to our method of questioning."[4]

Another way to think about this is through the well-known metaphor of the blind men and the elephant. As a group of blind men meet an elephant for the first time, each probes a different part of the animal (e.g., its tail, leg, trunk, or ears) and creates a unique image in his mind of what it may be (e.g., a rope, tree, snake, or rug).

Like the blind man who is convinced he beholds a rope, many disciplines held views, whether consciously expressed or not, of having a superior access point to truths on the mind. Many fields were also safeguarded by credentialed scholars and specialized terminologies, which limited their interactions with outsiders. Yet, as such scholars tightly gripped the elephant's tail, they often failed to see that they beheld a majestic creature that could take them on incredible adventures anywhere.

As I continued wandering at the edges of disciplines, I began to doubt if one could even arrive at a unified understanding of the mind. Then, one day, a deep sense of familiarity arose in my heart, which took me all the way back to childhood.

While growing up across continents, even though I was not conscious of this as a child, the feeling of being an outsider had become not just intimately familiar but oddly comfortable. I often felt as if I was both in a place and just an observer of it. Rarely content with a one-dimensional encounter with any elephant, I developed an innate curiosity to search for patterns everywhere.

Suddenly I realized that, in studying the mind, my perceived disadvantage of not being a scholar of any one discipline offered a distinct edge. Comfortable as an outsider, I could dive into diverse fields with a fresh, open mind, free of entrenched mental models, doctrines, and dogma.

Re-inspired, I combined my passion for finding universal patterns with my training in rigorous methods for evaluating ideas. I asked naive questions and often found insights hidden in plain sight. Whenever possible, I "rode" the elephant, free of norms on how to interact with it.

With time, I realized how sages millennia ago perceived the same insights on the mind that scientists are re-searching and

re-validating today. Although our terms and tools have evolved, all inner explorers eventually arrive at the same truth: To master our mind's potential, we can learn to turn its faucet rather than spend a lifetime mopping. To attain this, we don't need to gain extensive knowledge; we just need to find a way to experience and practice this within.

On my journey, such a path appeared in the form of a simple, universal pattern that wove through all disciplines on the mind through time. It revealed that most of our thoughts reflect three basic states of mind. When we understand how these states drive our mind, we can learn to transform our ways of being, thinking, and doing.

When I first stumbled on this idea, I shared it as a simple framework through a small book, *Enduring Edge*, published in 2014. From there, the idea took on a life of its own as readers shared it with colleagues, family, and friends and each wove it into their lives as made most sense to them.

A physician introduced it to her peers to tackle caregiver burnout. An inner-city high school teacher applied it to teach her students resilience. A graduate school dean wove it into her vision to foster creative thinking among faculty and students. A business leader used it for a workshop on diversity and inclusion. A university professor assigned *Enduring Edge* as a required textbook for her course on leadership. And a business school included the concept in its new student orientation to discuss mental agility.

Some shared it with partners at work and at home to transform their relationships. Others said it gave them renewed clarity on their sense of meaning and purpose and inspired job changes or even new career paths. Many said it catalyzed shifts—epiphanies, spontaneous breakthroughs, solutions to long-standing challenges, resolutions of inner conflicts, or even holistic healing—in often surprising ways.

Inspired by such stories and my own continued explorations, this book emerged. It reflects the collective wisdom of countless minds who played with the concept of the three states to become best friends with their own mind. Also, after reading *Enduring Edge*, many readers asked for more practical ways to apply its concepts. *United Mind* offers that. Yet this book is a standalone work that assumes no familiarity with *Enduring Edge*. If you are new to all this, *United Mind* will guide you to the same place: a way to rethink and transform how you live, work, and lead—in your life and in the world.

CLIMBING THE PEAK

By now, you may be wondering, *so what exactly will this book do for me?* That, dear reader, is up to you. The ideas here can serve any mind that aspires to venture within. Yet while we can easily learn a concept, it only serves us when used, which brings us to some critical caveats.

If you want quick tips or rules that tell you what to do, these pages may disappoint. While a predefined path may feel more comfortable, no one can tell you how exactly to best go within.

Also, if your mind seeks a rigorous intellectual workout, this will likely not meet your expectations. Rather than convincing you with abstract research, this book intends to help you experience real change. While studies suggest what may happen to you based

on what happened to others like you, your own experience shows you what actually holds true for you. Also, if you swiftly skim these pages to extract their gist, your experience may be like that of reading a travel brochure rather than going on the trip. Passive learning tends to transit through us. Firsthand experience, on the other hand, often transforms us.

Lastly, you may think, *I have no time.* Yet clarity in our mind creates more time in our lives. (Though time itself is just a construct of the mind—a topic for another day.)

Here is another way to consider all this: Imagine you have decided to climb one of earth's highest mountain peaks. A geologist can describe the terrain. A meteorologist can tell you about the weather. A historian can share tales of prior climbers. A mountaineer can map your path, and a Sherpa can guide your way.

Now, think of exploring your mind as climbing the mountain. A scientist can tell you about the brain. A philosopher can share wisdom from paths others have traveled before. A psychotherapist can help you untangle why your prior attempts failed, and a coach can motivate you to keep going when you feel stuck.

Yet no one else, no matter how skilled, can traverse your mind's peaks and valleys for you. No technology, no matter how intelligent, can know your truths as intimately as your own heart. You are the world's best expert on your mind. Others can point out paths but the work of walking them is yours alone. Also, there is no one-size-fits-all way to know our mind. The same "path" or practice can feel like a light, joy-filled stroll to one and a strenuous slog to another. Your best paths are ones that resonate within. The climb is hard enough. We cannot be forced or carried up a mountain. So think of this book as a guide to ease your way.

All you need to access your mind's potential is already within you. So is all that keeps you from it. When we lack clarity on why we climb, or we have fixed expectations on how our trip should go, we can easily get discouraged by setbacks or convince ourselves to quit. We may say, *I can't do this, change is hard, things will never change,* or *this is impossible.*

Such thoughts create inner stumbling blocks that make us believe we cannot climb, or don't want to even if we could. Yet such blocks are not made of rocks but of stories we can surmount anytime, as these words attributed to Sir Edmund Hillary, the first human to scale Mount Everest with Sherpa Tenzing Norgay, convey, "It is not the mountain we conquer but ourselves."[5]

There is a profound, lightning-strike level insight in this. The decision not to climb is a choice, like any other, even if at first your mind does not believe this to be true. Stories of why not to climb may be so well-trodden in our mind that we accept them as our reality. But just because such stories seem real does not make them true. We each have more power than we realize—or may dare to admit to ourselves—to scale and conquer our mind.

Since you are here reading this, you are already climbing. How far you go depends on what you decide at each step. One thing is certain. You will face steep crevices, dark caves, and spectacular edges where both danger and beauty reside. Sometimes, the joy will be in climbing, at other times in pausing to take in the view. Sometimes, the climb may feel so tough every fiber in your being wants to quit. Then remember this: the path and the peak are one.

If you keep going, you have already arrived, which will make more sense as we journey on.

While no one can promise you change, I do assure you this: By the end of these pages, you will know that, no matter what you think, you are the one who decides. With each thought, you choose between fear and courage, inertia and progress, and struggle and ease.

I am acutely aware that this bestows immense responsibility. It is one thing to believe you cannot climb and to reconcile yourself to base camp in the valley, which is how many spend their lives. Not that they don't see the peak; we all do. But, once you know you can climb—and since you are here, we know you can—staying in the valley becomes a conscious choice.

Thus, if after reading this, you stay in old routines and nurture the status quo, that is a decision you make. But it is also possible, just to forewarn you, based on what prior travelers have shared, that you reinvent your life, quit your job, or take a radical leap into the unknown.

Those who shared stories of change did not transform because of a book, even if that is what some returned to say. They changed because of what they decided for themselves. This is not just their truth, it is the truth, and is yours too.

PART II

Three States of Mind

Overview

Every morning, as we get out of bed and start our day, we move through many daily routines with little conscious thought. This is efficient. We don't need to weigh the pros and cons of brushing our teeth each dawn. We just do it.

Similarly, as we move through our day, habitual thought patterns launch in our mind to guide what we think, say, and do. They drive how we replay the past, act in the present, and imagine the future. By decoding these tendencies through the three states of mind, we can learn to use our mind as serves us best. The three states are:

1. the 1D (one-dimensional) mind,
2. the 2D (two-dimensional) mind, and
3. the 3D (three-dimensional) mind.

The terms for these states—1D, 2D, and 3D— are new, neutral, and reflections of each state's basic nature. They are meant to be easy to remember and free of any discipline's prior terminology. We will delve into the three states in detail in Chapters 3, 4, and 5 and explore their dynamic interplay from Chapter 6 onward. To begin, here is a brief overview of each state.

1D

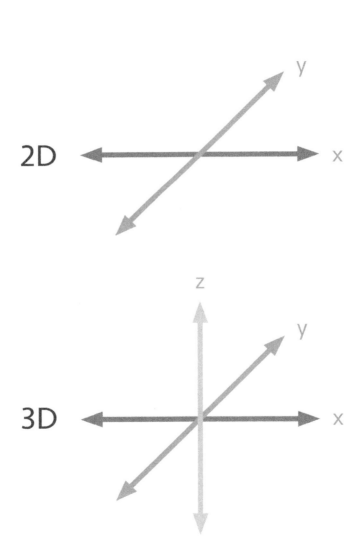

2D

3D

1. The **1D mind** focuses on our survival and safety. It reacts, or acts in response to, what we encounter in our outer—and inner—world. It is guided by primal impulses such as hunger, emotions such as fear, and our memories of past experiences. The 1D mind is rooted in our body or physical sense of self. We can also think of 1D as a **hands-on doing state**. It acts on what it perceives as urgent needs and thinks in linear ways that are sometimes highly efficient and, at other times, well, our worst-possible response.

2. The **2D mind** focuses on making sense of our world and defining our place in it. It is guided by our rational, analytical, and critical thinking abilities, also known as our intellect. The 2D mind is seated in our individual sense of self, or unique identity, also referred to as our ego. We can also think of 2D as a **head-based thinking state**. Its logical and systematic ways tend to serve us well—that is, until 2D forgets its own limits and walks us straight into trouble.

3. The **3D mind** is the seat of our inner sense of connection, contentment, and creativity. It is guided by our intuition, inner wisdom, and insights. The 3D mind is grounded in a universal, boundless sense of self. In this state, we are fully present in the moment and experience an expansive sense of interconnectedness that harbors the essence of our shared humanity. We can also consider 3D a **heart-centered being state** that fosters healing, resilience, kindness, and compassion.

Upon first reading these descriptions, the three states will likely seem familiar to you, as they should. They are a distillation of what we have always known. You may even find parallels to other frameworks on the mind you have come across. (Those most commonly mentioned by readers are included in this endnote.[6])

You may even wonder, *so what's the big deal? Why should I keep reading?*

The power of what we are about to explore rests not in an intellectual understanding of the three states but in our first-hand experience of each state in our own mind. While we each lean on all three states, only one can lead our mind at a time. When we are unaware of which state is in charge, we tend to abide by—and react to—its in-the-moment thoughts and feelings, often more than serves us.

This is how emotions such as fear (1D) override reason (2D), or rationalized arguments (2D) overrule our deeper wisdom (3D). To complicate matters, while each state's ways make perfect sense to it, they are counterintuitive to the other two, as if each speaks a different language. For instance, both impulsive actions (1D) and intuitive insights (3D) can appear irrational through a logical lens (2D).

When the three states are in conflict in our mind, it becomes like a space divided against itself, marked by inner confusion, struggle, and resistance. When the three states align in harmony instead, we experience a united mind and a deep sense of inner peace, joy, and resonance.

By decoding the interplay of the three states in our mind, we can learn to harness the talents and transcend the traps of each state. With time, we grasp which state is best to lead our mind from moment to moment. In this way, we transform unconscious, passive reactions into conscious, mindful choices.

At first, applying the concept of the three states may feel awkward, like learning to use a new tool. With practice, it becomes just as second nature. For example, if you have a hammer in your hand and come across a loose screw, you will likely just put down the hammer and find a screwdriver instead. Yet in our mind, we often "hammer" away in our in-the-moment state and then wonder why things don't go as we want—or unfold exactly as we don't want. By learning to use the state that serves us best based on what we face, we can move ahead with ease instead of struggling or, worse, ending up with a hole in the wall.

Many readers have shared how the concept of the three states becomes encoded in how they think and talk about their own and others' minds. Such as, "I was in the 3D mind and the answer just came to me," or "I felt stuck in the 2D mind and took a timeout," or "I realized he was in a 1D state, so I didn't take his words personally."

Table 1 at the end of this chapter provides a summary of the three states, including the contexts through which we will explore them in the rest of this book. Consider it a reference guide to which you can return as you journey on. (If you are reading this in paperback, you can also tear out the page and make it a bookmark for easy reference.)

Finally, to ensure we stay on the same page as we enter the abstract realm of the mind, let's briefly define a few key terms.

A WORD IS JUST A WORD

Words, beautiful words. We whisper, sing, and chant, as they flow from heart to heart. Words lend texture and meaning to our formless thoughts and feelings. As we strive to perfect their sequence and read their pulse, we confront both their magnificence—and brutal limitations.

Reductionist by design, words reflect impossible perfection, conveying ever more or less than they mean as they cast unique shadows on each mind. Yet, between us here now, they are all we have.

Over the years, some readers have shared how certain words such as "spirit" or "soul" can trigger strong inner reactions based on their prior encounters with them. While we delve into triggers later, it helps to remember that all words here, like the concept of the three states itself, intend to convey truths that transcend their literal definitions. Thus, try to hold these words lightly—in their spirit rather than their precise letters—to perceive their deeper meaning.

MIND

While our brain can be localized to the gray matter in our skull, we have no equivalent context to define our mind. Most disciplines that study the mind do not even agree on a unified definition of it. Here, we define our mind as the realm of our thoughts and feelings as experienced in our body and deeper being. While most disciplines on the mind focus on just its physical, psychological, or behavioral aspects, by exploring their dynamic interplay, we can gain a more holistic perspective on the mind.

MINDSTATE

This term will be used as a shortcut word for our "state of mind" in the moment. We will interchangeably use terms such as 1D mindstate, 1D mind, 1D state, or just 1D, to refer to the 1D state of mind (and likewise for 2D and 3D).

Mindstate is distinct from mindset, a term often used to describe our state of mind (e.g., positive and negative or fixed and growth mindsets). Mindset implies our mind gets "set" in fixed ways of thinking. But our mindset just reflects the mindstate(s) we are using in the moment, which we can change anytime.

FEELINGS

We usually describe our inner sensations in visceral ways such as, *I sense it in my gut*, or *I feel it in my bones*. Yet we sometimes confuse 1D's emotional reactions, such as fear, unease, or inner turmoil with 3D's intuitive insights, which harbor a deeper sense of calm and clarity. Here, we refer to the 1D mind's feelings as emotions and the 3D mind's inner perceptions as intuition.

Our emotions tend to be in perpetual motion—coming, going, and constantly changing form. In contrast, our intuitive feelings reflect an inner serenity and harmony that is deeply grounding, peaceful and restorative.

HEART and LOVE

Our heart has likely been the subject of more poems, letters, and songs than any other part of us.

In the 1D state, we tend to view the heart as the source of our emotions, such as when we feel our heart bursts with excitement or breaks with sorrow. In this state, our attention is focused on our own physical sensations.

In the 2D state, we tend to think of our heart as an exquisite anatomic pump whose rhythms we can measure and track. In this state, our attention is focused on our own thoughts.

In the 3D state, we tend to experience our heart as the essence of our being, spirit, or soul (as defined below), or as a portal into the limitless and timeless universe, as conveyed by mystics and masters through time. In this state, we sense a deep interconnectedness that transcends our sense of time, place, and self.

If we consider love, which we tend to locate to our heart, here is how we can think about it through the three states.

In the 1D state, love is a sensation of excitement or attraction that can evoke a strong inner physiological response (e.g., elevated heart rate).

In the 2D state, love is an abstract concept that appears confusing to define and describe.

In the 3D state, love reflects higher feelings of compassion, kindness, and caring that radiate outward and evoke a deeply calming inner state. In these pages, we mostly use the words heart and love in their 3D contexts.

BEING, SPIRIT, SOUL

We each experience an aliveness that reflects the essence of life in our being. We often refer to this as our spirit or soul. Since our grasp of this force rests beyond the realms of science, humanity has mostly explored it through our varied spiritual, philosophical, religious, and artistic traditions through time. Here, we use the words being, spirit, and soul interchangeably to refer to this inner essence or life force, without implying any religious, historical, or cultural connotations.

EXPLORING A CITY

Since the mind is abstract, another tool that can help us grasp it is visual metaphors, which these pages harbor in abundance, as you may have noticed by now. Given that each mind makes sense of itself in its own way, a variety of metaphors are included here, knowing that some will resonate more with you than others.

Many who read *Enduring Edge* said they found the following metaphor helpful, so we revisit it here. Imagine you have decided to visit a new city as a tourist.

1D

2D

3D

Being in the 1D state is like sitting in a tour bus or taxi. This is a fast and efficient way to go around town, and it allows you to look at many different landmarks in less time. Yet it also confines you to set routes and roads.

Being in the 2D state is like exploring the city on foot. You can stroll through alleys, visit shops and restaurants, talk to locals, and experience the city's culture and food in richer and more nuanced ways.

Finally, being in the 3D state is like taking a helicopter ride. As you rise above the city, you gain vast new vista views of its skyline and greater terrain.

Thus, each state offers a unique way to get to know the city, and together they reveal what no one state can alone.

MIND QUIZ

Before we dive into the three states, if you are curious about your own state of mind, you can take a short, anonymous quiz at www. vitamita.com/quiz. Its result reveals the mindstate(s) to which you tend to default. This can serve as a helpful guide as you journey on. If you cannot go online at this time, know that you will also naturally arrive at the answer as you travel through the next three chapters.

TABLE 1: THREE STATES OF MIND			
	1D MIND	**2D MIND**	**3D MIND**
Focused on:	Survival & safety	Significance & validation	Harmony & connection
Affirms:	"I am alive"	"I matter"	"I am"
Main mode:	Doing	Thinking	Being
Means:	Linear, rapid, reactive actions	Systematic analyses	Intuitive wisdom & insights
Rooted in:	Physical sense of self	Intellectual sense of self	Universal sense of self
Guided by:	Emotions & memories of past experience	Ego & logic, knowledge, and judgment	Deeper sense of unity, peace, joy, love, fulfillment
Traps:	Stressful, excitable, depletive	Controlling, judgmental, divisive	**None.** Healing, restorative, vast, open, inclusive
Ch 7. How We Become Who We Are	Act on impulses & emotions (reactive)	Follow ego, logic & reason (rational)	Listen to & trust inner wisdom (reflective)
Ch 8. How We Change & Grow	Short-sighted, resistance	Detailed plans, data, metrics	Enduring resonance
Ch 9. How We Decide Who We Become	Tangible & material assets, needs & greed	Achievements & accolades, validation	Inner meaning, purpose, values, contentment
Ch 10. How We Talk to Each Other	"Me" focused, emotional, impulsive	"You vs me" focused, cool, analytical	"We" focused, compassionate, understanding
Ch 11. How We Become Leaders	Dictate & rule by fear, scarcity	Delegate & govern by ego	Serve with love & abundance
Ch 12. How We Nurture Culture	Confrontational battlegrounds	Transactional marketplaces	Unifying, joyful playgrounds
Ch 13. How We Innovate	Reactive, safe, risk-averse	Incremental, systematic	Transformative, visionary
Ch 14. How We Create	To survive, self-maximize	To achieve, self-optimize	To thrive, realize shared humanity
Ch 15. How We Succeed	What we own, self gain	What we attain, show world	How we serve, give & love

CHAPTER 3

The 1D Mind

From the moment we are born, a deeper natural intelligence guides us. Primal instincts and impulses ensure our survival and safety. Hunger feeds us, fear protects us, and pain makes us cry for help and act. In short, if 1D does not perform its duty, 2D and 3D have no chance to be.

In many life circumstances, 1D's reactive ways are highly efficient to ensure swift results. If we are walking through a jungle and run into a tiger, we don't pause to study its stripes or ponder the origin of its species. Fueled by fear, we run as fast as we can, or fight, if we must. Or if we are starving and receive a warm meal, we don't stare at it for hours to contemplate its deeper meaning. We just eat, relieved to meet our stomach's needs.

Yet, in our modern lives, even when our basic needs have been satisfied, most of us default to 1D's impulsive reactions more than serves us. This can cloud our ability to bring 2D's reason and 3D's wisdom to our decisions and actions. By understanding our 1D mind, we can learn to prevent it from getting in our way and use it as serves us best. Just to alert you, since this chapter leads you into your 1D mind, it may at times feel difficult or uneasy to get through. But hang in there. The journey gets easier as we learn to transcend 1D's tendencies.

The 1D mind operates with a sense of urgency driven by reactions to outer stimuli or inner urges that it perceives as either threats or attractions. The term "one-dimensional" reflects this state's linear, single-minded ways, which are guided by:

1. inputs from our senses, which alert us to what is going on around us,
2. emotions such as fear, which are the fastest way to get our attention, and
3. memories of past experiences, which enable rapid, short-cut decisions.

Since we are each guided by 1D's instincts from the moment we are born, it is our most familiar mindstate. Many 1D impulses get etched into us below conscious thought and come to feel like a deeply familiar aspect of who we are. They lead us to think "on our feet" or to "jump" to conclusions. Curiously, the word emotion itself includes the word motion, reflecting 1D's focus on movement.

When we need to take urgent action, such as fleeing a tiger or meeting a deadline, 1D drives us into doing, which is vital in the moment. Yet when we come to spend our days in a state designed to save us from tiger attacks, we can feel constantly on edge, or allow emotional or impulsive urges to get the better of us.

The Prince we met in the Prologue was trapped in the 1D state when he was filled with despair. Dwelling in this state tends to overwhelm or exhaust us because we exist at the mercy of intense emotions, whether fears or desires, that seem to be beyond our control. Moreover, such sensations permeate our whole body and being. We don't just imagine fear in our head but may experience it as a spine-tingling, hair-raising, or gut-churning feeling. In fact, our body is the best starting point for decoding our 1D mind and its main operating mode—the stress response.

THE STRESS RESPONSE

When 1D senses danger, it launches intricate biochemical and physiological cascades in our body, also referred to as the "fight or flight" or stress response. Blood flows away from our gut and brain into our limbs to prepare them for action. Our heart rate increases, our blood vessels constrict, and our muscles tense to prepare for the looming battle. Blood glucose, insulin, cortisol, and adrenaline levels rise to serve as combat fuel. In parallel, activities that are less critical to our immediate survival, such as digestive and immune system functions, as well as, higher cognitive processes, such as critical reasoning, are deprioritized. There is just one problem with all this.

The 1D mind cannot tell an actual threat from one created in our head. Thus, it may "see" a tiger in a boss we dislike, a relative who gets under our skin, or a friend with whom we got in a fight. Then 1D proceeds to launch a full-on crisis response, led by fear and its loyal entourage, whose members often include impatience, anger, or irritation. All this can play out while we sit in a meeting, walk down a street, or lie awake at night with no foe to fight and nowhere to run.

Stress itself is a normal—and vital—part of our biological survival instinct. When deployed judiciously, as nature intended, it helps keep us safe. The challenge arises when we constantly unconsciously launch the stress response as our default way of being. Absent a physical threat to fend off, our body valiantly tries to discharge 1D's emergency brigade and its battle fuel stockpiles, such as elevated insulin and cortisol levels. Despite our body's best efforts, when stress becomes chronic or persistent, it depletes us.

Since our reactive tendencies often manifest below our conscious awareness, we can learn to notice how our 1D mind shows up in our body. Then we can de-escalate—and ultimately avoid launching—1D's combat mode when it doesn't serve us or may even cause harm.

We each experience stress in different ways, based on our unique biology and life experiences. Some sense muscle tension or chronic pain in areas such as the neck, back, or shoulders. Others notice its effects on their immunity through aggravated allergies, increased inflammation, or frequent infections. Some feel it in their gastrointestinal system as weak or disturbed digestion (e.g.,

The Stress Response

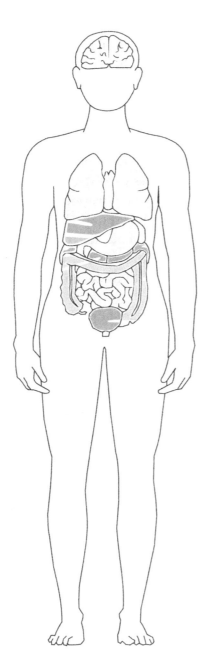

Anxiety, insomnia, lethargy, restlessness, or depression

Muscle tension or stiffness, e.g., in jaw, neck, or shoulders

Shallow breathing, rapid heart rate, or high blood pressure

Elevated cortisol or insulin secretion

Digestive issues, heartburn, cramps, or irritable bowel

Frequent urination or sexual dysfunction

Metabolic disorders, weight gain or loss, chronic fatigue

Weakened immunity, inflammation, allergies

Joint pain or inflammation, e.g., in knees, hips, or ankles

Muscle cramps and pain, e.g., in the lower back and legs

Vessel constriction, e.g. cold or tingling hands or feet

heartburn or stomach ailments). Still others sense stress in their cardiovascular system as high blood pressure or vessel constriction (e.g., cold hands or feet). Others experience its endocrine and metabolic effects, such as elevated insulin or cortisol secretion, which can, over time, lead to conditions such as diabetes.

Thus, chronic stress can corrode our well-being and lead to burnout, depletion, dis-ease, and eventually, often even disease. As increasingly also accepted by medical science, many chronic (and even fatal) diseases are caused or worsened by 1D gone wild.

Upon reading this, 1D may feel confused, or even defensive, and ask, *do you mean to say all my physical ailments and illnesses are my fault?* The short answer is, of course not. The origins of disease are complex and multi-factorial and include factors such as inherited genes, diet, lifestyle, environmental exposure, pathogen infections, and access to healthcare, among others. But no matter what else our body experiences, our state of mind plays a vital role in our well-being.

Beyond 1D's effects on our body, we can also learn to discern how it influences our thoughts. Since 1D guards our survival, its attention stays focused on the immediate and urgent. Uncertainty and the unknown terrify it.

In the face of a potential threat, 1D fixates on it with tunnel vision. When this tendency becomes a habit, it can feed thinking patterns such as negative thought spirals, rumination, worrying, or constantly imagining worst-case scenarios. Over time, 1D can also foster short-sighted, rigid, or closed-minded ways of thinking that are marked by dramatic or absolutist thoughts such as: *This is my reality. This always happens to me. Things will never change. I will always be this way.* Or, *I am ruined forever.*

Thus, in one of the great ironies of the human mind, when trapped in 1D's linear ways, we fail to think straight. Dwelling in 1D can also lead to mental tendencies such as obsessive or compulsive behaviors, phobias, insomnia, anxiety, or depression.

At one extreme, a mind may feel ever restless or nervous, as if always in a rush yet never able to catch up. At the other, a mind may feel so overwhelmed it enters a "self-protective" stance of paralysis, inertia, or apathy (also known as "freeze," a third response beyond "fight or flight"). At both extremes, 1D remains ever on edge, scared that even the slightest added stressor may push it over the brink.

The 1D mind succumbs to these patterns for one simple reason. It cannot see beyond itself. When we are in the 1D state, we come to believe its thoughts represent our whole reality. Then we blindly act on its impulses, whether in relieving discomfort or seeking pleasure. For instance, 1D would rather scratch an itch than bear its unease until it subsides, even if doing so may eventually abrade or harm our skin. Or, 1D can lead us to run away from a potentially good situation if it becomes scared of the unknown. This is how 1D leads us into rash or impulsive deeds that leave us later scratching our heads or regretting our actions.

Even when we satisfy a 1D desire (e.g., an urge for excitement or pleasure), we often find its satisfaction is short-lived. Today, 1D craves one thing. Tomorrow, bored of what it got, 1D seeks a new source of excitement to chase. Or, scared it does not have enough, or that it may lose what it has, 1D seeks ever more yet remains unfulfilled. In the extreme, this can lead us to face the world with a scarcity mindset, ever focused on maximizing what we can get.

The toll of defaulting to 1D's ways extends beyond our own lives. In relationships, 1D can fuel reactivity, tension, conflicts, or avoidance that leads to grudges or rifts. In organizations, it can foster stressful, toxic cultures marked by high burnout, increased turnover, and reduced productivity. In communities and nations, 1D drives fear-driven leadership that can stoke instability, violence, and unrest.

While 1D's reality may feel real when we are in it, 1D does not—and cannot—know the whole truth about our mind. By decoding when 1D's reactions threaten our capacity to thrive, we can learn to release them when they hold us back. Then, we gain space to access 2D's reason and 3D's wisdom to attain clarity, see the big picture, and discover new possibilities. To explore how we can train our 1D mind this way, let's visit another metaphor: the museum of emotions.

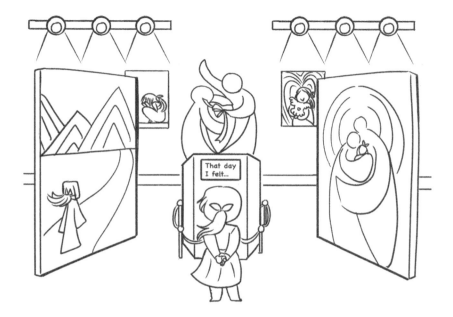

MUSEUM OF EMOTIONS

Although we are each intimately familiar with our emotions, we tend to have complicated relationships with them. Baffled by their origins, blindsided by their arrival, and bewildered by their intensity, 1D gets easily uneasy around intense or difficult emotions (e.g., anger, guilt, or shame).

The 1D mind may fear getting engulfed by emotions in ways that threaten its sense of comfort and safety. One way to transcend this is to think of our emotions, and their associated 1D patterns, as exhibits in our own museum of emotions, which holds the archives of our memories of past experiences.

By viewing our emotions as exhibits, we can gain some distance from them and avoid 1D's inclination to get wrapped up in itself. Then, like a curious curator, we can stroll through our museum to observe, learn, and grow. Guided by 2D's reason and 3D's wisdom, we can look at each exhibit we come across with a sense of curiosity and wonder. Instead of fearing what we may find—and how that will make us feel—as 1D might, we bring courage and compassion to discover new insights. Then we can consciously dismantle and release outdated exhibits that still take up precious space in our mind.

The alternative, which is how our reactive tendencies become permanent exhibits (such as inner triggers), is to avoid walking through our museum, to rush past exhibits we fear, to skip entire floors, or to pretend whole wings of our museum don't exist. Yet, as every child learns, closing our eyes does not make the world disappear.

To 1D, the prospect of facing and sorting through what seem like endless clutters of artifacts feels daunting, even impossible. For instance, anger may be woven with shame, guilt, sadness, and fear, creating a jumble 1D struggles to untangle. Thus, 1D's approaches toward unpleasant or painful emotions include varied forms of resistance such as, rejection, denial, suppression, repression, or disassociation. These responses are like locking the doors to a museum wing that 1D finds too painful to walk through.

Yet 1D's coping mechanisms often have the opposite of their intended effects. They lead us to inhabit a museum in which we gingerly tread. We may feel haunted by hidden artifacts or be on edge about triggering unexpected dust storms from old archives.

Further, as 1D tries to keep certain emotions at bay, its efforts consume our attention, energy, and thoughts. This reinforces and intensifies the very emotions 1D desperately seeks to dodge. These 1D tendencies explain how triggers, traumas, or phobias hijack our mind. As we develop reactive ways of facing the world, old exhibits, which may once have served to protect us, continue to exert control over our life.

To explore how we can renovate our own museum, let's walk through a simple practice to help you experience this directly. If you prefer to engage in this exercise later, just read through it for now to get a sense for its underlying principles.

1. Take a few moments to think of an emotional memory or experience that lives in your mind but you would like to release (e.g., anger toward someone or a fear of

something). Start with a less intense experience (i.e., on a scale of 1 = least to 10 = most intense, start in the 1 to 5 range) to gain comfort with this practice without feeling overtaken by emotions.

At each step of this exercise, feel free to close your eyes and breathe deeply to give yourself space and time to sink into the questions that follow and to allow answers and insights to emerge.

2. Recall the emotional experience and observe what happens in your body as you remember it. Stay relaxed and allow its sensations to flow through you without fear of how they will make you feel. *Where in my body do I feel the emotion? What does it feel like?*

    Just observe what feelings arise without resisting or analyzing them. Simply witness with compassion and ask, *how do my emotions shift as I sit with the experience?* As we learn to be with our emotions this way, we begin to sense how emotions continually shift, change shape, and slowly diminish in intensity or even disappear.

3. You can tap into 2D's reason to ask simple, unemotional questions to help you learn from the experience. *What makes me feel this emotion? When did I first feel it? How does that experience reflect my current reality? What is on the other side of my anger or fear?*

    Such questions help us switch from unconsciously repeating and reinforcing an emotion's patterns to gaining new perspectives that slowly transform our relationship to it. For instance, we may recognize how an emotion embodies a past experience that does not reflect our current reality. This helps shift our thoughts from ones such as, *I am so angry* or *I am really scared* to, *I reacted with anger to what happened* or *my fear was trying to protect me.*

This reduces the grip such emotions hold on our mind. At the same time, we guard against 2D's tendency to judge 1D (which we cover in Chapter 4). Instead, we trust 3D to guide us toward insights with compassion.

4. The 3D mind (as we explore in Chapter 5) reveals wisdom to help us evolve and grow. It offers kind, loving words such as, *forgive yourself—we are all human,* or *you reacted as best served you in the moment.* This creates space for deeper reflection and insights such as, *I sense fear or sadness beneath the anger,* or *I sense a longing for love beyond the fear.*

    We can then ask ourselves deeper questions such as, *what lessons does this experience bear? How can its wisdom guide me in the future? What becomes possible when I transcend this emotion?*

This exercise gets at the essence of how to master our 1D mind, which is why it is introduced here. You may want to revisit this practice after reading the next three chapters as you deepen your grasp of how the three states work together in our mind.

VISITING OUR MUSEUM

As we reflect on our emotions, we create space to transform them. We learn to make peace with and release exhibits that no longer serve us. We come to see how 1D's linear and limited ways can turn little stones in our path into what seem like insurmountable mountains. Yet often they are just pebbles that we can learn to kick aside anytime. Such insights often appear in simple ways.

A reader of *Enduring Edge* once shared how understanding her 1D mind changed her relationship with food. She said she realized this when, about fifty pages into the book, she had lost five pounds.

Becoming aware of her 1D tendencies shifted her default eating habits from mindlessly satisfying cravings to mindfully meeting her body's nutritional needs.

In another example, a retired executive once pulled me aside after a talk I had given. He shared how understanding his 1D mind helped him make sense of the depression associated with his recent diagnosis of Parkinson's disease. He realized that the despondent thoughts that had come to occupy his mind were 1D's fear-filled reactions to his changed health status. Yet such thoughts did not define him or his whole reality, a simple realization that brought peace into his heart and lifted his spirits.

At times, when we face a deeply entrenched or painful exhibit, such as a trauma, it can be helpful to have an experienced guide, such as a therapist, counselor, coach, or wise listener accompany us as we go within. Such guides can help us enter dark, hidden spaces, uncover artifacts that rest in basement vaults, or gain new insights on exhibits we have circled for so long that we no longer consciously "see" them.

Regardless of how we tour our museum, eventually we come to see how our struggles with emotions reside mainly in 1D's reactions to them. This is how a fear of change can keep us stuck in a status quo (i.e., a job or relationship) even when it no longer serves us. Or fear of facing the past can ensnare us in it. Fear of the future can lead us to write imaginary scripts about it. Fear of failure or rejection can keep us from taking a chance. Or fear of facing our fears can lead us to be driven by perpetual procrastination or restless avoidance. For instance, we may engage in activities that keep us "busy" but feel meaningless at a deeper level.

As we rush around outside, inside we stay stuck exactly where we don't want to be. Some minds may even conclude that living in a gloomy museum is as good as it gets. Yet, such thoughts sustain because 1D cannot see a deeper truth: We are the only curator of our museum, and all our exhibits are of our own making. As we shine light into dark corners of our museum, we learn to face all our exhibits, even ones that lurk down musty halls or surprise us when we least expect it.

As we witness the mysteries of our deeper being unfold before us, we come to accept, and eventually even appreciate, all emotions as part of the human experience. Instead of avoiding them, we realize each harbors lessons and insights to grow our wisdom and resilience. With time, as we release old exhibits, we come to inhabit a museum we love to stroll through.

We gain a sense of inner freedom that leads us into bright, airy galleries we cherish. We learn to take life in stride. When we stumble across artifacts from old exhibits, we sense how they have lost their power over us. Sometimes, we may even laugh at the truths they reveal. Ultimately, we realize how the power to create the museum of our dreams is entirely in our own hands—and minds.

TRAINING THE 1D MIND

As we befriend our 1D mind, we transform how its instincts guide us. We think before we act or react. When we see a tiger, instead of launching into a jungle brawl, we more easily recognize when it is not real. We realize that, absent a physical foe to fight, 1D's combat mode is a counterproductive exercise in futility.

Though all this sounds simple in theory, remembering—let alone practicing—it in the heat of the moment can feel difficult or even impossible. When intense emotions overtake us, logical arguments or wise words often fall flat.

Even while reading this chapter, 1D may at times want to put down the book, take a break, eat a snack to soothe itself, or give up on reading further. It may even seek to go hide in a place where it feels safe. Or, scared of being alone with its thoughts, it may look for outer distractions to avoid the very solitude that leads us to realize there is nothing to fear.

To release such 1D tendencies when they crop up, we can engage in simple practices to shift our ways of doing, thinking, and being. Like training a muscle, with regular practice, we strengthen our capacity to transcend 1D's defaults when they don't serve us. Here, we cover a few such practices. Most of these are well-known and more details are easily accessible through other books and resources.

DOING

At the action-based level of our body, a powerful way to reverse 1D's reactivity is through the simple act of **deep breathing**. Slow, long, deep abdominal inhales and exhales fill our lungs with oxygen, soothe our nerves, relax our muscles, and slow our heartbeat to revert our physiology from a state of inner war to inner peace. The beauty of this simple practice is that we can do it anytime and anywhere since we are each always breathing already. It doesn't even take up time. A physician once shared how she cultivated a habit of pausing to take three deep breaths each time before she entered an exam room for a patient visit. This made her feel more present and less rushed through long, busy workdays and even helped her get more done in less time.

Another powerful way to counter 1D's stress cascades is through **physical exercise**, such as going for a walk, run, swim, or bike ride. At a physiological level, exercise helps burn off the stress response's battle fuel, such as elevated blood glucose or cortisol. By exercising outdoors in fresh air, we help nourish and oxygenate our lungs. Also, spending time in nature evokes a sense of wholeness and connection that restores us in deeper, holistic ways.

When our body is so depleted or drained that we feel we are literally fighting for survival, such as when we face an intense crisis or a tragedy, a simple way to reduce 1D's reactivity is to ensure our most basic needs—for nutrition, hydration, and sleep—are met. Furthermore, finding brief moments or breaks to practice **deep relaxation** can help us consciously release stress and experience restorative tranquility within. Some practices that evoke this state are yoga nidra, yin yoga, or guided meditations that take our whole body into a state of deep inner calm. Whether we are feeling restless or drained, such practices help restore our energy and foster a sense of wholeness and well-being.

THINKING

At the level of our thoughts, we can calm 1D with simple practices that help us transcend its tendencies to indulge in worry, negative thought spirals, rumination, or imaginary worst-case scenarios. While the above-mentioned practices can help with this, the next three are direct ways to shift how we think.

Visualization is the simple practice of creating vivid, positive mental images that soothe, relax, and uplift us. For example, in facing fear of a "tiger," we can imagine it retreat into a distant prairie or visualize it as a cute, cuddly cub that can do us no harm.

Many guided meditation and guided imagery practices help shift our thoughts from indulging 1D to transcending it. For instance, some studies have shown that guided imagery helps patients experience greater calm before a surgical procedure and better post-surgical recovery.[7] As we envision healing energy flow through and relax our whole body, we can consciously release and reverse the harmful effects of the stress response.

Affirmations are simple statements that help us consciously switch 1D thoughts that don't serve us into more positive and uplifting ones. When facing a fear, we may say, "I am brave" or "I can do this" or "the tiger has no power over me."

A recent study showed that in people who experienced anxiety, "the replacement of worry with different forms of positive ideation, even when unrelated to the content of worry itself, seems to have similar beneficial effects, suggesting that any form of positive ideation can be used to effectively counter worry."[8]

While some positive affirmations can at first feel far-fetched or unrealistic, repeating them to ourselves over time helps quiet 1D in remarkably powerful ways. **Appendix A** includes suggestions for some simple ways in which you can ponder, play with, and practice affirmations to calm and soothe your 1D mind.

Finally, **gratitude** is a way to consciously shift our attention from negativity, pessimism, and gripes to positivity, optimism, and appreciation. We can think, *I am grateful for...* and list all that we treasure in our lives, despite the "tigers" that appear from time to time. Gratitude does not dismiss life's challenges, as 1D may fear. Rather, it helps us release 1D's tendency to feel consumed by its own thoughts. As we practice an attitude of gratitude, we reduce the space we give to any "tigers" to freely roam our mind.

BEING

At the being level, we can release 1D by directing our full attention to the present moment. This gives our body and mind a break from doing and thinking. Even when we face a crisis, we stay focused on what we can control—how we react in the moment. The following three practices are timeless paths to cultivate such inner calm.

Self-compassion is about giving ourselves the same caring love we would extend to a close family member, little child, or dear friend. Instead of responding to 1D's emotions with judgment or harshness (i.e., *you should not feel this way*) we bring patience and kindness to comfort them. We may say, *it is understandable you are nervous. Tigers can be scary. Let's explore how we can befriend this tiger or else how we can bid it farewell.* As we cultivate greater compassion for our own 1D mind, we also bring such a way of being to others' 1D thoughts.

Mindfulness is a conscious practice to bring our whole attention to the present moment. Being mindful helps us direct our thoughts to where we are here and now. We can release 1D's tendency to restlessly hurry and worry and be more peaceful and thoughtful as we move through our days. No matter what we are doing, we bring our full attention to it. While eating, we focus on the taste, smell, touch, look, and feel of our food. While walking, we observe the world around us, such as the leaves on trees, the songs of birds, and the sights and sounds that surround us. While talking to others, we are fully present, without any distractions.

Even while reading this book, you may notice 1D getting restless at times. It may want to get to the "point" or to quickly finish and move on to the next thing. Being mindful reminds us that knowing ourselves is not a task to complete in a rush but a lifelong journey of contemplation.

Finally, **meditation** is a timeless, universal practice that allows us to directly still our body's doing and our mind's thinking to embody a state of pure being. With regular practice, as we release thoughts and emotions, we viscerally experience their departure from our body, mind, and being. Ultimately, we realize that most tigers are not real and simply creations of our mind. We gain a sense of deep inner freedom and serenity as tigers—both outer and inner—lose their power over us.

While the above section provides a brief overview of some practices to train the 1D mind, we will revisit several of them in greater depth as we explore the 2D and 3D minds. **Appendix B** includes a summary chart of all the practices to train the mind described in Chapters 3, 4, and 5. It also provides some self-reflection questions you can use to explore your own three states of mind.

To identify practices that resonate most with you, play with as many as you can. Find ones that can be effortlessly folded into your daily life, ideally as regular habits or rituals, like brushing your teeth. Remarkably, by working on taming any 1D tendency (e.g., boredom snacking, mindless screen scrolling, or an inner trigger), we help discipline other 1D impulses. Over time, as we learn to train 1D, we experience profound ripple effects across all dimensions of our lives.

Before we end this chapter, it is important to acknowledge that sometimes life thrusts us into survival mode beyond what seems humanly bearable. Examples include a patient dealing with serious illness, a caregiver supporting an ailing loved one, a healthcare provider tending to endless streams of patients, a frontline worker upholding overtime shifts, a breadwinner struggling to make ends meet, a refugee fleeing home for a foreign shore, a trauma survivor rebuilding a life, a soldier bearing the weight of war, or a planet battling a pandemic.

Yet, even in the depths of darkness, there is always a light within us. Amidst unbearable sorrow and tragedy, it helps us find calm in chaos, heal through pain, and sustain hope. It lights our path, cradles our heart, and connects us to our shared humanity. Ultimately, it leads us to trust that we can always find our way, whether we are wandering through museums or far beyond them into the great unknown.

CHAPTER 4

The 2D Mind

While tigers mostly prowl earth's tropical jungles and grasslands, our species has settled into nearly every corner of this spinning rock, from Amazon rain forests and Arabian deserts to Arctic shores. In our multitudes—our diverse customs, cultures, and ways of life—we confront both the grandest glory and greatest limitations of the 2D (two-dimensional) mind.

In contrast to 1D's focus on our physical survival, 2D directs its attention to existential matters of a different kind: making sense of the world and establishing our unique sense of self, also known as our identity or ego, in it. Guided by our intellect and its critical reasoning abilities, the 2D mind:

1. studies, analyzes, and logically organizes what it encounters in the world to make sense of it, and
2. strives to define and validate our place in it, as individuals, communities, or nations.

Unlike 1D's rapid, reactive ways, 2D prefers to rely on data and reason to guide our actions and decisions. Like a meticulous museum curator, 2D methodically researches and catalogs artifacts to attain knowledge and establish facts.

The term "two-dimensional" reflects 2D's inclination to explore a terrain in detail. After reading the prior chapter, entering this one may feel like walking into a museum's spacious courtyard, having survived its most crowded and cacophonous exhibit hall. *All is well, sanity has been restored,* 2D thinks to itself as it regains its much-needed sense of order and control.

While we rely on our 1D mind from birth, we tend to cultivate our 2D mind through lifelong learning, such as educational and professional training that imparts specific skills (e.g., reading and critical reasoning) and knowledge (e.g., math and science). If we consider 1D's instincts as "street smarts" to help us survive, we can think of 2D's intelligence as "book smarts" to help us navigate the world.

The 2D mind likes to learn and organize information, make plans, and create systems and processes. It guides us to develop expertise in specific fields, which often serves us well. When we encounter a leaky faucet, broken car, or hurting tooth, we are grateful for skilled plumbers, mechanics, or dentists who can fix such issues.

Guided by 2D's intellect, we have untangled the mysteries of science, attained awe-inspiring feats of engineering, and created technological marvels to transform and save lives. In light of its many talents, it is no wonder that 2D takes—and deserves—credit for much of human progress through time. Yet in this we also face its greatest paradox.

If we think our relationship with 1D's emotions is complex, that with 2D's ego is even more so. If 2D had its way, it would always lead our mind, convinced it is the best mindstate. The 2D mind takes great pride in its unemotional, methodical approaches. It cherishes the sense of control they give it, especially as antidotes to 1D and 3D's seemingly haphazard ways. Yet like 1D, the 2D mind can also not see beyond itself, which is hard for it to swallow, let alone accept.

To explore how 2D's talents can turn into traps, we examine three of its most common tendencies—siloed, binary, and circular thinking. Since 2D likes concrete details and realistic examples, we will explore these thought patterns through one of the most universal challenges we continue to face as diverse tribes across time—that of divided minds, or when we see others as separate and fail to see eye to eye. (In the rest of this book, we explore the 2D mind's tendencies through myriad other contexts.)

Also, just to alert you: just as exploring the 1D mind can be exhausting, reading about 2D may, at times, leave your head spinning. But trust that it gets easier as you learn to transcend its ways.

SILOED THINKING

Our sense of self, or identity, begins to take shape with the name we receive at birth and continues to be defined by elements such as our ethnicity, gender, religion, and culture. Our uniqueness is further refined by our education (e.g., degrees and fields of study), societal status (e.g., access to power, wealth, or fame), profession, relationships, and, ultimately, a legacy that outlives us.

As we strive to stake our own special place in the world, we straddle a delicate line between affirming our uniqueness and creating silos that divide us. The 2D mind falls into this tendency because silos offer it a way to organize the world.

A silo, per its literal definition, is a tall, cylindrical structure used to store grains. These days, the term mostly refers to unique realms of knowledge (e.g., specialized disciplines), expertise (e.g., departments in an organization), or experience (e.g., the cultural heritage of a community).

Here, we expand the definition of a silo to encompass all the ways in which we label ourselves and others. Beyond tangible aspects of our identity, our silos can include our ideologies, beliefs, and stories about ourselves, each other, and our world.

As we move through life, we each encounter countless silos of others' and our own making. Some silos have open doors (e.g., social movements) while others are confined to certain groups (e.g., race-based experiences) or overseen by gatekeepers (e.g., academic tenure). Some silos reflect shared histories (e.g., attending the same college) and others divergent ones (e.g., how our socioeconomic background shapes our college experience).

Today, most large organizations and systems consist of vast mazes of silos that those in them must learn to navigate to survive and rise through them. In a way, this makes perfect sense. How else do we organize the billions of members of our species to get things done? Well-defined structures, ranks, and laws help us maintain a sense of order and control.

Yet, when hierarchies and policies come to rule over us, we can get trapped in siloed thinking. For example, in large organizations, silos can foster bureaucracies that stifle creativity, productivity, and innovation. Siloed thinking can also lead to the creation of exclusive or elitist establishments—such as ones based on race, gender, politics, or religion—that see those who don't "belong" in them as being separate or outsiders. Such divides mark the heart of most struggles for justice, equality, and freedom around the world today.

Thus, while silos offer order, they also constrain human potential. When minds become isolated in silos of their own kind, they can fall into groupthink, a term used to describe a group of minds who all come to think alike. Or, as silos confine us within their walls, they can narrow our perspective and foster blind spots and biases. Ultimately, we lose countless potential ideas and solutions that tend to emerge when diverse minds mingle and learn from each other.

Minds trained in fields built on 2D's talents, such as academic or technical disciplines, can be more prone to siloed thinking since 2D's ways mostly serve them well. Yet in some form, we each harbor silos in our mind.

For instance, when we define ourselves by a story we accept as our reality, we wall ourselves into its silo. When such a story gets woven into our identity, we may even fiercely defend it, blind to how it potentially limits us. We may assume that a story's labels define who we are and fear treading beyond its bounds. At times, we may live by such a story for a long time—even a lifetime.

Hence, the silos so masterfully crafted by our 2D mind can become among our greatest barriers to living our best life. Yet, guided by our 3D mind, we can see how all silos are ultimately just

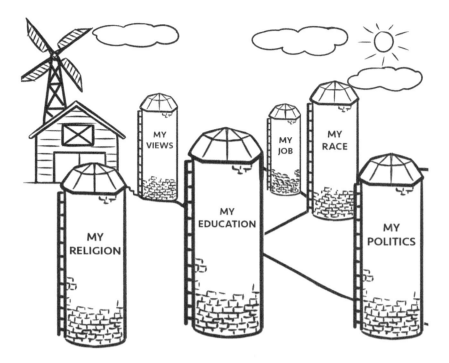

small structures built in our heads. Although they may feel real when we sit inside them and stare at their walls, as we rise above them, like a helicopter that ascends into the sky, we see how they are simply creations of another 2D tendency: binary thinking.

BINARY THINKING

Just as 1D's impulses are inherent to its nature, 2D's thought patterns are not its "fault" and simply its default ways. This notion itself is a leap of mind for 2D, since it is quick to judge everything, even itself. To decode this, let's look at 2D's tendency for binary thinking, also referred to as black and white thinking, an all-or-nothing mentality, or seeing the world in duality.

The 2D mind engages in binary thinking for one simple reason: to establish our unique identity, it needs an "other" against whom to compare and contrast us. Yet this boxes us into its labels, judgments, and definitions. Binary thinking may be the 2D mind's most common yet least recognized trap because it tends to hide in plain sight.

In its attempts to define and protect our uniqueness, 2D is quick to see differences or to defend who it thinks we are. Yet, limited to what it can concretely analyze, 2D focuses on tangible factors such as appearances, gender, or ethnicity.

Further, in its attempts to feel special or unique, 2D can slip into feeling superior, judging those unlike it as inferior (and vice versa). This can magnify differences and feed 2D's tendency to stereotype or judge others based on its own stories.

The 2D mind easily reduces nuanced layers to binary labels such as better or worse, good versus bad, or us versus them. Yet as 2D confidently defines the world around it, we confront an inherent paradox. For, while we are quick to judge others, we do not like to be judged ourselves, knowing we harbor deep, invisible, layered, and often contradictory multitudes.

In the extreme, binary thinking can foster prejudice, intolerance, or polarization, whether in a community, family, or heart. For instance, 2D can lead a mind to isolate itself in a silo of its own making, driven by either pride or shame, two sides of the same coin: the ego's focus on itself. This can fuel separation, estrangement, or the loss of a sense of having a tribe—whether in raising the young, healing the ailing, or caring for the aging—leaving everyone with a shared sense of being on their own.

As we become aware of 2D's binary thinking tendency, we start to see it all around us. When a family or community gets entrenched in binary thinking, it can become like a house divided against itself, in which both sides suffer from losing a sense of unity and belonging. When an organization or nation is driven by binary thinking, divisive tendencies lead everyone to experience higher stress and reduced well-being.

In such dynamics, while each "side" of a divide may be convinced it is right, both forget that feeling united is not built on being "correct" but on understanding the other side. Although 2D may judge minds that don't think like it as inferior, ignorant, or ill-informed, 3D reminds us that the bridge to unity is paved with humility and compassion. Guided by 3D, we value our collective welfare above our own interests and positions. We bring an open

Binary Thinking

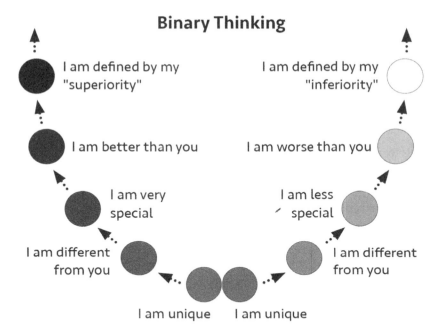

mind to truly listen to each other. We humbly acknowledge that we all harbor biases and prejudices, just on different matters.

Ultimately, we come to accept that there is more to being human than 2D can know. Its logical explanations and labels cannot tell our whole story, whether as individuals or as nations. We come to see that what often limits our perspective is another 2D tendency: circular thinking.

CIRCULAR THINKING

Driven by its analytical talents, the 2D mind loves to think. It likes to collect and dissect data, link what it finds to its archives, compare and contrast, weigh pros and cons, and curate and define preferences. While such methods often help us make better decisions than following 1D's impulses, when we stretch this talent too thin, we can fall into its trap of circular thinking.

For instance, in many contexts, data are unattainable, imperfect, or meaningless. When we want to be innovative and creative to imagine a new reality, we cannot build precise predictive models to guide us. When we limit ourselves to what we already know, we end up with marginal solutions that miss possibilities beyond the limits of our knowledge.

When we evaluate a person (e.g., as a potential job candidate), 2D tends to focus on what it can see and analyze, such as their resume and concrete skills. This can lead us to miss invisible aspects of who they are, such as their deeper intentions, guiding values, and character virtues, all of which play vital roles in how they will perform on the job.

As 2D faces its analytical limits, not knowing what else to do, it enters circular thinking, which is like spinning in circles, as if we are running on a hamster wheel, chasing our own tail, or generating spirals in our head. This usually plays out in predictable ways.

Instead of admitting it is confused or doesn't know the answer, 2D seeks control by digging deeper into its ways. For instance, it may search for clarity in the outer world by asking others what they would do in its place. Or, scared of making the "wrong" decision, 2D may seek ever more data, research, or studies. This can lead us into analysis paralysis or down slippery slopes of sophisticated yet futile reasoning.

Often, 2D is quick to rationalize. Once 2D makes up its mind, it may create compelling arguments to justify its decisions. Or, it may selectively search for "objective" data that validate its positions, a tendency also known as the confirmation bias.

Sometimes, 2D may even rationalize 1D's impulses by saying, *I didn't have a choice—I behaved that way because of another person's behavior,* or *I didn't want to be judged—I did that to protect my image,* while neglecting deeper 3D wisdom that could have led to other outcomes.

At other times, 2D may link what it encounters to its stored knowledge archives. For example, it may say, *this person I've just met is exactly like my old boss, former partner,* or *in-law.* Yet the "person" has likely never met the boss, partner, or in-law, and the only place where the two co-exist is in the mind that has brought them together. This is like constructing an entire museum exhibit with a few artifacts to craft a story about someone that makes

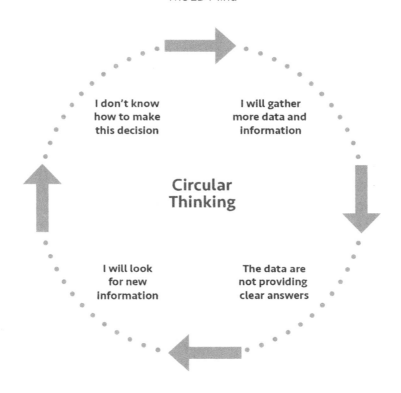

perfect sense to its curator but may ring utterly false or foreign to the one it is about.

By now, as 2D begins to question its own ways, it may start to analyze why it is the way it is, and why it overanalyzes, analyzing its way into a paralyzing state, without taking a pause to see where it is going. The path to escape these tendencies is always there, just not where 2D goes looking.

TRAINING THE 2D MIND

As we default to the 2D mind, we are inclined to think about everything we encounter. When this tendency doesn't serve us, we can learn to recognize when 2D gets in our way.

At first, this can be tricky to spot given the double-edged nature of 2D's talents. Further, 2D is quick to discount 1D's fickle and emotional and 3D's free flowing and intuitive ways, viewing both as inferior to its own. To complicate matters, 2D prefers to be in denial about its limits, both because it truly struggles to see them, and because admitting its limitations feels like a threat to 2D's self-constructed sense of self. Finally, 2D would much rather extensively analyze others' minds and behaviors (e.g., *how can they be so judgmental?*) than to take a brutally honest look at itself (e.g., *when do I become judgmental?*)

Just as observing 1D's effects on our body helps us train our 1D mind, noticing 2D's tendencies in our thought patterns helps us master our 2D mind. Instead of getting caught up in their content, we simply notice their underlying patterns, such as when we get trapped in siloed, binary, or circular thinking. The practices mentioned in the prior chapter can help quiet 2D's inner chatter. Here are a few more potential practices to train 2D directly.

DOING

At the physical level, when we notice an unproductive thinking pattern, we can engage in an activity that helps us consciously shift out of the 2D state. An executive once shared how he would go for a daily lunchtime swim to give his mind a break during busy workdays. While swimming, he often gained insights on how to solve challenges at work.

Others have described how going for a walk in fresh air, or engaging in a hobby, such as playing an instrument, helps shift their mind when they notice futile 2D thought patterns appear. Many creative minds through time, such as writers, composers, and scientists, have credited such daily rituals, such as long, solitary walks in nature, with nurturing their creativity and insights.

For instance, Albert Einstein often solved complex physics challenges while playing the violin. As his son once described, "Whenever he felt that he had come to the end of the road or into a difficult situation in his work, he would take refuge in music. That would usually resolve all his difficulties."[9] Einstein himself also often described how the flow of music guided him to epiphanies on theorems that had stumped him when he actively thought about them.

THINKING

At the thinking level, when we realize a train of thoughts is taking us nowhere, we can proactively shift our perspective. A simple yet powerful way is through deep, open **curiosity** that is free of 2D's judgments and biases. By being sincerely curious to learn, we encourage our mind to see what is before us in a new light, untainted by our preconceived notions.

The intention of such curiosity is not to satisfy 2D's inquiries but to access 3D's insights. Whether in talking to someone with radically different views, or in solving a challenge in our lives, we ask open-ended, non-judgmental questions to expand our understanding. When we notice 2D's labels or judgments crop up, we remind ourselves that they neglect not just shades of gray but all other colors in the palette.

Guided by such curiosity, we can shatter silos, remove binary labels, and transcend analysis paralysis. We come to see the limitations of thoughts such as: *How dare she say that? He is so irrational.* Or, *these are our only options.* Instead, guided by deeper curiosity, we can ask: *I wonder what made her say that? I am curious, what motivated his behavior?* Or, *how can we expand our options?* In this way, we train our 2D mind to accept contradictions and ambiguity in ways that broaden and expand our view.

BEING

At the being level, to transcend 2D's ways, we can engage in practices that help us consciously enter the 3D mind, as we explore in detail in the next chapter. A guiding principle for such practices is **humility**, which helps us transcend 2D's focus on our sense of self or ego.

In essence, we remember not to take ourselves so seriously. This releases us from the ego's focus on itself. Else, when 2D rules over our mind, it tends to keep us on ever-shaky ground. Since 2D derives its sense of validation from external factors, it gets swiftly swayed by outer approval or critique. One moment, 2D asserts our superiority: *I am so smart. I know best.* The next, it slides into inferiority: *I am so dumb. I am not good enough.* This leads it to swing on a perpetual pendulum between feeling invincible and perfect or feeling irretrievably broken and worthless. All the while, 2D makes us believe that our ego, whether grounded in pride or shame, decides who we are. Then, when 2D comes across a potential threat to its sense of self, it becomes easily defensive.

Even in reading this, 2D may question the authority or challenge the audacity of words that point out its limits. It may say, *I don't have these issues. I am not egotistical (though I can think of others who are). I don't brag (or even humble brag) to seek others' validation.* It may even assert, *I don't see any issues with my mind. Why should I change who I am? I don't want to lose myself.*

As 2D fails to see the irony in its words, it sinks further into its ways. Sometimes, it may even isolate itself in silos built on stories that help it feel in control. Yet, when we define our life by 2D's notions of who we are, we often miss deeper truths.

For instance, in facing a challenging situation, 2D may point fingers or shift blame while denying its own role. It may say, *you made me angry; that's not my fault.* Or, in attempts to cover its self-identified "flaws," 2D may project a facade of outer perfection, oblivious to how the only one it fools is itself.

When we let our 2D mind define us, no matter how diligently we strive to satisfy its needs, we still often sense an inner void. We may feel as if something is missing, such as a deeper sense of contentment or calm.

Led by our 3D mind, we can bring humility to let go of our ego's endless needs. We come to see how 2D's yearning for significance bears an inherent paradox. We realize that pleasing our ego, like satisfying 1D's impulses, is an endless game and not one our heart longs to play.

Guided by deeper wisdom, we recognize how, so often, there is no clear right and wrong or better and worse. Ultimately, we realize that, no matter how lofty or well-defined, all our silos—in the world and in our minds—are simply creations of our 2D mind.

We humbly accept that, while 2D has many talents, it does not have all our answers. This shifts how we view ourselves, each other, and our world. We realize that no one part—whether in our self, family, community, or planet—can thrive in isolation without being in harmony with the whole. Ultimately, we come to realize that who we are is much greater than who 2D thinks we are.

❉   ❉   ❉

A few years ago, after a talk I gave on *Enduring Edge* at a law firm, a young man sitting in the back raised his hand to pose what is one of the most commonly asked questions on the book. "So, what is the ideal ratio that we should strive for in using the three states of mind?"

My response, which tends to elicit chuckles of familiarity, is always the same: "That is a perfect 2D question."

Eager to be flawlessly optimized, 2D easily misses the point. (It may still be scratching its head about what was wrong with its question!)

As may be apparent by now, the concept of the three mindstates is itself a 2D construct that labels three distinct states, each with unique talents and traps. This way to describe the mind made most sense since we tend to rely on our 2D mind to study and understand our world. But it is vital to keep 2D's limits in mind.

For instance, 2D will tend to dissect the three mindstates in great detail and compare them to each other or other frameworks with which it is familiar. Further, when 2D encounters statements that appear confusing, it may rush to conclusions on what they mean based on what it knows.

To transcend such tendencies, instead of thinking of the three states as precise, prescriptive concepts, consider them guiding principles to help deepen your understanding of your mind. And instead of honing in on the precision of words, focus on their deeper meaning.

By holding these ideas lightly this way, we can transcend 2D's "by the book" nature, which tends to focus on literal definitions. Instead, we let 3D guide us to grasp the deeper meaning or "spirit" behind words. Ultimately, as we come to know our 2D mind, we realize how, in using it, often less is more.

When we release what we think we know, such as norms that say, *this is how it has always been, this is how it should be,* or *this is how things work,* we are able to discover what else may be possible.

All this is disconcerting to 2D. When a path is uncharted or unclear, 2D searches for clarity and control. Yet there are no set manuals for how to raise a child, motivate a student, retain an employee, or live your best life. There are no boxes that, once checked, guarantee lifelong happiness. There is no set amount of money, power, or fame that signifies lasting success.

While precise instructions or outcomes may make 2D comfortable, they also confine us to its ways. Although learning "Ten Tips for Finding Your Purpose" or studying "Five Steps to Happiness" may satisfy our 2D mind, neither our sense of meaning nor deeper contentment emerge from meticulously following tips or steps.

Ultimately, we realize that what we seek in our hearts rests not in a world that 1D and 2D can see, but in a way of being that only 3D knows. For, its wisdom leads us to discover beauty in what 2D deems imperfect. Beyond that, 3D guides us to see how the very essence of beauty rests in life's imperfections in a perfectly beautiful way.

CHAPTER 5

The 3D Mind

Within each of us, beyond the commotion of emotions and the chatter of thoughts, another dimension speaks to us in quieter ways. We hear it in whispers that nudge us to follow a calling or explore a new path. We experience it through epiphanies that seem to appear out of nowhere to transform our perspective. It infuses an artist's creativity, a pioneer's passion, an inventor's hunches, and a poet's soul-stirring song. It embodies what we mean when we say we feel something in our bones, know it in the depths of our being, or sense it in our hearts.

This is the 3D (three-dimensional) mindstate, which is the source of our inner wisdom, intuition, and insights that guide us toward our truths. While 1D strives to keep us safe in the world, and 2D establishes our place in it, 3D reflects our deeper connection to everything around us.

For even after 1D has satisfied our needs and 2D has validated our existence, we sustain a longing that only 3D understands—for love and belonging in our hearts, for meaning and purpose in our lives, and for peace and contentment in a turbulent world.

The term "three-dimensional" reflects this state's sense of limitless expansiveness across space and time. Returning to the metaphor of visiting a city, while we can drive (1D) and walk

(2D) through it to learn more about the city, when we soar above it (3D), we see the big picture and gain whole new vista views.

Here is another metaphor to think about this. If 1D is like a cube of ice, solid and confined, then 2D is like water, free to flow across a surface, and 3D is like steam that expands in all directions. In the 3D state, we experience:

1. deep presence in the moment that connects us to a sense of universality as reflected by our shared humanity, as well as, a sense of unity with all in the universe,
2. inner wisdom and truths that harbor our sense of meaning, purpose, and values, and
3. creativity, intuition, and insights that light our path and guide our way with inner harmony and resonance.

When the Prince we met in the Prologue absorbed the Sage's wisdom, he sensed deep serenity ascend in his heart. While prior teachers had tried to change the Prince's mood with persuasive arguments (2D), they failed to grasp his deeper turmoil (1D). The Sage, in contrast, asked intuitive, compassionate questions (3D) that guided the Prince into his own heart. There, the Prince found deeper truths that grew his inner peace and understanding.

While sages through time have described the 3D state in myriad ways, like the Prince, we come to know it best through direct experience. Then, all definitions and explanations become superfluous.

Most of us sense being in the 3D state in what seem like mysterious and random ways we struggle to articulate. We feel a joyful aliveness that inspires us. We hear an inner voice that guides us. Artists speak of it as being in a state of flow, writers as inspiration from a muse, inventors as eureka moments, and athletes as being in the zone. Even scientists, though their instruments cannot measure it, attribute many of their greatest breakthroughs to it.

We may experience the 3D state as a sense of deep connection or oneness that echoes our shared humanity. We may express it as kindness toward a stranger, compassion for the suffering of fellow beings, selfless acts that serve a higher purpose, or a deep sense of caring for the welfare of all.

Guided by our 3D mind, we see our life in relation to all other beings as part of an interdependent whole in which we each play a role. We recognize how we all share the same basic needs—for safety, security, and belonging—and seek the same ultimate truths—connection, contentment, and love.

Some describe being in the 3D state as experiencing the limitless consciousness of the universe. Others ascribe it to a mystical, magical, or holy realm—a form of the divine—that flows through all (but cannot be claimed by any one) of the world's spiritual traditions and religions. Some give it form as faith in a higher power, whether they name it Nature or God, or in a way of being that holds and unfolds the secrets of the universe. Still others see it as a dimension that transcends the three dimensions of space and the fourth one of time.

Masters on the mind through time have described the 3D state as sensing the essence of life, whether we call it our spirit, soul, or inner being. Experiencing this state is the ultimate intention of deeper contemplation and meditation. Ultimately, regardless of which of these descriptions resonate with us, and whether we accept them or not, they all lead us to the same place within.

As 1D and 2D follow along in this chapter, they may feel baffled or confused. The 1D mind may wonder, *if I can't see, hear, taste, smell, or touch 3D, how do I know it's real?* The 2D mind may label 3D as woo-woo, hokey, or new age. It may state, *if I can't study and validate it, why should I accept 3D exists?*

Here is how 3D might respond: These questions are like asking, how do we know we love those we love? We can engage in acts that show our love, or describe the depths of our love, yet both our actions and words fall short of fully encompassing a much deeper sensation. But we don't doubt or deny our love just because we cannot concretely prove its existence. We just trust the certainty and clarity we carry in our heart. Thus, no matter how 1D feels about it, or how 2D thinks about it, 3D reflects the deepest essence of our being.

The Relaxation Response

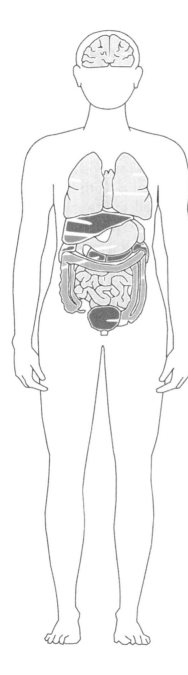

Mind becomes peaceful
and still as thoughts quiet

State of complete presence
in the present moment

Muscles and nerves relax
and release tension

Breathing becomes steady
and calm, heart rate slows

Biochemistry of the stress
response is reversed

Blood vessels relax and
blood pressure lowers

Deeply restorative state that
fosters a sense of well-being

Although 1D and 2D can both not see beyond themselves, 3D can grasp all three states and their dynamic interplay. It is the very source of the deeper courage and compassion that help us befriend and train our 1D and 2D minds. It knows that each mindstate plays a vital role and that no one state is better or worse than the other two.

As we learn to bring the best of all three states to whatever we face, 3D leads us to a united mind. Guided by 3D's wisdom and insights, we learn to reduce the grip of 1D's emotions and 2D's ego on our mind. We come to see how one of our worst fears is the fickle nature of our emotional reactions, and one of our greatest foes is the ego's tendency to seek control.

While being in the 3D state can appear mysterious or fleeting, we can each learn to access it anytime. With practice, we come to trust 3D to guide our ways of being, thinking, and doing. To decode this, let's first explore what *being* means.

THE RELAXATION RESPONSE

While the 1D mind is the seat of the stress response, the 3D mind harbors its opposite, also known as the relaxation response. In this state, our breathing becomes steady, deep, and calm. Our heart rate slows, and our muscles and blood vessels relax. The relaxation response soothes our nerves and lets all systems know that they can be at ease. In this way, it reverses the effects of the stress response and leads us to experience a state of pure being.

Since dwelling in 1D without rest drains our body, and over-using 2D without a break exhausts our mind, being in 3D gives us a chance to recover from both. Without the need to watch out for potential threats, or to analyze thoughts running through our head, we can be fully present in the moment.

We may refer to such ways of relaxing as "letting off steam" (discharging stress built up by 1D and 2D), "unwinding" (from the tight coils into which they can twist us), or "re-centering" ourselves (in the 3D state). We experience an inner harmony, balance, or wholeness that some describe as coming home to ourselves. This is a deeply healing and restorative state.

In the 3D state, we lose track of time and place and our sense of self. This creates space in our mind for wisdom and insights to dawn. We feel more content and at peace and sense an inner clarity and calm that is unconditional, no matter what else is going on around us.

Several stories from readers reveal the power of this. A lawyer once shared how, after learning about the three states, she started giving credit to her 3D mind for the first time in her life. Since the legal field is driven by 2D thinking, she tended to dismiss the power of her intuition, not knowing how to judge its value and contributions. Yet, upon reflection, she recognized how her 3D mind's wisdom and insights actually played an invaluable role in guiding her decisions and her relationships with clients and colleagues.

A physician once shared how she had practiced meditation for years but still sometimes found herself going through her mental "to-do" list or other tasks while thinking to herself, *well, at least I am sitting in meditation right now*. She said that reframing meditation as a path into the 3D state transformed her perspective—and her practice. She could quiet her thoughts more easily, which helped her feel more centered throughout the day.

Finally, a research scientist once shared how learning about the 3D state inspired him to dust off his long-neglected trumpet. As a graduate student, he had often played the instrument to relax. Now, he realized how playing his trumpet could help him not just unwind at the end of long days but also become more creative in the lab.

By now, 1D and 2D may be wondering, *all this sounds nice (almost too perfect, if 2D might add), but how exactly does playing a trumpet unleash creativity?* So, let's address that head on.

TRAINING THE 3D MIND

In our day-to-day lives, our experiences of being in the 3D mind can appear so fleeting they seem surreal or even unreal. Yet just the opposite is true. If we think of 1D's emotions and 2D's thoughts as clouds passing through the sky, 3D is like the sun. Although clouds appear to make the sun disappear, even amidst dark, raging storms, it is always there. If you wake up one rainy morning and think, *it's so gloomy outside,* such a thought does not mean you will have a dreary day, as 1D may fear, or that you have a negative attitude, as 2D may label your mood. The thought is just passing through your mind and defines neither your whole reality, as 1D believes, nor who you are, as 2D concludes.

Unlike the patterns in the skies, we can change the "weather" in our mind anytime, as 3D knows. Upon reading this statement, 1D may reject or resist it and 2D may try to disprove it with data from its archives. Yet, while 1D and 2D are correct to point out a dark sky, its shadow on our mind is of our own making.

Here is a simple thought experiment to explore this. Read through the three statements below and pick the one you think is most true:

1. I have no or little power or control over my mood.
2. I sometimes have some power or control over my mood.
3. I have substantial to total power or control over my mood.

The statement we choose reflects the "weather" in our mind. If we believe the first two statements, our mind gets easily overcast by 1D or 2D clouds. If we believe the third statement, we trust 3D is always there. No matter what is going on outside, we focus on the sun despite the clouds.

This concept can be hard for 1D and 2D to accept, especially if they have lived in exhibits (1D) or silos (2D) built by the first two statements for a long time. Learning to trust 3D when 1D cannot see it and 2D cannot validate it is deeply counterintuitive to both.

Curiously, while 3D can appear vague or mysterious to adults, it is naturally intuitive to children who are effortlessly carefree, playful, and creative. As children, we look at the world with a sense of awe and wonder, unclouded by beliefs on what is realistic or how things should be. As we grow into adults, we learn to abide by societal norms and rules that can sometimes make us feel as if our 3D mind gets 2D'd out of us. Thus, mastering the 3D state is not about learning new ways of being but about unlearning acquired 1D and 2D ways that cloud 3D's wisdom and truths. This is so vital it bears repeating. Instead of focusing on how to get into our 3D mind, we direct our attention to getting out of our 1D *and* 2D minds, which, by default, leads us into the 3D state. Once the clouds disappear, the sun shines clear.

How you can best learn to bring more sunshine into your life, is yours to discover by exploring different paths. Just like training our 1D and 2D minds, we each have our own best ways into the 3D state. There is no way that is fastest or most efficient, as 1D may desire, and none that is superior or more proven, as 2D may want to believe. The same activity, such as writing, gardening, or playing the trumpet, can bring deep joy and peace to one person and feel like a laborious or frustrating chore to another.

The practices covered in the prior two chapters can help us learn to quiet 1D and 2D so we can experience the 3D state. Deep breathing, physical exercise, and deep relaxation help us release the stress response and enter the relaxation response. Visualization, affirmations, and gratitude shift our attention away from the clouds. Self-compassion reminds us that the sun is always there. Mindfulness and meditation quiet 1D and 2D so we can experience 3D. We can also think of 3D as the curator in our museum who helps us renovate and dismantle old exhibits. It is also the source of our curiosity and humility to help us rise above 2D's siloed, binary, and circular thinking.

3D PRACTICES

As you explore different paths that easily lead you into the 3D state, as with training 1D and 2D, it is helpful to have several tools in your toolbox. Sometimes, the same activity, such as cooking, can relax us one day but tire us the next, based on what else is going on. When you feel restless, try a practice that relaxes you (e.g., meditation). When you feel tired, tap into one that energizes you (e.g., walking). Practices that easily lead us into the 3D state tend to share some basic principles, which are helpful to keep in mind:

First, a 3D practice allows us to release the stress response *and* **evoke the relaxation response**. Some activities can release 1D or 2D without creating space for 3D. For example, sleeping or napping helps us rest and relax, especially when we are exhausted, but these activities are not paths into a conscious 3D state.

Taking a warm shower or bath can help us both relax and be in the 3D mind (assuming we stay awake). Deep breathing, mindfulness, and meditation are 3D practices. Consuming alcohol or mind-altering substances to "release" our mind are not. Although such chemicals appear to temporarily soothe or numb 1D's stress and 2D's thoughts, they do not train us to consciously access the 3D state.

Here, if your 2D mind disagrees with the above sentence, it may try to convince you otherwise. Yet, while it may fool our mind, it cannot fool our deeper self. The secret to mastering our mind rests in the inner freedom we gain when we realize we are not at its fickle mercy. When such empowerment hinges on an external substance or stimulus to get us there, we may come to rely on it or fear its absence, which paradoxically disempowers us with dependency.

Second, a 3D practice allows our mind to **suspend thinking** so we can be fully present in the moment. When we learn a new skill, such as playing a musical instrument, we need to engage our 2D mind. Once we know how to play it, we can effortlessly get immersed in its music to enter the 3D state.

Activities such as walking or biking on a nature trail, or in a safe, tranquil space, can take us into the 3D mind. We can take in the fresh air, be present to what is around us, and sense calm enter our being. When we engage in the same activities while using a mobile device or on a congested city street, we cannot so easily release 1D and 2D since we need them to navigate.

Third, a 3D practice is **easily accessible** so we can train our mind to access the 3D state anytime. Such practices need not take up much time. For instance, they can be moments we design into our day, such as closing our eyes for a few minutes to take some deep breaths and re-center our attention. Or they can be creative activities or hobbies we enjoy so much that we decide to engage in them regularly with the intention of being in the 3D state. The more we engage in 3D practices, the more easily we learn to embody the 3D state as our natural way of being.

Finally, 3D practices are often best **practiced in solitude**. This gives us space for contemplation and reflection so we can hear our inner voice. Sometimes, uplifting music in the background can be a wonderful companion. But if our attention tends to focus on lyrics, those can become distractions.

When we engage in a 3D practice with another being, we may more easily slip into 1D or 2D when engaged in conversation. The exception is when we interact with the mutual intention of going inward, as happens in deeply resonant conversations from the heart in which both beings feel transformed.

Now, you may wonder, how do you know which 3D practices are best for you? One way to discover them is to reflect on moments in your life when you engaged in activities that naturally took you

TABLE 2: SOME 3D PRACTICES	
Meditation	Listening to relaxing music
Yoga	Playing an instrument
Taking a pause to breathe	Composing music
Writing, journaling	Singing
Reading poetry	Gardening
Being in nature	Knitting
Watching a sunrise, sunset	Creating arts or crafts
Stargazing	Drawing, painting, coloring
Hiking through woods	Designing, making jewelry
Biking on trails	Photography
Going for walks	Creating scrapbooks
Spending time at the beach	Woodworking
Sailing, boating, kayaking	Home projects
Swimming, floating	Organizing
Golfing	Cooking or baking
Spending time with pets	Sitting still in contemplation
Grooming a horse	Practicing deep relaxation
Birdwatching	Taking a warm bath or shower

into a 3D state, when you sensed a state of pure being, felt deep joy and peace, or lost track of time and even yourself.

Try to come up with activities that you can weave into your daily life and practice regularly. In case inspiration might help, **Table 2** includes some practices shared by readers through the years. Do keep in mind that each of these can be "practiced" in a 1D, 2D, or 3D state of mind. As you cultivate your own practices, look for ones that feel joyful and effortlessly take you into the 3D state.

Ultimately, all our practices are paths to a destination that does not depend on them. The more we embody the 3D state, the more we learn to let it guide our way of being. This calms our emotions, brings clarity to our thoughts, and frees up immense mind space. As such a way of being guides our thinking and doing, we unlock the power of a united mind.

A UNITED MIND

By this point, 1D may be losing its patience, and 2D may be biting its tongue as both are itching to ask: *It's nice 3D has all these talents but what about its traps? Is it (gasp!) perfect? What happens to us when 3D is in charge?* The 1D mind may fear for its existence and the 2D mind may feel threatened and seek to reaffirm its importance.

What both need to grasp, which can be hard for them to accept, is that 3D has no inherent traits that can entrap us. Yet, to unlock our mind's potential, we need all three states.

This is a vital point. No one state can attain alone what all three can together, when they unite in harmony. To explore this, we briefly look at what happens in our mind when any one state goes missing.

NO 1D DOING

Our mind can have incredibly creative ideas (3D), and even build detailed plans around them (2D), but until we act to make our ideas real (1D), they remain figments of our imagination. When we neglect 1D's doing, we may spend our days lost in thoughts—

dreaming up new ideas, perfecting plans, or waiting for inspiration to strike—while forgetting to get up and act. Thus, 1D's doing state is vital to help us take action to realize the potential of 3D's ideas and 2D's plans.

NO 2D THINKING

When we face a complex challenge or difficult decision, 3D's big picture perspectives, wisdom, and insights can be invaluable. Yet, 2D's talents are also vital to help us gather data and gain knowledge to inform what we do. Else we may take action driven by blind faith in 1D's impulsive instincts or 3D's intuition, without the benefit of 2D's intellect and reason.

While many experienced professionals, such as police officers, social workers, or surgeons, talk about developing a sixth sense or intuition to guide their work, they gain expertise first, driven by 2D's talents.

NO 3D BEING

Although doing helps us get things done, and thinking helps us know how, it is our state of being that guides why we do what we do and what we ultimately want. In the hurried pace of modern life, marked by constant doing and thinking, we can easily come to neglect 3D's being, viewing it as less vital to surviving day-to-day.

Yet 3D reminds us why all our doing and thinking matters in the first place. Without clarity on our sense of meaning, purpose, and values, much of our doing and thinking can eventually end up feeling meaningless as we sense a deeper void.

❉   ❉   ❉

After learning about the three states of mind, readers often respond with a common question: *This sounds great. I want to be more 3D. Who wouldn't? But how can I be 3D in what feels like a 1D/2D world, filled with crises and complexity?*

You will likely now recognize that such a question is asked by 1D and 2D as they look at the world through their own frames of reference. Yet, while 1D gets easily stressed, and 2D seeks control,

3D reminds us that how we perceive the world depends on our state of mind.

When we face a challenge, 1D may call it a crisis that defines our whole reality and then conclude we live in a world filled with chaos. But 3D can see how 1D's thoughts and emotions are like clouds that hide the very sun over whose loss 1D worries.

The 2D mind can be more rational to help us see beyond the challenge of the moment. Yet 2D gets easily wrapped up in complexity, driven by siloed, binary, and circular thinking, which create their own inner confusion. Then, 3D can gently guide us to look up and remind us of the essence of life's deeper simplicity.

In this way, 3D leads us to answers to life's restlessness and confusion. It looks at the world with a sense of lightness and intuitive delight, as if in on a cosmic joke on how silly 1D and 2D are in taking themselves so seriously. Thus, 3D leads us to a way of being that is grounded in a wholeness beyond what 1D and 2D can perceive.

As 3D's light enters our being, it transforms how we know ourselves, interact with each other, and view the world. While 1D tries to protect us from danger, and 2D defines its details, 3D transcends all this. With a single kind act, caring gesture, or humorous insight, it unites us in laughter and love, returning us to what we share. Thus, 3D finds beauty, joy, and peace in the same world that 1D and 2D may see as riddled with crises and confusion.

We reflect rather than react. We meet others, no matter how different from us, with harmony in our hearts and seek to understand them from their perspective. We see each life as deserving of equal dignity and respect and trust that we are all doing our best based on what we know.

We consider the holistic, long-term, big picture impact of our actions. We keep humanity at the center of what we think, say, and do, and live by intentions that serve our shared well-being. When challenges arise, we face them with courage and resilience. When complexity confounds us, we trust our heart's wisdom to guide us. Above all, at each step, we step into the power and freedom that rests in staying true to our deepest selves.

❖   ❖   ❖

As we conclude this chapter, I will leave you with one of the most beautiful lessons I stumbled upon during these explorations. Over the years, I met many well-known minds who widely shared their journeys and how others could follow in their footsteps.

Yet, across fields, I also observed that the wisest teachers often toiled in relative obscurity, humbly focused on the purest intention of their work, undistracted by the glow of spotlights or the din of sound bites.

They did not follow in anyone else's footsteps, yet all walked the same path—into their own hearts. They lived with an unshakable confidence that rested not in who they were in the world but in who they knew they were within. In this way, they attained a way of being that made them who they became.

As teachers, they generously shared knowledge from the heart. They did not prescribe preset paths as the best (or only) way to journey within. They taught by living their teachings and sharing the essence of their experiences. Though they lived varied lives, they had all arrived at the same truths—ones we each carry within yet forget in the hurry and worry of getting through busy days.

They trusted in the power within each of us to arrive at our heart's truths in our own way. Like the wisdom the Sage shared with the Prince, they simply inspired others to light the candle of such wisdom in their own being. They had each realized, in their depths, how life is not about the candle, or even its wax, color, shape, or scent, which all melt and burn away. Life lives in the flame.

CHAPTER 6

Uno, Duo, Trio

Our mind becomes our best friend in life's journey when the three mindstates align in harmony. By working together as a united team, they can lead us from where we are to where we want to be.

One way we can explore their dynamic interplay is to think of the three states of mind as three friends who go on a trip together. This idea was inspired by a talk I gave at a high school one winter evening. While explaining the three states of mind to students and their parents, I began to impersonate 1D, 2D, and 3D, as if they were engaged in a conversation. Afterwards, several in the audience said that they found this example helpful in understanding their mind, which eventually led to this chapter.

Our three friends' names are Uno (1D), Duo (2D), and Trio (3D). In the following story, we join them on a weekend road trip. While all three are always in the car, only one can be in the driver's seat, as is also true with the three mindstates. The one in charge decides how we "drive" wherever we go.

We each let some mindstates drive more than others. Some default to 1D (e.g., rushing to action), others to 2D (e.g., conducting detailed analyses), and still others to 3D (e.g., trusting their intuition). To ensure the best driver is at the wheel in each moment, we can use a simple tool, AAA, which stands for Awareness, Acumen, and Agility:

1. Awareness is about observing which mindstate we **Are** using in this moment (i.e., **A**).

2. Acumen is about assessing whether that state is best for this moment's context, or else, in which state we want to **Be** (i.e., **B**).

3. Agility is about switching from **A** to **B**, so we can be in the state that is best from moment to moment.

Table 3 at the end of this chapter, provides a summary of AAA and can serve as a reference guide as you journey on. At first, using AAA may feel awkward, like learning to drive a car. With practice, like any habit, it becomes second nature and a natural part of our way of being. We learn each state's tendencies and how the three can best work together. To see how this plays out, let's begin our road trip.

One late summer day, Uno, Duo, and Trio decide to go on a weekend camping road trip to enjoy the scenic beauty of the Blue Ridge mountains in Virginia. On the morning of their trip, Uno excitedly rushes around, eager to get on the road. Nervous about roughing it outdoors, Uno packs extra blankets to ensure everyone will be warm and comfortable in the tent.

Meanwhile, Duo double checks its list to make sure nothing is missed and packs an umbrella to be prepared for all possible weather forecasts. Duo also studies a map to plan out the best route. Uno urges Duo to rush so they can arrive before dark and then runs to the pantry to grab an extra bag of chips, recalling the pleasure of snacking while listening to music on the road.

Trio calmly observes the two and reminds Uno not to feel so hurried and worried. "I know driving those winding mountain roads at night can seem scary, but we have time and will make it to the campground before sunset," Trio says. It also gently reminds Duo not to over-plan, knowing road trips can hold many unpredictable adventures.

When they are finally ready, Trio gets in the driver's seat and Duo in the passenger seat to navigate. Uno opens the back door, relieved to get on the road. Now, you may ask, if Uno is the "doing" state, focused on rapid action, shouldn't it drive, with Trio in the back seat?

Uno suddenly realizes that too and says, "Listen, you two, let me drive. I'll get us there faster. You will waste time along the way." Uno senses irritation rising as it recalls their last road trip on which Trio stopped at every scenic lookout while Uno impatiently stewed.

As Uno talks, Duo and Trio nod at each other in agreement. Uno's concerns about arriving on time make sense and they promise to honor them. Yet both concur that Uno in the driver's seat would make for a stressful ride since its rushed and impulsive ways tend to get the better of it.

Trio says, "Uno, your excitement is infectious, and I know you will ensure we have fun along the way. Why don't you relax in the back and take charge of snacks and music? That way you can enjoy yourself and not be bothered by the stress of driving. If we needed to get somewhere in a hurry, it would make sense for you to drive."

Uno sighs, disappointed, yet also feels a sense of relief about not needing to take charge.

At the same time, as Duo analyzes the situation, it starts to wonder if it might be the best driver? It weighs its own methodical approach against Trio's love for random exploration. "Actually, I've thought it through and think I should drive," Duo declares with firm determination. "I am an expert on the route and have it all mapped out."

Trio responds, "I get your logic. I am grateful for your attentive planning, which will ensure we have a smooth journey. Duo, if we were navigating complex city roads, it would make sense for you to drive. But our intention for this weekend is to relax, take in nature, and enjoy new adventures. With me at the wheel, we stay open to endless possibilities. Who knows how the majesty of those mountains will unfold? I hope you can both trust me on this."

Duo rolls its eyes and mutters to itself, *there goes Trio again with those sentimental, cheesy words. What do they even mean? Why can't it be practical and get to the point?* Though Duo does not fully follow Trio's logic (well, there is none), it reconciles itself to the decision, knowing it can revisit their plans anytime. Duo also reasons that this way it can give directions on the optimal route, which means, it rationalizes to itself, it is actually the one in charge.

Belts buckled, they get on the road. Within minutes, hungry from the morning's frenzy, Uno is happily snacking. Duo settles in with its maps. Trio relaxes as it takes in the golden morning sunrise and glides onto the highway.

AWARENESS: WHERE AM I NOW?

As Uno, Duo, and Trio coast along, let us pause to explore the concept of awareness. In simplest terms, awareness is being conscious of what is going on in our mind. It leads us from thinking in—or about—a state to becoming an observer of it. We watch our inner "conversation" to notice which mindstate is "driving" in the moment.

To master this, we learn to ask ourselves, *in which mindstate am I now?* Since we cannot be both in a car and see it drive by, awareness shifts us from embodying our thoughts to witnessing them.

Though simple in concept, awareness has a transformative effect in practice. It creates space between our thoughts and our reactions to them so we can be like a curator who observes an exhibit. Rather than judging or jumping to conclusions about what we sense (e.g., *this is uneasy, I need to escape*), we bring curiosity, humility, and compassion (e.g., *I sense discomfort, I wonder what I can learn from this*).

We come to see how our default reactions are not our only options but among many possible ways of being. Guided by reason and wisdom, we can identify emotional triggers, diffuse inner

grenades, and dissolve judgmental cascades to dismantle exhibits and shatter silos.

Then, we can consciously decide which state serves us best. For example, both 1D's impulsive instincts and 3D's intuitive insights seem to appear instantaneously, which can lead us to confuse them. Awareness helps us see how 1D's emotional reactions bear restlessness. When 1D gives us a "gut" answer it is often accompanied by confusion and doubt. When 3D leads us to an intuitive insight, it harbors a sense of clarity and certainty that is peaceful and grounding.

To master awareness, we let 3D drive to become unemotional, nonjudgmental observers of our thoughts without reacting to (1D) or analyzing (2D) them. If we let 1D drive, we are likely to feel constantly on edge or on guard, which can lead us to obsess over our state of mind. If we let 2D drive, we are likely to judge or label what we observe, which can lead us to siloed, binary, or circular thinking. When we let 3D drive, we can observe our mind's state without fear of what we may find and without judgment of what that may mean. Thus, to master awareness, we keep 1D and 2D in the back, as quiet as they can be. To explore this further, let's rejoin our road trippers.

A few hours into their drive, Uno, Duo, and Trio stop at a highway rest area. After stretching, using the restroom, and catching some fresh air, they hop back in their car. As Trio starts to pull out of the parking spot, a loud thud jolts them.

All three jump out to find that another car just rear-ended theirs. Moments later, an elderly woman emerges from the other car, visibly shaken and distraught.

Uno panics and gets tense, unsure of what to do. It remembers the last time it was in an accident and worries about the delay this will cause. *Why does this always happen to me, I am so annoyed,* it mutters in frustration.

With awareness, we can notice when 1D's stress appears. Instead of reactively acting on emotions, we can say, *I feel agitated. I am in the 1D mind. I don't want to be here, but at least I now know what's going on.* Then we let 2D and 3D lead.

As Duo looks at the accident scene, it is concerned about the damage caused and wonders, *how could the other driver be so sloppy? Why is she even driving at this age?* Duo justifies Uno's anger and generates a list of arguments to defend Trio's innocence. At the same time, Duo recalls the steps to take after a collision and asks the lady for her insurance information.

With awareness, we can see how pointing fingers, shifting blame, getting caught up in details, or rationalizing our views, are all 2D attempts to gain control over a situation. By noticing such tendencies, we can pause and learn to lead with curiosity and humility. We can reflect on what may be going on beyond what we can see, and we avoid projecting our own stories onto others. This creates space for 3D to guide us.

As Trio gets out of the car, it walks over to the other driver to ask, "Are you okay?" Wise and compassionate, Trio cares about everyone's welfare. It stays calm, knowing this helps others around it relax. It gives others the benefit of the doubt and trusts that they are, just like us, vulnerable and fallible and also trying to do their best based on what they know.

"Thank you for asking," the lady responds as she catches her breath. "I am so sorry. I did not see your car while pulling out. I was distracted. My husband was just taken to the hospital, and I am on my way there. I stopped here to call my sister so she can meet me there. Please take my insurance information. I will take care of your car. I hope it is still drivable?"

Trio reassures her the collision likely just caused a bumper dent and reaches out to give her a hug. She sighs with relief. Trio asks Uno to bring her a bottle of water and sits down on the curb with the lady to help her calm down. After chatting for a bit and learning her name (it's Mara), Trio offers, since the hospital is nearby, that they can help her get there. Still feeling shaken, she accepts their kind offer with gratitude. Soon, Duo joins Mara in her car to help her navigate and Trio and Uno trail them in theirs.

When they arrive at the hospital, Mara walks in to check on her husband and asks the three to wait for her. A short while later she reappears with a relieved smile and says, "I talked to the nurse. My husband will be fine. I don't know how to thank you. You appeared as if out of nowhere. I am so glad we bumped into each other." Realizing what Mara just said, everyone bursts out laughing (though Duo faces a slight delay in catching the pun).

They continue chatting, and Mara shares that she and her sister own a cozy bed and breakfast inn not far from where Uno, Duo, and Trio plan to camp. She insists they stay there, as her guests. Reluctant yet grateful, they accept her offer for the second night of their trip.

As our road trippers return to their car, Trio says, "See how the wonders of the universe unfold. Both cars need just light work. We met such a beautiful soul, and our trip just got a huge upgrade. Thank you, both. This was a team effort, as always."

Uno grins in delight, recalling its worries about roughing it outdoors. Duo feels embarrassed it was so judgmental. Uno resolves to listen to Trio when it doesn't know what to do. Duo promises to trust Trio when it feels confused. Both are thankful they let Trio lead.

✻　　✻　　✻

Awareness helps us realize how our reactions to what we face—within or in the outside world—are more a reflection of our inner state than of what is going on outside. Guided by such insights, we can shift our responses from default reactions to wise decisions. Sometimes, this simple shift can make us feel as if we have just met our mind for the very first time.

ACUMEN: WHERE DO I WANT TO BE?

While awareness helps us know our mindstate in the moment, acumen helps us assess if that state is best for what we face or if one of the other two may serve us better. To master acumen, we ask, *in which mindstate do I want to be?* For example, in making a decision, we can consider these questions:

1. Should I take immediate action (1D)?
2. Can I get data to inform or expand my options (2D)?
3. How can my intuition guide me here (3D)?

The first question takes us into doing, the second into thinking, and the last into being. While 1D can grasp awareness, because it focuses our attention on the moment, with acumen, it is at a loss. When an instant reaction is not required, 1D does not know what to do. Thus, to master acumen, we let 1D nap in the back of the car.

For the 2D mind, acumen is its comfort zone. It can apply its analytical skills to carefully evaluate which mindstate is best for the moment. Here we can draw on 2D's ability to gather data to inform our decisions. We just need to beware that 2D can fall into judging mindstates as being better or worse when they are just so in the context of a moment. Also, absent 3D's wisdom, 2D can fall into doubt or second-guessing, afraid of making mistakes.

Hence, while awareness is best led by 3D, acumen is best led by 2D with 3D by its side. This helps 2D distill gathered data into wise insights. For instance, when a complex decision or challenge has no easy black and white answers, we can collect and study data to expand our knowledge. But the final answer often appears from an intuitive knowing that gives us clarity on how to proceed. To see how this plays out, we return to our road trippers.

❊   ❊   ❊

Back on the road, our friends are bopping along to Uno's favorite songs as they coast up winding roads into the spectacular Blue Ridge mountain range. Suddenly, as they make a hairpin turn, they see cars on the road ahead screech to a halt.

"Oh no, not again!" Uno exclaims. "We've already been delayed once. Road trips are such a pain. Argh!"

A moment ago, Uno was listening to music and having fun. Now, back in crisis mode, it focuses on all that is (or can go) wrong, as a new "reality" takes over its mood.

Seeing Uno's reaction, Duo says, "Wait a minute, we don't know what is going on. Before you get upset, give us a chance to find out."

"Okay, but I don't know what to do," Uno says as it fidgets, starts to breathe faster, and restlessly bounces its right leg.

Trio notices Uno's physical reaction and adds, "How about you sit back and take a few deep breaths to relax and calm down. You can roll down the window, enjoy the view, and take in the crisp, cool mountain air. I understand your concerns, but we don't need your help right now."

Duo scans the maps on its mobile device for traffic alerts. "There seems to be an incident a few miles up the road, but I can't figure out what happened," it says.

"If your device doesn't have the answer, maybe you can find out in other ways?" Trio asks, as it sees drivers up ahead get out of their cars. "How about you ask them?"

As Duo ventures out, Uno mumbles, "Be careful. It's a very narrow road."

After a while, Duo returns to report, "There has been an accident a few miles ahead on the two-lane mountain road."

"I hope no one got hurt?" Trio asks.

"A truck overturned. The driver is fine, but the truck needs to be towed," Duo says, wondering why a truck was driving on this narrow road in the first place. *Why didn't the driver take the wider highway?*

Duo adds, "We might be here for hours. The drivers ahead said towing the truck from this steep cliff is no trivial matter."

Uno worries about reaching the campground before dark. Trio looks in the rearview mirror and notices cars making U-turns through a lookout point they just passed.

After studying alternative routes, Duo says, "If we stay on this road, once it opens, we'll be two hours from our destination. If we make a U-turn, we can take another route that looks clear. It will double our driving time to four hours but is supposed to be a beautiful drive. We have five hours until sunset."

"What if there is an accident on the other road?" Uno blurts. Duo starts evaluating the odds of that as a back-and-forth dialogue ensues. Dilemmas, uncertainty, and the fog of confusion brew.

Finally, Uno proclaims, "Let's decide already. We need to act, or it will be dark before Duo is done deliberating."

Trio adds, "Uno, you are right. It is time to decide. Duo, thank you for your research. There are no right or wrong answers here. We don't know when this road will clear. The purpose of our trip is to enjoy nature and have a good time. Since we can make a U-turn, let's take the alternate route and see what adventures it holds. Although anything can happen on either route, we will likely make it to the campground by sunset."

Uno and Duo look at each other, scratching their heads at how Trio, mysteriously, almost magically, seems to get its way. They recall their earlier insistence on avoiding lookouts, and now Trio gets to lead them on a four-hour scenic drive! Yet they agree to trust Trio's decision, knowing they have said and done all they can.

As they settle into the new route, Trio reflects on their day: "I just want to say how grateful I am for our trip together. It has revealed so many precious gifts."

Uno and Duo look at each other with the same thought: *Oh no, there goes Trio again.* Yet curiosity gets the better of them, and they ask in unison, "Like what?" Trio responds with words often quoted as the serenity prayer: "Grant me the serenity to accept the things I cannot change, courage to change the things I can, and wisdom to know the difference."

Duo proceeds to analyze the words: "I guess 'serenity to accept' is Trio's strength, guided by inner calm. 'Courage to change' is Uno's, when it acts without fear. And 'wisdom to know the difference,' is mine, when I don't overanalyze. You're right, Trio. We make a fantastic team."

Uno chimes in, "But how can I be courageous, and Duo be wise?" Trio stays quiet. Then Uno and Duo look at each other with sheepish nods. "Of course, courage is guided by Trio," Uno says with delight.

"Wisdom is too," Duo adds. "I get it now. We let Trio drive, and each bring our best as a united team. Wait, that's what we are doing now!"

Trio smiles, knowing that such self-realization is much more powerful than any lectures it might have given.

❧   ❧   ❧

Acumen helps us decide how to best act on what awareness reveals. Instead of focusing on what we cannot change, we shift our attention to what we can, guided by the talents of all three minds. We see how our default thinking patterns are like well-traveled roads in our mind but not our only possible paths. We realize that, often in life, U-turns and detours are not just possible but can reveal stunning, new vista views that transform us.

AGILITY: HOW DO I GO FROM A TO B?

Agility is the ability to shift from where we Are (i.e., point **A**) to where we want to **Be** (i.e., point **B**), based on what awareness and acumen reveal. Thus, agility is acting on our insights. To master agility, we engage in two simple acts:

1. We let go of where we are when it doesn't serve us (e.g., releasing a hammer when we face a screw).
2. Then, we decide where we want to be and act on it (e.g., picking up a screwdriver and using it instead).

If we hold onto what we should let go, we stay stuck. If we let it go but fail to pick up the best "tool" or mindstate for the moment instead, we also make little progress.

While awareness is best led by 3D and acumen by 2D with 3D by its side, agility is best led by 1D, given its focus on action. Yet 1D also needs 3D by its side to ensure it acts with wisdom and avoids impulsive reactions. Also, 2D is best off in the back seat since its analytical tendencies can lead us to second-guess and delay acting on what acumen has revealed.

As with any habit, practice makes perfect. As we consciously learn to shift our state of mind, doing so becomes more effortless and intuitive over time. The principles and practices discussed in the prior three chapters help us master agility. As we learn to train each mindstate's talents and avoid its pitfalls, we gain comfort in switching across states based on what we face.

Agility explains how two minds can face the same or similar situations and have divergent reactions to them. When we lack agility, we may stay in the "wrong" mindstate for the moment. Then we tend to feel trapped, as if we have few options or no control. When we shift into the "right" mindstate instead, we can make progress with ease and trust the path forward. For instance, in the face of uncertainty, 1D seeks comfort and 2D wants control. When those needs cannot be met, we learn to trust 3D's wisdom to guide us toward a path we cannot yet see.

As you read on, if your mind says, *this is really hard*, or *I don't know if it will work*, such thoughts are like holding onto a hammer simply because 1D and 2D doubt the existence of a screwdriver or don't know how to use one. This reflects both our greatest barrier (holding onto the hammer) and breakthrough (using a screwdriver) in mastering our mind. Here is another way to explore this.

Upon first encountering the concept of the three mindstates, readers often responded in three basic ways, which you will now recognize.

Some said, "Okay, I get it. Now tell me what to do." Driven by 1D, they focused on what actions to take. Others said, "Why is this better than frameworks I already know?" Guided by 2D, they would analyze the three states and how they compared to what they already knew. Yet others said, "This resonates with my truths. It reminds me of wisdom I forgot I knew. I trust it to guide my way of being."

There is no judgment here of any one reaction being better than others, as 2D may conclude. Ultimately, agility is about 1D and 2D learning to trust 3D's way of being so we engage in doing and thinking as serves us best. As 1D and 2D loosen their grip, we learn to keep 3D in the front of the car, leading or guiding the way, a theme we continue to explore as we journey on. For now, we return to our road trippers for the final stretch of their trip.

❖　　❖　　❖

Once Uno, Duo, and Trio get on the longer, scenic route, their journey proceeds uneventfully. A few miles before their destination, Uno spots signs for a local country fair.

"Trio, please let's stop here. It looks like so much fun," Uno exclaims as it sees colorful Ferris wheel lights on the horizon.

Duo adds, "We are close to the campground and have made good time. I agree, let's take a break."

Trio agrees and slows down to switch lanes to exit the highway. In that instant, Trio has another epiphany: Awareness is observing the traffic in each lane. Acumen is knowing there are other lanes and deciding in which lane we want to be. Agility is giving the turn signal, and swiftly switching into that lane. *There truly are lessons everywhere, even in driving on a country highway*, Trio muses.

Once the three arrive at the fair, they buy entry tickets, which each include five coupons to use as they choose. Then they split up.

Uno sets out to find cotton candy, its favorite fair pleasure. Duo wonders how to make the most of its coupons and looks for a stall with an easy game with a good chance of winning a big prize. Trio strolls around the fairground and takes in the scene: children laughing and playing, friends chatting, and staff enjoying the warm, golden summer evening.

Trio passes by a stall for a local animal shelter and is drawn in by the caring compassion its staff have for the rescue animals they brought to the fair. After chatting with them for a while and learning more about their work, Trio drops all its coupons (and some cash) into their donation box.

Our three friends meet some time later and walk back to their car. Uno feels queasy, realizing it may have had too much sugar. Duo is carrying a stuffed tiger toy, not as big as it had hoped, but pleased it is the only one with something to show. Trio returns with a contented smile that leaves Duo wondering if it missed out on something better.

"What did you do with your fair coupons?" Duo asks with nonchalance tinged by nosiness.

"I gave them away at the animal shelter booth," Trio responds. "Those animals need caring love, like all beings. I hope the shelter staff can have some fun at the fair with the coupons."

Uno and Duo scratch their heads. They spent their coupons to satisfy themselves. Trio gave its coupons away yet seems happiest. "How do you always manage this?" they ask in unison.

Trio responds, "When we live from the heart, we serve to bring joy to others without expecting anything in return, which enriches both the giver and the receiver. In connecting to our shared humanity, we gain more than we give."

This doesn't make complete sense to Uno and Duo, but they don't doubt its truth. By now they know better. Once they get back in the car, after a short while, Uno spots the exit for the campground.

They reach there just in time to catch the sunset over a cliff. As the cool night settles in, they pitch their tent and prepare to make a fire in the pit. Uno goes off to fetch wood. Duo arranges graham crackers, chocolate, and marshmallows for s'mores.

Trio gazes at the sky, awed by how brightly the stars shine in the dark. Here, where all devices have gone silent, with cell towers left behind, nature serves as a steady guide whether in walking through the woods or the vastness of our inner space.

"Isn't it amazing that the same North Star has guided all humans since the start of time?" Trio says to Duo. "We are not alone. The stars watch over us. Our nearest one, the sun, sustains us."

Duo ponders this and then says, "I just realized that when we insert love and space into alone, we are all one."

"What do you mean?" Trio asks. "That sounds like something I would say."

"Take the word alone and add another "l" for love to form allone," Duo responds. "Then add a space in the center to spell: all one."

"Now you are being the cheesy one," Trio says, as both burst out laughing. "I love it. There is profound truth in your clever play on words."

You see, dear reader, Uno, Duo, and Trio are all one in our mind, always together as we journey through life. We decide, in each moment, who leads our mind, whether we are traveling on a road or looking at the stars. As we befriend all three, they dance together in harmony to lead us where we want to be. How that can transform our lives—and our world—is the story of the rest of these pages.

TABLE 3: AWARENESS ACUMEN AGILITY (AAA)		
	1. AWARENESS	**2. ACUMEN**	**3. AGILITY**
Ask yourself	Where **A**m I right now?	Where do I want to **B**e?	How do I go from **A** to **B**?
Intention	Be led by 3D **being** to observe your current state of mind	Be led by 2D **thinking** to evaluate your current state of mind	Be led by 1D **doing** to act on what awareness and acumen reveal
Mind Driver	**3D** (with 1D / 2D in the back seat)	**2D** (with **3D** by its side and 1D in the back seat)	**1D** (with **3D** by its side and 2D in the back seat)
Example	"I notice I feel nervous and stressed about this decision. I'm in my 1D mind…"	"…I would like to reflect on my options and tap into my intuition and inner wisdom…"	"…I will do deep breathing to shift from 1D to 3D and then revisit the decision…"
Wrong Drivers	"I'm frustrated about feeling so stressed!" (1D led)	"I don't know what to do so will do nothing." (1D led)	"I'm busy; I'll rush through deep breathing!" (1D led, no 3D)
	"Feeling this way is wrong; I should know better." (2D led)	"How will I be sure that I make the best decision?" (2D led, no 3D)	"What if deep breathing doesn't help?" (2D led)

PART III

How We Lead Our Lives

Tara's Triathlon

One mid-May morning in Annapolis, Maryland, Tara awoke to her 4:30 a.m. alarm in pitch darkness. As a healthcare executive with a passion for triathlons, she looked forward to taking part in that day's competition, the local Columbia Triathlon. That is, until she checked the weather forecast.

Conditions were usually ideal at this time of the year for the Olympic-distance race in Ellicott City, Maryland, "one of the most challenging and longest running triathlons in America" that attracted athletes from all over the world.[10] Usual temperatures in the mid to high 70s Fahrenheit promised a comfortable 0.93-mile swim in Centennial Lake, followed by a 25-mile bike ride through rolling suburban farmlands and a 6.2-mile run with a finish line in the scenic park surrounding the lake. This morning, it was 47 degrees Fahrenheit outside!

I don't think I can do this, Tara thought as she looked at the forecast. She winced at the thought of wearing a wet suit. She also recalled articles on the potential health risks of such cold race conditions. Jumping into frigid waters could increase some athletes' risk of life-threatening medical conditions driven by rapid blood vessel constriction in the cold combined with exertion in the race setting.[11] Tara loved triathlons, but no race was worth her life.

Tara shared this story with me a few days after the event. "I have to tell you something," she said with excitement after a talk I had given. She had patiently waited for everyone else to leave.

"When I woke up and had thoughts of quitting the race, I took a deep breath and paused," she said. "Then I realized they were 1D's fear-based reactions."

That simple insight, Tara shared, allowed her to shift from reacting to her thoughts' content to understanding their context. She also added she had just finished reading *Enduring Edge* and was more aware of her states of mind.

"I decided to drive to the park to assess the conditions," Tara said. Once there, she talked to other athletes getting ready for the race. She weighed the pros and cons of the weather and concluded it was not as bad as she had feared. *At least it's not windy*, Tara thought. Her tension eased. She decided to compete and pulled out her wet suit.

A short while later, Tara stood at the edge of the lake, poised to jump into the water. She shared how she began to repeat a simple mantra to herself: *I am one with the elements.*

This helped her breathing become steady and calm and allowed her mind to release thoughts racing through it. By the time she entered the chilly waters, she was in "a state of complete focus and clarity," Tara said.

"Although this triathlon had among the least favorable conditions in my many years of competing, it was one of the most joyful races of my life," she added.

Tara's face lit up as she recounted the day's event. "I made peace with what was—and come what may—knowing I was doing my best," she said. "This helped me release inner resistance and struggle. I didn't worry about or analyze each step of the way."

"It was a simple yet remarkable shift," she added. "I realized that day, even when things seem really tough, you can still find a way to stretch your potential. This was a profound lesson for me. We can turn any challenge into a way to grow."

❖   ❖   ❖

While we may not all be triathletes, Tara's story is an inspiring example of how a united mind can transform our experience, no matter what we set out to do or what we face along the way.

When Tara first saw the outside temperature upon waking up, **awareness** that her fears were driven by her 1D mind allowed her to pause and reflect before acting on them. This prevented fear from taking over her mind and created space for her to consider other possibilities.

Then, **acumen** helped Tara evaluate other options besides quitting the race. She could gather more data on the race conditions. Once Tara had a plan, her tension subsided. Guided by **agility**, she shifted from feeling stuck to taking action and drove to the park.

Since Tara's 1D mind had alerted her to potential health risks, she kept them in mind while assessing the race conditions guided by 2D. Once she decided to compete, Tara realized that being led by her 3D mind would not only improve her physical performance but also make for a more enjoyable experience.

Tara's visualization and affirmation of being "one with the elements" helped her evoke a deep sense of harmony and oneness with nature and calmed her nerves. As she later described, she gained greater comfort in pushing herself to excel outside her comfort zone. In the 3D state, which athletes also refer to as being "in the zone," she could be fully immersed in the present moment in a relaxed yet focused way.

This was brilliant all around. By releasing 1D's tension, Tara relaxed her muscles, reduced her risk of injury, and supported her body to strive for peak performance. By letting go of 2D's analyses, she focused on being fully present in each moment rather than replaying just-finished parts of the race, predicting outcomes of upcoming segments, or comparing herself to her peers.

In this way, Tara harnessed the best of all three minds so they worked together as a united team. As she jumped into the water, Tara said she felt strong and at ease, ready to face any challenges that might arise. This created a win-win-win, for her physical performance, her inner experience, and her race results. She raced against herself as her best self.

�֍   ֍   ֍

Tara did not tap into awareness, acumen, and agility as methodically as this narration may suggest. The concept of AAA did not even exist in *Enduring Edge*. It emerged in the years since, from stories like Tara's, which offered powerful insights on how readers united the three states in their minds to attain success across varied dimensions of their lives.

In this part, we explore these themes further as we look at **how we become who we are** (Chapter 7), **how we change and grow** (Chapter 8), and **how we decide who we become** (Chapter 9), whether we are pedaling through country roads or riding through life.

How We Become Who We Are

Before undertaking any change—in our lives or in the world—it helps to know our starting point, or who we are here and now. This transcends the name we are given at birth and the face we see in the mirror each morning. It reflects our deeper, invisible being, which decides the expressions we see on the face and the underlying thoughts that create them.

WE ARE MADE BY NATURE AND NURTURE

From our embryonic beginning, we are formed by a dynamic confluence of forces, both etched and ethereal. The etched, such as the genes we inherit, are like cards we are dealt. As our genetic code is transcribed into proteins and tissues, it shapes the physical structures and biochemical reactions that create our unique body.

While the sequence of our genes is fixed, our pulsating, living self is shaped by deeper forces that drive how we play our cards. We tend to refer to them as nurture. They encompass the physical environments—such as the womb, families, and communities—in which we grow up. They also include factors such as education, socioeconomic status, and the habits, cultures, and stories we absorb from others around us. Nurture also reflects our early life experiences. Childhood memories—of both nurturing, loving care and painful, stressful events—mold how we react to and come to view the world.

The debate over how much nature versus nurture shapes us continues to fascinate scientists and sociologists alike, mostly because of how little we know. Recent research in fields such as epigenetics suggests nurture's influence may extend down to the level of how our genes are expressed and passed on.[12] Some studies further suggest that such changes may be dynamic, and that we harbor the capacity to reverse their potentially harmful effects.[13]

For instance, the endcaps of genes, known as telomeres, which are associated with lifespan, can be shortened by intense, chronic stress. Yet studies suggest that such effects may be reversible as we develop resilience and harness a 3D state. In essence, to what extent nature shapes our destiny may be more under our control than science has traditionally believed.

Our power over nurture (and, hence, nature) emerges from our capacity to consciously decide how we respond to what we face in life. A fascinating example of this comes from clinical science, though not as researchers intended, through phenomena known as the placebo and nocebo effects.

PLACEBO NOCEBO

When researchers develop a new treatment, such as an oral pill, they first test its safety and effectiveness in clinical trials. Such studies often compare the potential therapy to a harmless control, such as an identical-looking sugar pill, called a placebo. Patients enrolled in such trials are blinded from knowing whether they are receiving the therapeutic drug or the placebo.

Such carefully designed trials can cost up to tens of millions of dollars and take years to complete. Yet, much to the dismay of drug developers, they often fail—not because the novel therapy doesn't work but because the placebo seems to be just as effective. Thus, the novel treatment offers no meaningful advantage to justify its costs and side effects.

This phenomenon, known as the placebo effect, is pervasive in clinical trials for medical ailments such as those of the central nervous system (e.g., anxiety, depression, or pain) and the digestive system (e.g., irritable bowel syndrome).[14] It has also been observed in surgical procedures (e.g., for knee or back pain) where superficial incisions on placebo patients can lead to similar long-term outcomes as in patients who undergo more invasive surgeries.[15]

Curiously, the placebo effect is further validated by its opposite, known as the nocebo effect. In clinical trials, when patients are told they may experience the side effects of a treatment, such as headaches, dizziness, nausea, or pain, some report such symptoms even while just receiving a placebo.[16]

Drug developers and investors tend to write-off the placebo effect as an expensive nuisance. Yet it reveals fascinating insights on our mind's capacity to both heal and harm us, guided by either positive or negative expectations. In recent years, some research studies have even shown how consciously evoking the placebo response in patients can help improve health outcomes.[17]

Beyond clinical trials, caregivers across healthcare settings, such as in trauma and rehabilitation centers, also offer fascinating insights on how the mind influences healing. Many share stories on how patients who are fiercely determined to get well, and who sustain positive, uplifting thoughts, can experience better recovery (at times even from worse conditions) than those who fall into negative or defeatist thinking patterns or lose the will to live.

It is important to qualify (because this often comes up as 2D analyzes the above paragraph) that such observations are not a judgment on patients who confront terminal illness despite a fierce will to live. Rather, they suggest how shifting our mind from 1D to 3D helps foster healing and well-being in ways beyond what clinical science tends to measure and treat.

Even among humans in peak physical shape, such as Olympic athletes or elite special forces in the military, coaches and generals alike share how differences in performance—between those who reach the top of their field and those who fall just short—have less to do with the state of their bodies than that of their minds.

Thus, these fields complement intense exercise regimens with equally rigorous mind training practices to cultivate mental focus, resilience, and calm—no matter what the body may face. For example, an athlete may tap into visualization, guided imagery, and affirmations to mentally rehearse positive outcomes in vivid, multi-sensory detail. A skier may simulate repeatedly racing down a course, rehearsing each move with exquisite precision.[18]

Recent studies suggest that such mental practice activates the same regions in the brain as when an athlete is actually moving on a course, and improves physical performance in tangible ways.[19] (Though this does not imply we can each just go to "the gym" in our mind, however tempting that may be.)

The mainstream adoption of mindfulness and meditation practices in the U.S. in recent decades—from schools and work-places to sports teams and the military—has been accompanied by extensive new research to validate the benefits of mental training.[20]

For example, studies on regular meditators show reduced reactivity in regions of the brain associated with primal, impulsive, emotional reactions (i.e. the amygdala).[21] Other studies suggest that meditation may reduce activity in the brain's Default Mode Network, which harbors tendencies such as mind wandering, rumination, and obsessive "self-referential" thinking.[22]

Some studies also suggest we retain the capacity to rewire existing neural pathways (i.e. neuroplasticity), and create new ones (i.e. neurogenesis), throughout life. In short, our brain is less fixed than we once thought. Or said another way, an "old dog" can learn new tricks.

In essence, cutting-edge neuroscience is re-searching and re-validating ancient knowledge on how training our mind helps us shift from reactive (1D) to reasoned (2D) and wise (3D) responses. Nonetheless, even neuroscientists admit that their understanding of our mind remains in its infancy and our best proof of its power often emerges from our own first-hand experience.

WE ARE FORMED BY EXPERIENCES

Beyond nature and nurture's lifelong dance, a deeper, invisible force guides us. It drives not just how we play our cards, or when we wager or fold, but how our lives unfold. It is reflected in how we weave our life's experiences into the stories that come to define us. This guides how we see—and what we believe about—everything we encounter, including our own mind. Its power is often much greater than both nature and nurture's forces.

During our early, formative childhood years, the innocent, impressionable space of our inner being is like a pristine, empty museum that is filled with exhibits for the very first time. Since every experience is new, even mundane events take on importance and form vivid imprints on us, often in ways of which we remain unaware when young.

Such experiences can shape our life trajectories in profound ways. We become a doctor because we loved how our pediatrician made us feel. We enjoy cooking because of the pleasant childhood memories it evokes. We love reading because of inspiring books we read as a child. We keep our sense of curiosity and wonder alive because of the joy it brought us while growing up. Or we meet a hero, imaginary or real, and see ourselves in them.

Other early experiences can leave darker footprints to shape a life with equal force. Studies on adverse childhood experiences (ACEs) show how abuse, bullying, neglect, violence, and other forms of trauma—such as loss of a parent, racism, discrimination, or migration—can leave powerful imprints on a young mind, often with lasting effects.[23] Such experiences can lead a mind to feel ever on guard or on edge, defaulting to 1D more than serves it. This can lead it to re-live a trauma for years, sometimes even a lifetime, and to suffer from mental distress or even physical disease.

Yet, beyond what we experience, how that comes to define our reality is shaped by the stories we tell ourselves about it. As children, we are mostly unaware of this. As adults, we have a choice. We can consciously revisit our stories and their emotional memories with reason and wisdom. We explored this in brief in the exercise on visiting our own museum of emotions in Chapter 3. Here, we delve deeper.

While disciplines such as biology help us know nature, and ones such as sociology help us study nurture, in deciphering our inner stories, we often don't know where to turn. We may naively assume our stories define who we are, oblivious to their lasting effects on us. We may attribute our attitudes to early life environments or conclude our habits were formed by tendencies over which we had no control. Or, we may accept limiting beliefs (e.g., on being weak or powerless) as our truths, unaware of their power over us.

Sometimes, we even allow the destiny of our lives to be defined by stories created by others' minds—about who we should be, what we should do, or what the world is like—without pausing to question how such stories gained a stronghold in our mind.

We end up in these patterns because our mind's evolution does not always follow our body's linear maturation. As we grow older, we learn to discipline impulsive reactions (1D) with reason (2D) and wisdom (3D). Toddlers tend to throw tantrums when they don't get what they want. Most adults know that shouting and crying are not the best ways to get our needs met. With experience, we also gain greater wisdom that we don't always get what we want, and that this may be for the best in the long run, even if it does not appear so in the moment.

Although 1D's reactive ways tend to help us survive as a young, helpless child, when we stay stuck in them, they can become an adulthood trap. Each time we replay an old story it can feel like our current reality, driven by intense emotions. But, as we continue to dwell in childhood emotions that no longer serve us, they can hold us back and make us feel divided within.

When we experience intense suffering (e.g., from a trauma, loss, separation, or death), we may turn to fields such as psychology and psychotherapy to help us untangle and release painful emotions. Yet, in our day-to-day lives, most of us seldom pause to ponder how we became who we are and how our stories shape us.

Even less often do we revisit our deepest stories to consider if we should hold onto them or can release or rewrite them. While such self-reflection may appear to be a frivolous endeavor amidst busy days filled with urgent tasks, when we don't know our deepest selves, we move through our days out of touch with our hearts. For, our inner evolution and growth is guided by how we process and make peace with the stories of the experiences of our lives.

WE ARE SHAPED BY STORIES

Why do stories have such a powerful hold on us? The human mind loves stories. In telling a story, we tap into a magical ability likely bestowed on no other species on earth, at least as far as we know. We may forget data and facts or ignore danger and risks, but we always remember a good story.

Before we wrote them down, stories infused campfires and bedtimes as fables and songs. Though storytellers turned to dust, their stories often outlived them, passing on from heart to heart. Even a brief story, such as the one below, becomes easily embedded in our mind. In fact, if you have heard this story before, you will likely recall its ending by the end of the first sentence.

One day, a young girl was walking along a beach and saw hundreds of starfish scattered across the sand. She started picking them up and tossing them into the water. A passerby, upon seeing her effort, remarked she was wasting her time. Her work would not make a difference. There were many more starfish than she could save. To which the girl replied, "I made a difference for this one," as she tossed the starfish in her hand back into the sea.[24]

Stories weave vivid imagery with meaning to create powerful memories we easily recall. They help us archive the past, find meaning in the present, and imagine the future. Some stories inspire minds for generations, while others lose relevance with time. Centuries ago, we thought the earth was flat and that thunder and lightning were acts of angry gods. New knowledge has since roundly deflated those myths.

Similarly, while our own stories are intimately familiar to us, not all of them deserve space in our mind. By deciphering which of our stories enlighten us, and which ensnare us, we can release ones not fit for posterity. To learn how, let's first explore why we hold onto our stories.

HOW 1D THINKS ABOUT OUR STORIES

An oft-repeated story comes to feel real to our 1D mind. Like watching a movie rerun, 1D finds comfort in the familiarity of its plot, whether it serves us or not. As we replay a story, we focus our attention on it. Like repeatedly walking a well-trodden path, we reinforce its neural pathways, which shapes our default thoughts, as reflected by the saying: *neurons that fire together wire together.*

But just because a story feels real, does not make it true. The next time you are on the road, if you consciously decide to look for red cars, you may suddenly feel as if there are many more red cars than ever before. You may even proceed to tell yourself a story about how red cars have suddenly multiplied. Yet, most likely, a shift in the focus of your attention, rather than an increase in red car production, explains your perceived new reality.

While such storytelling is harmless with red cars, when it infuses our mind, it can profoundly affect how we lead our lives. As we believe stories based on where we focus our attention, we can unknowingly let them define our reality in ways that limit us. Driven by 1D's tendencies, we may come to believe that the world is a scary place, or that our life bears permanent pain. At times, we may share our beliefs about the world, or even ourselves, with no one else but retell them to ourselves constantly (e.g., *things will always be this way, I am doomed,* or *there is no better future*).

Sometimes, 1D can lead us to believe in linear stories that the only thing keeping us from a better life is getting—or getting rid of—X. Here, X can stand for a person, a relationship, a possession, or even an experience. Yet such stories are easily disproved by the simple fact that, as soon as we get—or get rid of—X, we sense that 1D is still not fully satisfied.

Then we may conclude that the missing link to our happiness actually rests in Y or Z, leading us down an endless path of restless dissatisfaction, driven by a 1D story that has taken hold of our mind. As we become aware of 1D's ways, we can discern whether our stories simply meet its needs or truly serve our deeper being.

HOW 2D THINKS ABOUT OUR STORIES

The 2D mind also loves to preserve our stories in its archives. To it, our stories form the scaffolding of our unique sense of self, or identity. Further, they offer 2D a semblance of structure in making sense of a complex and often confusing world. Thus, 2D creates stories about our work (e.g., *I am a nurse* or *I am a police officer*), our relationships (e.g., *I am a son* or *I am a sister*), our views (e.g., *I am liberal* or *I am conservative*), and our cultures and faiths (e.g., *I am Native American* or *I am Irish Catholic*).

Not only is 2D unable to fathom who we remain without our stories, it fears their dissolution threatens our very existence. *If I am not my work, relationships, views, or culture, then who am I?* To 2D, contemplating this is like gazing at the night sky and accepting its insignificance in an infinite universe. Terrified of oblivion, it snaps back to earth and seeks to revalidate its existence.

❊   ❊   ❊

In light of their attitudes towards our stories, 1D and 2D are not inclined to explore, let alone challenge, the origins and credibility of our long-standing narratives. They may resist with avoidance (e.g., *don't go there, you will feel awful*), distraction (e.g., *there's no point, focus on something else*), or denial (e.g., *I like my stories and myself; I don't want to change*).

Sometimes, we may be so oblivious to a story's sway over us that we don't even realize how it runs our life. For instance, when a mind goes through a traumatic experience over which it had no control, it may try to "cope" with the trauma by trying to control everything around it—its environment, its circumstances, and even people around it—blind to how the only true control in its life is the control the old story has over it.

HOW 3D THINKS ABOUT OUR STORIES

While 1D and 2D get easily caught up in a story's emotional drama or complex plots, 3D leads us to face our stories with courage, humility, and compassion. Guided by 3D, we come to see how every story harbors wisdom and insights to help us learn and grow, even when 1D and 2D find this hard to admit or accept.

For instance, 1D may fear facing a story that triggers intense emotions. It may be scared of how it will feel as it viscerally re-lives the story, as if for the first time, sometimes for a lifetime. In parallel,

2D may not want to rewrite a story it has established as part of our identity, biased by tendencies that 2D can't transcend.

In contrast, 3D can face the story like a calm curator walking through a museum. Instead of getting triggered by fear or trapped in an identity, 3D leads us to learn and grow. In this AAA can help.

Awareness creates space to be with a story. As we realize that our default ways are not our "fault," we recognize that we need not fear what they reveal (as 1D may) or judge ourselves by them (as 2D might). **Acumen** brings curiosity and humility to help us discern how a story may once have served us, and to evaluate whether it still does. Finally, **agility** guides us to bring courage to release a story when it can go, as we explore through Jay's story below.

As we reflect on our stories this way, we come to realize that, no matter what any story tells us, it is just one perspective. A dozen minds can witness the same event and create hundreds of unique stories about it, as each connects the dots in its own way. Even one mind can revisit the same experience and continuously revise its story about it, either consciously, based on new insights, or unconsciously, since human memory is inherently fuzzy and fickle. Ultimately, we come to realize that we are all fiction authors.

WE ARE ALL FICTION AUTHORS

Before 1D reacts to this statement, or 2D takes offense at such an assertion, let's clarify what we mean by "fiction" here. Every story we have is about a past that is gone or a future yet to come. No matter how real the past and future feel, they exist in our present only if we allow them to appear.

Now, 1D may exclaim, *my memories of my emotions are valid, they are my reality, you cannot deny them.* And 2D may add, *you cannot invalidate what I experienced. I am not being emotional. I am reporting facts.* Yet 3D helps us see that how we recall and experience a story simply reflects our state of mind.

Although, even when we realize that an old story no longer serves us, it can feel hard to dismantle, especially if it has been a permanent exhibit in our museum for a long time. We may not know what to replace it with, or wonder who we are without it, or

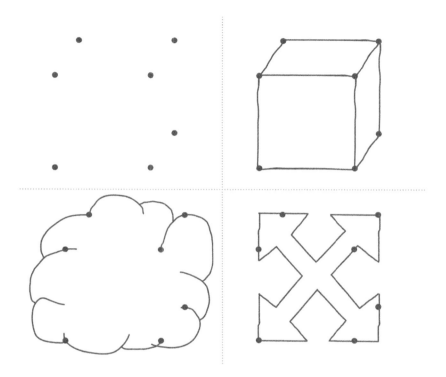

fear the emptiness it will leave behind. Since a new story has not received equal "space" or attention in our mind, a better future can feel impossible to imagine, like an uncharted trail still invisible in the woods. But, as we take our first step, we help a new path or story come to life, first in our mind and then in the world, as we explore through this next story.

Jay had been an entrepreneur for as long as he could remember. His earliest memory went back to a lemonade stand he had set up at a local park with his elementary school friend, Troy. Jay still vividly recalled his first customer: a deaf and mute girl who stopped by with her mother. When she took her first sip of their lemonade, her face lit up with a burst of delight that Jay never forgot.

Though they did not make a profit that day, the girl's joy made the experience more than worth it for Jay. As a teenager, Jay spent many late afternoons working the cash register at his parents' gas station. He loved chatting with customers from all walks of life about how their day was going. He often cheerfully whistled his favorite songs and loved it when a rushed customer looked up with a smile upon recognizing a familiar tune.

A few years after college, Jay decided to pursue his lifelong dream of opening a kabob and falafel shop in his hometown. It would feature several recipes that had been passed down through generations in Jay's family. Jay was thrilled when Troy agreed to join him.

Not long after opening, the shop grew a loyal following. Many patrons came from afar and viewed a visit to the hole-in-the-wall eatery as a special treat. Each time Jay talked to a satisfied customer, he thought back to the girl who had visited his lemonade stand years ago.

Yet, a few years into running the startup, the stress of managing a small business began to wear on Jay. Since the eatery opened, he had not taken any time off. Jay struggled to juggle the day-to-day challenges of managing a staff, sustaining through long, tiring days, and helping Troy open a second location across town. In addition, Jay's aging parents needed more of his help, and his friends complained about his frequent absences from social events.

While restlessly awake one night, Jay realized that he could not remember the last time he had whistled while he worked. He resolved to take a few days off and, the next day, called his cousin to accept her long-standing offer to visit her timeshare at a nearby beach.

The following weekend, as Jay relaxed and took in the warm breeze by the sea, he felt grateful he had carved out this time for himself. He pulled out his copy of *United Mind*. He realized that, in recent months, his three mindstates had been at odds with each other, which often left him feeling drained. Now, he finally had space to ponder what was going on.

WHAT ARE MY 1D MIND'S STORIES?

What are my 1D mind's stories? Jay wondered. While his struggle for financial survival was real, Jay realized his 1D mind would often spin worst-case scenarios late into sleepless nights on all the ways in which he might fail. Jay pondered why such fears loomed so large in his mind. He suddenly recalled the laundry service startup that he and Troy had launched in college to help pay their way through school. Though Jay's parents had little money to spare, they had lent him seed funding to get started. A year later, the venture went under, and all the money was lost. Jay had felt guilty, frustrated, and filled with shame for years over losing his parents' hard-earned income.

Even today, when the risk of failure arose, it instantly took Jay back to the intense emotions of the failed college business. Jay's 1D mind would remind him, in excruciating detail, of what had happened and how much pain it caused. *If this new eatery doesn't work out, you will feel awful. You will let people down. Remember last time? Maybe you should just get a job. This is not worth the risk.*

Jay's 1D mind would then proceed to drum up a parade of all his prior failures, including the smallest stumbles. Each time, he felt tension build within as his shoulders and back got stiff.

Now, while relaxing at the beach, Jay could revisit those 1D stories guided by 2D's reason and 3D's wisdom. He realized that he had come a long way from his college days and was much smarter and wiser about building a business. Most of his old 1D failure stories just took up precious mind space, drained his energy, and distracted him from focusing on the future he wanted to see.

WHAT ARE MY 2D MIND'S STORIES?

Then Jay asked himself, *what are my 2D mind's stories?* He realized how his 2D mind's tales were less emotional but often offered clever rationalizations for his 1D fears. *Think of the humiliation that failure will cause you. What will people say? How will it affect your reputation?* Such stories drove Jay to worry about how failure would diminish his standing among his family and friends.

Jay also realized how his 2D mind could lead him to become overconfident and, if he was truly honest, arrogant. He now saw how this had contributed to the failure of the college laundry startup. Whenever Troy suggested ways to improve the business,

Jay tended to dismiss them, thinking he knew better. When the startup failed, Jay proceeded to blame Troy for not pushing back harder with his ideas.

As Jay pondered how his 2D mind had come to be this way, his thoughts wandered back to his middle school days. He remembered how he was often bullied by other boys who made fun of his foreign looks and accent. Ever since, Jay had been highly sensitive to how he came across to his peers and had placed high value on fitting in. His worst nightmare was to embarrass and make a fool of himself.

Jay smiled as he realized his current colleagues and friends were polar opposites of the middle school bullies he had long ago feared. Troy and the kabob shop staff were fiercely supportive and loved him. When crises arose, they always had Jay's back, as he had theirs. They were like his second family. Several had left higher-paying jobs because they believed in Jay's vision of serving great food to bring together their local diverse community.

Jay laughed out loud as he realized the absurdity of continuing to give those schoolyard bullies undeserved space in the playground of his mind.

WHAT ARE MY 3D MIND'S STORIES?

Then Jay mused, *what are my 3D mind's stories?* Jay sensed deep tranquility enter his being as he realized how his 3D mind helped him make peace with his 1D and 2D stories. His deeper wisdom reminded him that fear was a passing emotion of the 1D mind and that failure was just a label of the 2D mind.

Jay also saw how, in hindsight, every experience had taught him something valuable. Instead of getting wrapped up in a story's emotions or defending his own views, guided by 3D, Jay harnessed patience, humility, and compassion to discover its deeper teachings.

When Jay returned to work the following week, he noticed how his insights at the beach shifted his thinking patterns and transformed his thoughts. Over the weeks that followed, when a 1D or 2D story knocked on Jay's mind, he would be aware of its appearance and open the door to acknowledge it. He would assess, with acumen, what lessons it held. Then, guided by agility, he would swiftly bid the story farewell and close the door. Earlier, Jay might have not only invited such stories into his mind but also indulged them in a fancy feast, allowing them to outstay their welcome and bring along uninvited cousins. Or he might have slammed the door in their face and plugged his ears trying to pretend he could not hear their ever-louder knocks.

As time passed, Jay noticed how releasing old stories freed up significant space in his mind. Many challenges that had overwhelmed him before now felt easier. Solutions came to him more naturally. When old thinking patterns returned for a visit, since Jay did not entertain or indulge them, they gradually lost their power over him. Jay also felt less tired and had more energy, as if he had a "new" mind.

When challenges arose, instead of rushing to quick fixes, Jay would step back and reflect on their deeper root causes to find enduring solutions. With time, he noticed crises abate as he became better at anticipating them before they blew up in his face. Jay also felt more productive and sensed a deeper peace within, no matter what he faced. This not only led the business to thrive but also gave him more time for family and friends, transforming all dimensions of his life.

WE CAN WRITE NEW STORIES

As we revisit and rewrite our life's stories, like Jay, we realize how our reality does not exist in what happens but in the stories we tell ourselves about it. We come to see how every experience—even if painful or difficult—bears wisdom to help us grow our courage and resilience. Along the way, we gain new insights on how our stories shape and guide us.

Ultimately, we realize timeless truths that transcend all our stories. What happens just happens. While 1D may build an emotional exhibit out of it, and 2D may add its own labels to it, 3D helps us see how all 1D and 2D stories—about ourselves, others, and the world—are riddled with fears, biases, exaggerations, judgments, and rationalizations. Guided by 3D, rather than holding on to such stories, we open up to truths we may not have considered—or even rejected—before. We gain clarity to help us confidently forge new trails through the woods, and we let shrubs grow over old paths until they disappear.

As we deepen our understanding of our own stories, we come to recognize how most conflicts, divides, and wars—within and between individuals, communities, and nations—simply represent clashes between alternative stories on what we believe about ourselves, each other, and the world. As we discover deeper wisdom and truths that transcend all our stories—others' and our own—we gain a deep inner freedom and sense of harmony to guide how we change and grow.

PLAY, PONDER, PRACTICE:

WHAT ARE MY STORIES?

The next time you face a challenge, consider exploring Jay's approach by taking some time to pause and reflect on it at a deeper level.

Ponder what stories you harbor about the challenge and what roles those stories play in your mind. Here are some questions to help guide your exploration:

1. What are my 1D mind's stories? What insights do they reveal? How do they help me? How do they hinder me?

2. What are my 2D mind's stories? What lessons do they hold? How do they help me? How do they hinder me?

3. What are my 3D mind's stories? What wisdom can they teach me? How can they help me transcend 1D and 2D stories that hinder me?

CHAPTER 8

How We Change and Grow

Change is inherent to life—the only constant—as the saying goes. Throughout our lives, our body's cells churn through continuous cycles of birth, growth, and death. Our families, friendships, communities, and countries form and transform with time.

Ever-changing weather patterns dance across our skies as tectonic plates prance beneath our feet. The universe itself, as far as cosmologists can tell, continues to expand into a void whose edge we may never find.

In this timeless, boundless space, we each appear as a fleeting flicker on a temporary planet that orbits a star with an inevitable end. Hence, it remains one of the great mysteries of life why we still struggle with change so much.

In the brief blip of our existence, we desperately long for stability, permanence, and belonging. We strive to hold onto those we love, to protect our communities, and to preserve our cultures and ways of life. We seek anchors to ground us, traditions to root us, and connections to sustain us.

When we face change we do not want, we often resist it or try to make it go away. Even when we pursue change we want, we often struggle to attain it. Most New Year's resolutions are abandoned after a few weeks. Weight loss remains an ever-expanding industry. And countless ideas rest unexplored, books unwritten, and dreams unrealized.

In our attempts to master change, we often search for solutions in the world. We listen to motivational stories on how others changed, in hopes of learning their secrets. We read books and articles to get advice. We attend workshops, take assessments, and seek out mentors or coaches. Organizations spend billions each year on experts to help "facilitate" transformation. Yet, lasting change still often remains elusive.

By shifting how we think about change itself, we can transform how we lead it across all dimensions of our lives. We can learn to create lasting change in ways that cost nothing and are entirely in our own hands—and heads. Because, whether change is easy or hard, or fades or lasts, depends less on what we want to change than on the state of mind in which we lead it.

THE START OF CHANGE

Often, our attempts at change start in the 1D and 2D minds, driven by actions and tasks guided by tactics and plans. While these two states are invaluable in guiding change, they are rarely our best starting points. Change that lasts tends to emerge from the 3D mind, which harbors our deeper intentions and our sense of meaning and purpose (as we explore in the next chapter). These 3D elements motivate us in more enduring ways than 1D's carrots and sticks or 2D's metrics and milestones.

Even when we face unwanted change, such as a devastating crisis, 3D helps us sustain courage and patience to persevere. Rather than feeling overcome with despair, we bring self-compassion to give ourselves the space we need to process and make peace with what has happened. We bring humility to release the ego's need for control and connect to something greater than ourselves. We take time to grieve what was lost, come to terms with our new reality, and sustain hope and resilience. With time, we transform overpowering, painful emotions into inspiration to guide us forward.

In contrast, in the face of a crisis, 1D is easily overtaken by intense feelings, such as sadness or anger. Scared of its own painful emotions, 1D tends to resist change. This leads us into counter-productive responses, such as denial or avoidance, as discussed in Chapter 3.

While 2D can be unemotional, the ego's ways also harbor limits in facing change. When things don't go as planned, or we encounter unexpected setbacks, 2D can be at a loss for how to move ahead. Devoid of 3D's wisdom, it can lead us to move through the motions of change, while neither making peace with the past nor finding deeper meaning to guide us forward. Also, in making sense of what happened, 2D tends to blame outer circumstances, other people, or even the state of the world. This further walls us into 2D's ways and limits our capacity to evolve and grow through a challenging experience.

The 3D mind reminds us that change need be neither scary or uncomfortable, as 1D may fear, nor confusing or complex, as 2D may think. Guided by 3D, we can bring the best of all three states to navigate any change with a united mind. This is a vital point. Lasting change is led by all three minds aligned in harmony.

For instance, we cannot compete in a triathlon, no matter how inspired we feel, without preparation (2D) and practice (1D). Yet the passion that drives us to train, day in and day out, even when we may not feel like it, or try to talk ourselves out of it, emerges from the 3D mind. To explore this, let's return to our opening story of Tara's triathlon.

❧　　❧　　❧

On the morning of Tara's race, beyond the mindstate shifts she described, Tara was guided by a deeper force. For Tara, training for and competing in triathlons held a profound sense of meaning and purpose that reflected her deepest values.

She loved the sense of connection and community with fellow athletes. She cherished spending time outdoors in beautiful natural surroundings. And she enjoyed striving for excellence and training her body to peak performance, especially in challenging natural terrains. Each of these values infused Tara with a positive force that guided and sustained her.

It inspired her to get out of bed and go for practice runs on cold, dark mornings, even when she was tempted to turn off the alarm and pull the covers back over her head. When work got too busy or she felt tired, it encouraged Tara to make time for bike rides, nonetheless. When she got a cold, the prospect of being able to go for a swim motivated her to make time to rest and recover faster. When Tara's older brother passed away suddenly, long runs on wooded trails helped her find a semblance of peace in her heart.

This powerful positive force, a deep inner passion that fueled Tara, emerged from her 3D mind. When negative thoughts to derail her showed up, Tara noticed how they were mostly 1D's concerns (*it's cold outside, you should stay comfortable inside*), or 2D's reasoned analyses, which often sounded right (*you don't have time away from work*), yet felt wrong within (*I can bundle up and make time—I work to live, not live to work*).

Tara also shared how training for triathlons through the years helped her cultivate resilience, discipline, and endurance in other dimensions of her life. During the Covid-19 pandemic, when all her races were canceled, Tara continued training for her favorite kind of race—the Half-Ironman, which consists of a 1.2-mile swim, followed by a 56-mile bike ride, and a 13.1-mile run—as if she were going to compete. This helped her sustain positivity, connection, and a sense of camaraderie with fellow athletes.

For Tara, the greatest reward of participating in races was not how she performed in them but who she became through them. She often thought to herself, *triathlons have saved my life.*

THE HEART OF CHANGE

The positive force that drove Tara decides the fate of most change in our lives—how we face it, what meaning we find in it, and who we become through it. Its essence is guided by two dueling forces:

1. **Resonance**, which is a positive, uplifting, and serene sense of flow that moves us forward, guided by deep inner harmony, joy, and an effortless ease (3D); and,

2. **Resistance**, which is a negative, heavy, or tense feeling of pushing or pulling back, driven by inner conflict or friction (1D and 2D).

When we harness resonance, we are led by a united mind. When resistance arises, it reflects the myriad forms of a divided mind. The force that leads our mind from moment to moment decides the momentum and trajectory of our lives.

Given their intangible nature, resonance and resistance can baffle 1D and 2D. Yet we can grasp them in our deeper being in powerful ways. Most of us can relate to the feeling of meeting someone, or walking into a gathering, and sensing a natural, uplifting, effortless connection. Even with a stranger, we may feel as if we have known them all our lives. Most of us can also easily distinguish such encounters from ones that evoke inner unease or discomfort, driving us to search for distractions, or even an escape route.

Another way to consider these forces is to think of resonance as beautiful music that inspires us and envelops us in its splendor. Resistance, in contrast, is like music that grates on us, feels out of tune, or drives us to plug our ears.

At the deepest level, resonance evokes a sense of inner freedom that energizes and empowers us and reflects our deepest passions. Resistance, in contrast, feeds a sense of inner confinement that builds friction, depletes our energy, or leads us to feel stuck. By discerning how these two forces guide us, we can learn to transform situations when we struggle or shuffle along into ones marked by lightness, joy, and ease.

Whether we seek to change a habit, a culture, or a community, led by 3D resonance we gain clarity on why the change we seek matters to us. Then, when 1D or 2D resistance arises, it holds less power over us. Stumbles and setbacks turn into lessons instead of excuses to quit. Goals and rules become helpful tools rather than regimens to dread. Even when change feels hard, or presents seemingly insurmountable odds, we persevere, trusting 3D to guide us.

When we drive change led by 1D or 2D, we may take actions and make plans. But when resistance crops up, it tends to win the day. Absent the power of resonance, change can feel forced or seem to require significant exertion of effort or willpower. We may feel unmotivated, or view taking action as a forced obligation we would rather avoid. We may engage in extensive internal debates, be filled with doubt, or move through the motions of change in half-hearted ways.

Tara shared how she once had an epiphany on the dynamic between resonance and resistance during her weekly yoga class. While trying to sustain tree pose, a one-leg balancing posture, she noticed, as she stood still, how her breathing became steady and her thoughts slowed down. When she lost her balance, she gently let her foot touch the ground, took a deep breath, and rebalanced herself on one leg. It was no big deal, and she did not berate herself for losing her balance.

Faltering did not make Tara a "failure" at yoga. She did not create elaborate, emotional, resistance-filled stories about why she had lost her balance, or what that said about her as a person. She simply observed what happened to learn how she could improve her practice.

Tara said this made her realize how such a way of being could transform how she approached many other aspects of her life. When she faced any failure, setback, or rejection, rather than feeling dejected, she could just think of it as stumbling during yoga class, trusting she would find a way forward with patience and resilience.

To explore how we can each harness the power of resonance, and release the persistence of resistance, we briefly delve into both below. As you read the rest of this chapter, try to become aware of your own inner experiences with these two forces, noticing when each appears in your inner being.

THE POWER OF RESONANCE

In stories that survive the ages, the same universal truths prevail. We hail the triumph of good over evil, of light over dark, and of peace over war (in our hearts and in the world). We celebrate the resilience of the human spirit and admire journeys of heroes who persevere against the odds. We cherish a sense of connection and belonging and celebrate kindness and love. In short, our timeless stories connect us to the essence of our shared humanity.

Even though our outer world has transformed since the days of the Prince we met in the Prologue, his inner journey still offers precious insights that can help guide us today. The Sage's wisdom remains as, if not more, relevant to our modern lives. This is the timeless power of resonance led by the 3D mind.

When we are in a state of resonance, we connect to our heart's truths. We feel guided by our sense of meaning, purpose, and values. We experience a natural ease that inspires us from within. We tap into an inner joy that motivates us to take on challenges, or even the seemingly impossible. Yet we also sustain a grounding inner peace that gives us the courage to persevere, to shatter inner and outer walls, and to even reach for the edges of the universe.

When we are led by 1D, in contrast, our attempts at change remain at the mercy of fickle forces, driven by 1D's impulsive needs. While those can sometimes serve as catalysts for taking action, they often fail to sustain momentum in driving change. For instance, 1D may be excited to act today but then become bored or unmotivated tomorrow. Thus, 1D's impulsive urges can lead us to exist in an ever-restless state that becomes exhausting and often counterproductive.

For example, news headlines often try to grab our attention with alarming, worst-case scenarios that evoke fear, which is always the fastest way to get our attention. Thus, the news often focuses on dangers (e.g., violence and threats), or warns us with cautions (e.g., smoking can kill you, or loneliness is as deadly as smoking).

Heeding 1D's instincts is invaluable in an urgent crisis (e.g., in a fire, when alarms urge us to rush outside, or in a pandemic, when orders urge us to stay apart). But fear is an unsustainable long-term motivator for change. Since it evokes resistance, fear eventually depletes us. In our attempts to cope, we may tune out, unable to take in more. Or we may become habituated or numb and need ever higher thresholds to evoke a response. Along the way, existing in a perpetually reactive state, we often neglect deeper truths that can guide us toward the change we seek in more enduring and meaningful ways.

Led by our 2D mind, we can be less erratic and more systematic in driving change. Guided by reason and logic, 2D draws on data to convince us why change is important (e.g., research studies on the dangers of smoking, loneliness, or pandemics). Yet such approaches also often fail to provide lasting motivation. Absent deeper meaning, data can feel hollow or have limited impact. We may struggle to apply abstract probabilities to our personal decisions. Or, we may rationalize that taking a risk just once won't make a dent in the overall odds, as we slide down slippery slopes.

To overcome the limits of 2D's ways, we often create strict rules or plans to drive compliance. But unless our intention for change is guided by deeper resonance, resistance often prevails. For instance, in education systems around the world today, an emphasis on scores and metrics can lead students and teachers to feel forced to focus on tests and results. This leads to a neglect of nurturing education's deeper mission—to cultivate curiosity and a lifelong love of learning—which naturally fosters the very excellence that tests try to coerce through 2D ways.

When guided by resonance, we excel because we love to learn, and not just to get a high score on a test. We let go of unhealthy habits because we care about our health or being there for our loved ones. In a pandemic, we sacrifice our own comfort to help save the lives of those we may not even know. In this way, as we learn to let resonance guide us, we release resistance in all its forms.

THE PERSISTENCE OF RESISTANCE

While releasing resistance may sound straightforward in theory, it is not always easy in practice. To explore this, let's consider another metaphor. Imagine you have decided to go on a trip to visit a friend in a nearby town. Here, the "trip" can stand for any change that matters to you. It may be personal (e.g., changing a habit, career, or relationship), or professional (e.g., leading a team, movement, or culture). To plan your trip, you call your friend, decide on a date, and make plans for the day.

In many aspects of our lives, we move through this sequence with relative ease. We decide to do something and get it done. Yet most of us have at least one domain in our life where we struggle with change. A reader once described how she could easily run 10 miles every day, yet felt unmotivated to apply for a new job, despite her frustration with the status quo. Another shared how he had made rapid progress in his career, yet perpetually struggled to sustain an exercise regimen.

Returning to our trip metaphor, this is what happens when resistance scuttles our plans: We walk out the door and get in our car but, as we turn on the ignition, decide we don't feel like driving and walk back inside. Or we get on the road but, as soon as we encounter some traffic, turn around. Or we see an exit for a shopping mall and decide to go there instead. Or we arrive at our friend's place but stay in our car. Or we go knock on their door, say hello, and then leave.

While such derailments may sound absurd in the context of visiting a friend, we end up approaching change this way more often than we realize. Unaware of how we get in our own way, we may blame outer factors such as terrible traffic or an enticing mall, for sidetracking us. We each harbor our own unique forms of derailing resistance. Here are some common ones:

1. Feeling overwhelmed or stressed, driven by incessant fear or worry about our lives, the future, or the state of the world.
2. Existing in a state of anxious alertness, making detailed contingency plans for everything that can go wrong.
3. Focusing our attention on self-critical, belittling, or berating thoughts, or indulging in limiting beliefs.

4. Complaining, holding grudges, weaving grievance stories, harboring resentments, or constantly venting gripes about others or the world.

5. Replaying the past in endless loops, with each retelling amplified by new stories and emotions, or by creative associations made in our memory archives.

6. Feeling paralyzed, disempowered, helpless, or like a victim of circumstances out of our control (e.g., pandemics) or in others' hands (e.g., lockdowns).

7. Avoiding unpleasant or uncomfortable truths with tactics such as procrastinating, being in denial, searching for distractions, overcompensating with perfectionism, or even engaging in reckless acts.

8. Striving for order and control in all parts of our lives—such as routines, environments, or relationships—blind to how control itself is just an illusion of the mind.

9. Allowing our own moods and attitudes, or even our sense of self, to be defined by others' views.

10. Projecting our thoughts and stories onto others or the world by judging, pointing fingers, or claiming expertise in reading others' minds or knowing their truths.

11. Fixating on fixing others or our outer circumstances while ignoring the one place where we hold all the power to actually drive change—within.

12. Depending on others' opinions for making our own decisions and then blaming them when we feel discontent with the outcomes.

13. Striving for perfection or seeking approval or validation from others, forgetting that we are each always whole.

The list goes on and on, but hopefully this gives you a sense for resistance's many forms. In fact, just reading through this list can evoke inner resistance as 1D and 2D find associations to their own ways, stirring up intense emotions or analyses.

When our trip to visit our friend is guided by resonance, we keep our intention for seeing them at the top of our mind. We know

why the visit matters to us (i.e., we cherish and want to nurture the friendship). And we don't allow trivial factors (i.e., an urge to visit the mall or an aversion to traffic) to tempt or derail us.

Resistance is like a box built by our mind, whose walls we mistake as real. Thus, we sit inside the box and think it defines our world (e.g., *I am depressed and this is my reality*). Sometimes, we get so used to the box's walls, we become oblivious to how they constrain us. Or, we may feel as if resistance is a weight or burden we carry, giving it power over our mind and life (e.g., *I have depression and depression has me*).

To shatter its walls and release its weight, we learn to recognize resistance for what it is—a creation of our mind that we can let go of anytime. As we call its bluff, we come to see how resistance loses its power over us, diminishes, and ultimately fades away. In short, the secret to releasing resistance is to stop holding onto it. As we cease resisting it, which is like no longer sitting in the box, or carrying it on our back, we can move on and leave it behind.

While facing a persistent source of inner resistance may be the last thing we want to do, that is the only path to releasing it. If we sense that a form of resistance is deeply entrenched or long-standing, it can be helpful to get support from a therapist or coach. They can help us unblind ourselves from blind spots that lead us to hold onto resistance, often without conscious thought.

A powerful way to deepen your practice of releasing resistance is to become aware of when you experience resonance or resistance throughout your day, and to notice what evokes each. As we attune to our inner sensations, such as lightness versus heaviness, constraint versus freedom, or serenity versus stress, we learn to acknowledge what we feel in the moment. Then, we can allow it to pass through us without resisting or holding onto it. In this, AAA can be of help:

1. **Awareness:** As we learn to observe resonance and resistance within us, we can notice when resistance arises (e.g., *I sense I am tensing up*). Guided by awareness, we simply observe it. We acknowledge and face resistance that appears but do not indulge it or dwell in it. We just let it be and observe how it shifts and transforms.

2. **Acumen:** With acumen, we can also discern what insights a resistance may harbor. We can ask ourselves: *What wisdom or lessons does this resistance bear?* (e.g., *My tension harbors a deeper fear of loss.*) *How can I learn to be with it?* (e.g., *Don't offer this fear a feast. Put it on a fast. Fear has not seen the future. Trust courage to guide you.*) As we use reason and wisdom to calm and soothe resistance, we slowly learn to quiet its inner chatter.

3. **Agility:** Next, we can consciously allow resistance and its associated emotions, thoughts, and stories to flow through us. We often sense this in visceral ways as releasing resistance naturally leads us to experience resonance. We may feel a sense of lightness or relief, as if a weight or dark cloud has been lifted, and a renewed sense of joy enters our being.

As we recognize and release resistance, we gain immense inner freedom. We feel increasingly carefree, light, and at ease. Even when the going gets tough, we sustain courage and hope in the face of fear and doubt. We confidently walk ahead guided by an inner, resonant light that emerges from the heart. At times, we may even feel as if we live surrendered to the peaceful ways of a greater force that we fully trust to hold and guide us.

Writers and artists often describe this as feeling that their work emerges from the natural flow of a higher power that moves through them without conscious effort on their part. The words seem to write themselves. The essence of this experience rests in the simple yet powerful act of surrender.

THE ART OF SURRENDER

The notion that surrender can lead us to freedom appears deeply counterintuitive to 1D and 2D. They tend to think of surrender as giving up, capitulating, being passive or apathetic, or becoming uncaring or indifferent. Yet, as 3D knows, surrender is a deeply empowering act in which we consciously release resistance to allow resonance to flow.

❖   ❖   ❖

On the morning of her triathlon, when Tara's 1D mind urged her to stay home, she shifted from following its tales to questioning their trails. She realized that all her resistant thoughts had the same goal—her survival. As Tara acknowledged and accepted their presence, their intensity declined, which freed and opened her mind to consider other possibilities.

When Tara later resolved to be "one with the elements" as she jumped into the lake, she consciously surrendered to nature to harness the power of resonance.

Surrender is flowing, and being in harmony with, the eternal changes of the universe without trying to resist or control their natural course. We learn to accept—not endorse or embrace but just face—any resistance we come across. This creates space for resonance to guide us.

Surrender is an act of immense courage and the deepest source of inner clarity, healing, peace, and freedom. We get out of our own way and let our wisdom and truths guide us. We engage in an act of total trust that rests beyond 1D and 2D's grasp.

In facing surrender, 1D may fear what happens when we let go of resistance, even when its pull holds us back. Yet, as we resist resistance we feed its persistence. We tightly hold onto that which we desperately want to let go. This is how, when we are afraid of our fears, we give them power over us. Or, when we fixate on feeling stuck, we get more entrapped.

Writers literally refer to this as writer's block, which can feel like being in a swamp or walking through molasses. We expend significant energy yet feel we make little or no progress.

The 2D mind can be a sophisticated accomplice in all this. It may lead us to analyze that which we are resisting in such exquisite detail that we continue giving it undeserved mind space, furthering its persistence. Or 2D can lead us to become so obsessed with letting go that its chatter drowns out our ability to follow deeper 3D wisdom on how to simply do so.

Sometimes, 2D may even create well-rationalized arguments on how our resistance serves a useful purpose, such as, *you are not a pessimist, you are a pragmatist. An optimist ignores all that can go wrong. You are not like that.* Yet, both 1D and 2D fail to see how their ways just uphold resistance.

All along, 3D's deeper wisdom reminds us that resistance has no power over us unless we empower it. By embracing surrender, we do not deny or become passive before the realities of our life or the world. Rather, instead of focusing on resistant thoughts that entrap us in their limited ways, we direct our attention to resonant ones that can guide us toward new possibilities.

Instead of pushing back on resistance, we accept and transcend its existence with patience and compassion. We forgive our 1D and 2D minds for their ways, realizing that they do not—and cannot —know better. Thus, guided by surrender, we cease resisting change and courageously step into its flow, trusting resonance to guide us.

❅   ❅   ❅

A few years ago, during an early afternoon in late spring, I visited a high school in Washington, DC. A teacher there had asked if I would spend some time with her students to whom she had recently introduced the concept of the three states of mind. I readily agreed and enthusiastically arrived with prepared PowerPoint slides.

As I began talking, the class soon became disengaged. Eyes rolled, and yawns rippled across the room. I sensed the energy in the group sink and swiftly closed my laptop. We decided to sit in a circle and just started talking.

The students began to share their daily life challenges—broken homes, violence, trauma, despair about the future, and a sense that, as one of them said, "No one out there cares about us." After listening to their experiences of struggle and pain for some time, I asked, "What brings you joy?"

Suddenly, the energy in the room shifted, as if sunlight rushed in. Their faces lit up as the students excitedly started sharing their passions. A young girl, Hope, who had earlier talked about the difficult circumstances of her home life, became quiet.

She had been crying as she described the desperate hopelessness and depression that engulfed her. While several of her classmates, the class teacher, and I had all offered motivating words to lift her spirits, I sensed she struggled to internalize them.

Now, as we talked about sources of deeper joy and resonance, Hope spoke up and shared that her favorite activity was writing poetry. It made her feel as if she entered a different world. She could be creative and free in expressing herself. She felt like it gave her a voice. Hope shared how it made her otherwise suffocating problems feel more bearable. Her eyes sparkled as we asked her if she would read us a few of her poems.

We spent just a few hours together that day, yet laughter and tears flowed. Weeks later, Hope wrote me a note to say she still thought of that visit. A year later, she emailed to ask how she could publish her poems—she had continued writing and was on her way to college.

＊   ＊   ＊

Hope's story has stayed with me ever since. The shift she experienced is available to each of us. As our thoughts shift from negative to positive, hopeless to hopeful, and depressed to uplifted, we transform from the inside out.

We come to understand why we are as we are, accept who we are, and learn how we can grow from it. With time, we gain confidence to not only listen to our heart's song but also share it with the world. We experience, firsthand, how our minds, lives, and world transform as we consciously decide who we become.

PLAY, PONDER, PRACTICE:

RESONANCE & RESISTANCE

As you move through your days, play with observing your inner sensations of resonance and resistance in response to what you face.

As we learn to tune into these two sensations, we can access vast new realms of insight on both.

The following questions can help guide your exploration of this practice:

1. When do you experience inner resonance? What evokes it? How can you grow its flow in your days?

2. When do you experience inner resistance? What provokes it? What can you learn from it? How can you reduce its appearance or practice releasing it when resistance shows up?

CHAPTER 9

How We Decide
Who We Become

On most evenings, we have options for how to spend our time. Some may be rare opportunities (e.g., a special celebration or performance) and others available almost anytime (e.g., cooking dinner or watching television). While we often deliberate on what to choose, our most crucial decision is often not as conscious a choice. It is the mindstate we bring to whatever we decide to do.

When we are unaware of our mind's state, we tend to obediently follow its thoughts and feelings, assuming we are beholden to their arrival, tenure, and departure. As we come to know our mind, we realize that what we think is as conscious a decision as any other we make. Thus, not changing anything is as much a choice as changing everything.

We decide who we become as we choose between living in the past, focusing on the future, or being in the present from moment to moment. Although our mind mostly exists in, and thinks about, the past and future, it is our presence in the present that determines how we experience both.

When we are fully present in the moment, 3D leads our mind. This evokes resonance to guide our thoughts, words, actions, and, ultimately, our way of being. We create space to be with ourselves and listen to the whispers of our heart. We can make peace with the past and gain clarity on the future. We grow courage and confidence to transcend fear and doubt. Ultimately, we arrive at a deeper sense of meaning, a higher purpose, and the guiding values that define us. To explore how we decide who we become, in this chapter, we look at how our meaning, purpose, and values shape how we live, work, and lead in the world.

THE MEANING OF MEANING

Meaning, in simplest terms, is a sense of connection to something that transcends us. It helps us rise above the needs of our 1D impulses and 2D ego and connects us to our 3D essence. One of the most powerful examples of this is described in *Man's Search for Meaning*, a book written by psychiatrist and Holocaust survivor Viktor Frankl.

Frankl shares deep reflections on how he and his fellow Nazi concentration camp victims and survivors coped with their brutal circumstances, which were marked by unbearable suffering, traumatic separations, profound loss, and often certain death.

Even in the depths of despair, Frankl observed how those who sustained a sense of meaning—something to exist for beyond their own lives—were better able to cope with, and at times even survive, the painful psychological toll of the camps.

The sources of people's meaning varied—loved ones, a project or mission, or acts of selfless service—yet they had the same effect. They evoked a deep sense of commitment to something that gave them a fierce will to live. In contrast, those who lacked such an inner force often felt hopeless, despondent, or defeated—and often more easily gave up within.

Meaning harbors immense power because it leads us to live guided by resonance. Through the years, countless readers have shared inspiring stories on how their own sources of meaning gave them invaluable courage and strength in the face of seemingly unbearable challenges such as devastating diagnoses, deaths, or crises.

Meaning has such a powerful effect on us because we know why living matters to us. We don't succumb to the perpetual drumbeat of 1D's instincts, such as fear or anxiety, or to the fault lines of 2D's ego, such as doubt or insecurity. We also increase our immunity to resistance, trusting that our meaning's resonance is much stronger than it. We harness hope, courage, and light in the face of darkness, fear, and despair. To explore how we can gain clarity on our own sense of meaning, let's look at it through the three mindstates.

In searching for meaning, 1D tends to seek out sources of excitement or pleasure and 2D looks for what validates our uniqueness or importance. Yet such sources of meaning are fleeting, and leave us ever dependent on the outer world to deliver experiences or achievements that bring mostly short-lived happiness.

A sustained sense of meaning, in search of which we often follow many paths in the world, emerges from deep within, as 3D knows. For example, many people who share stories of undertaking radical change in their lives, such as giving up on unhealthy habits or addictions, talk about how what compelled them to quit—often cold turkey—was not grounded in 1D's fears (e.g., of premature death), or 2D's data (e.g., on the higher probability of death), but in a sense of meaning that arose from their heart.

One wanted to live to see his daughter graduate from college. Another did not want to cause more pain to her family. Many sought inner freedom—to be able to commit themselves to what truly mattered to them—without feeling like they were victims of urges they could not control. Each tapped into a deep sense of meaning that evoked resonance and made their prior unhealthy habits meaningless to them.

When we connect to a resonant source of meaning, it empowers us to overcome the pull of resistant forces. We remain grounded even before 1D's impulses or temptations and don't blindly obey 2D's rationalizations. In short, a cookie tempts more when we see it as a source of pleasure and less when eating healthy means more to us instead.

Living with a deep sense of meaning is the secret to the serenity we sense in those who own little in the world and yet seem to behold the whole universe in their hearts. Guided by 3D, they transcend

1D and 2D's unending needs for security and significance. Even those who diligently meet all the needs of their 1D and 2D minds still often talk about harboring an inner restlessness marked by a sense that there must be more to life than what 1D and 2D want. This is because, as 3D knows, our sense of meaning resides not in what we accumulate or attain in the world. Rather, it rests in how we live from the heart to honor our shared humanity with a deep sense of peace, love, and joy.

Sometimes, it takes a crisis to reveal what matters most to us, when all that we think matters is lost. As life forces us to pause (e.g., in a pandemic or in any situation that shakes up our lives), we get a chance to stop and listen to our heart. Like standing in the eye of a hurricane, when we enter a state of inner stillness, we realize what we truly care about amidst all the turmoil around us.

We discover the source of true security, which rests in a peaceful heart, and of true significance, which resides in living by its truths. We realize how simple it is to feel fulfilled and how little we need of what 1D and 2D have us chase, often for much of our lives.

We come to delight in simple acts of kindness. We give from the heart without needing anything in return yet gain a profound sense of fulfillment that nothing else can bring. We sustain gratitude for simply being, starting with the gift that we are here right now and able to breathe and read this. We sense a deeper connection to all we meet and realize there are no strangers. As we honor our sense of meaning this way, we naturally discover our purpose.

THE PURPOSE OF PURPOSE

If we consider our sense of meaning as living in resonance, we can think of our purpose as how we express it and share it with fellow beings. In essence, our purpose is an embodiment of our deepest intentions and passions. It guides what actions we take and how we show up in the world. Rather than defining a specific role, field, or path, our purpose reflects our way of being.

Since concepts around "finding our passion" or "living our purpose" can seem confusing or overwhelming to many, let's try to clarify them here. Mainstream advice on passion and purpose often leads us to search for them led by 1D or 2D. For instance, 1D may look for what excites us (e.g., composing music) and wonder if we can make a living from it (e.g., as a musician). Meanwhile, 2D may weigh how our purpose will make us look, what others will think, or how it validates our uniqueness. *Can I make a name for myself? What will my friends or family say?*

Some people have many interests or passions and struggle to select "the one" worthy of being their purpose. Others may have a hard time identifying even one leading contender. In both instances, the stakes can feel too high, or nothing may live up to 1D or 2D's lofty aspirations. In the morning, we dream of writing music all day; by the evening, we doubt if we can make a living that way, are daunted by the hard work involved, or wonder if we even want to do it.

Guided by 3D, we can shift our perspective and discover how, at a deeper level, our purpose is a commitment to an enduring passion and not a contract to satisfy 1D and 2D's needs. The true purpose of our purpose is to honor a way of being that serves and uplifts our shared humanity. Hence, we can live it through many possible paths. For example, if our purpose is to foster healing, 3D can lead us to discover many ways to be a healer.

Physicians can heal with treatments, therapists with talk, and teachers with heartfelt caring. A writer can heal with a story and a pastor or priest with wisdom that unites a community. A poet can mend hearts with soul-stirring words and a musician with uplifting compositions. A nurse can heal through bedside support and a librarian by sharing books that lift spirits. Thus, whether we focus on nurturing a child, a patient, a garden, a village, or a nation, we become a healer through our way of being.

One way to gain clarity on our purpose is by knowing what it is not. When we say we are passionate about something yet give up on it when we stumble (i.e., we do not get the job, promotion, or admission we desperately wanted), we were likely driven by 1D or 2D motives.

For example, we can discern a politician's commitment to their oratory of serving the people by observing what they do when they lose an election or do not gain a desired position of power. Do they sit back until their next chance to win or gain power, biding time and changing tracks, or do they sustain an unwavering commitment to service in other forms, especially ones that may be less lucrative or not as high profile? While 2D may rationalize the former paths with compelling arguments (e.g., *I need to focus on making money for my next campaign*), 3D reminds us that to truly serve the people we need not big money but a big heart.

When we stay true to our purpose, the journey becomes its own reward. We experience the same contentment at the start as along the way and at the end. We serve and pursue our daily work for its own sake, even when it feels difficult or challenging, as most meaningful work at some point does. We strive for excellence with an intrinsic passion that comes from the heart, rather than for outer recognition or rewards.

In this way, we experience how work becomes play or we sense we have found our calling. We may toil for long hours yet feel as if the time flies by. Sustained by resonance, we strive with an effortless ease instead of dreading our daily work as a forced grind we seek to escape. Thus, the purpose of our purpose is not to point us to a specific path but to give us a way of being no matter where we end up, trusting that the journey itself will show us the way. To ensure we don't get lost, our values guide us.

THE VALUE OF VALUES

Our values are the timeless, enduring principles and truths that guide how we embody our meaning and purpose in the world. If meaning defines our why, and purpose how we live it, our values clarify our way of being. For instance, we may decide to serve humanity (meaning) as a healer (purpose) guided by caring and compassion (values). Or we may educate children (meaning) as a teacher (purpose) to share and instill a love of learning (values).

Our values sustain and grow resonance in our lives and help reduce and release resistance. As we live in alignment with them, they come to guide how we make decisions, take actions, and face trade-offs.

By taking time to consciously identify and articulate the core values that matter most to us, we can learn to keep them front and center in our minds and lives. While some of our values shift as we evolve through life, many sustain as enduring guides, like a compass that shows us the way no matter where we are.

In a graduate course on *Leading Change* that I taught at Johns Hopkins for several years, the students engaged in an exercise each semester to create their own Values Compass. Many students said the exercise helped them gain clarity across many dimensions of their work and lives and urged it be added to this book. So, if you would like to try it out, the exercise is included in **Appendix C**.

While we may have clarity on some of our values, we can identify others by reflecting on moments in our lives that evoked a deep sense of resonance and meaning. Also referred to as peak experiences, such moments tend to form vivid imprints on us marked by deep peace, love, or joy. To recall them, we can ask ourselves:

1. When in my life did I experience a deep sense of peace in my heart? What values do those experiences reflect?
2. When in my life did I experience a deep sense of love in my heart? What values do those experiences reflect?
3. When in my life did I experience a deep sense of joy in my heart? What values do those experiences reflect?

As you reflect on why these experiences hold deep meaning for you, your values begin to emerge. Many who have engaged in such a reflection are surprised to find shared threads between what they viewed as different experiences (e.g., both traveling and cooking for friends can reflect the value of fostering connection).

Another way to distill our values is by reflecting on principles that we consider absolutely non-negotiable. For example, if integrity is among our core values, we strive to uphold it no matter what, and avoid situations that could lead us to potentially violate it. As we honor our values, we become more conscious of when we are out of alignment with them. We also come to realize that much of the resistance and friction we encounter in life results from experiences that challenge or are in conflict with our deepest values.

For instance, if we value freedom, we will sense harmony in a life that upholds it, and resistance in one that restricts it. If we cherish simple living, we may sense friction in relationships, partnerships, or friendships with people who focus on the trappings of material status. If we value health but work for a company that prioritizes profits over patients, we may feed our stomachs but feel sick in our hearts.

With clarity on our values, we confidently transcend resistance created by 1D fears or 2D rationalizations that could lead us into potential transgressions. For instance, 1D may say, *do it just this one time, there is no other way.* And 2D may add, *these are the rules of the game, you must play by them to succeed. Everyone else is doing this too.* Such slippery slopes are all around us. They are often bolstered by statements such as: *Don't challenge the establishment. It is too risky to ruffle feathers. You may ruin your reputation. First get to the top and then speak your mind.*

Yet, as we slide down a slope of inner resistance it can grate on us within. When we honor our values instead, we move ahead with resonant inner harmony and peace. Ultimately, we realize that, every decision we make is an opportunity to clarify and affirm our values since everything we face has trade-offs.

EVERYTHING HAS TRADE-OFFS

Returning to the example at the start of this chapter, for whatever we decide to do on a given evening, we leave all other options on the table, some for later, others forever. Every action we take and every decision we make has trade-offs. For everything we gain we give up something else. And with everything we lose, we gain something too, even if this may feel difficult to accept in the moment.

Much of our anguish in life emerges from how we face our life's trade-offs and what stories we tell ourselves about them. In facing potential trade-offs, 1D tends to be driven by scarcity thinking. It tries to have it all or frets about what to let go, gripped by a Fear of Missing Out (also known as FOMO), a modern term to describe

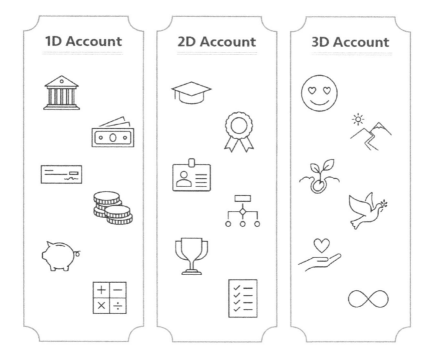

an age-old malady. The 1D mind also easily falls prey to emotions that can leave us feeling indecisive or confused.

The 2D mind tends to engage in extensive pro and con analyses to optimize decisions. While this can be valuable in weighing trade-offs, when data are limited or nonexistent, 2D's efforts can lead us into siloed, binary, or circular thinking.

Our 3D mind reminds us that there is more to trade-offs than 1D and 2D can know. We can explore this with a simple metaphor in which we consider our life as a portfolio of three accounts:

1. Our **1D account** consists of what we need for survival, such as access to money and resources to meet our basic needs. We can liken this to a traditional bank account.

2. Our **2D account** consists of non-monetary assets that mark our identity, such as skills, credentials, and achievements. Since we cannot easily put a numerical

value on these, we tend to "measure" them through titles, awards, ranks of power, and other such metrics.

3. Our **3D account** consists of assets that cannot be measured in 1D or 2D ways. We grow this account by living in resonance, aligned with our values. We fill it with acts that reflect our sense of meaning and purpose such as nurturing meaningful relationships, engaging in selfless service, or cherishing simple joys. The more we share this account's currencies of peace, joy, and love, the more we fill it up with contentment, fulfillment, and connection, attaining true wealth within.

The 1D account is zero-sum. When we give our money to someone else, we no longer have it. When we focus on this account, we can come to live by a scarcity mindset, scared of losing what we have or trying to accumulate ever more.

The 2D account offers some shared value. When we share our skills with others, they benefit and we improve our mastery of the skills. Yet 2D can foster a transactional mindset, focused on what it gains for what it gives. Also, to measure its own worth, 2D constantly compares its own balance to others' accounts. Hence, 2D's perceived wealth remains ever relative.

While 1D and 2D's accounts are filled with what we gain or attain in the outer world, 3D's account is generative, limitless, and self-renewing. It fosters an abundance mindset. Its currency is a way of being that builds resonance within and around us. As we give from this account, such as through caring, kindness, and love, we are enriched within.

Since our 3D account's currency is internal, only our own heart can tell us how full it feels. When our 3D account runs low, no matter how full our other two accounts, we feel empty and unfulfilled. When our 3D account feels full, we realize how little we need in our 1D and 2D accounts to feel content and fulfilled.

That said, we do need to fill our 1D account enough to meet our basic needs. Existing in perpetual survival mode is stressful and exhausting. For example, an artist may struggle to sustain 3D creativity when overtaken by 1D anxieties about paying bills. Often, filling our 2D account with an education and professional skills can, in turn, help us fill our 1D account.

But once our basic needs are met, when we mostly focus on our 1D and 2D accounts, we often come to neglect our 3D account, as this next story reveals.

As the clock on his computer hit 9:00 p.m., Peter, a partner at a firm in Washington, DC, sighed. He would again fail to leave the office at a reasonable hour. In recent months, Peter had been working late nights for a major project that was to decide his next promotion. He had missed spending time with his family and friends, barely visited his aging and ailing mother, and taken no time off, despite feeling burnt out.

Tired and frustrated, he had felt less creative and productive, as if missing from his own life, sensing it race him by. Commuting home on many late nights, Peter often wondered, *what is it all for?* In recent months, Peter struggled to get out of bed in the morning, and sensed tension and resistance run through his body.

One morning, while taking a shower, Peter decided to linger under the hot water just a little longer. He sensed deep relaxation wash over him. Suddenly, he had an epiphany that jolted him out of the feeling that he had been moving through the motions of life with a sense of resignation, as if stuck in a rut.

Peter realized the promotion he was working so hard to attain would take him further away from his family and friends and the simple, everyday joys he cherished. Meetings would engulf his life. The extra income would be nice—maybe for a bigger house or nicer car—but was not necessary to satisfy his basic needs.

The promotion would boost his stature at the firm and among his peers, but it would also put more pressure on him to bring in new clients and grow profits. Peter mused, *why am I so obsessed with this promotion? Is it because my boss praised me with how much potential he saw in me to lead the firm? Is it to show others that I am good enough to get it? What am I trying to prove to them—and myself?*

As these questions swirled through his mind, Peter was surprised to feel tears streaming down his face. He recalled the deep sadness he felt when he lost his father as a teenager. He had always wanted to make his dad proud. His father worked hard all his life and Peter rarely saw him besides weekends.

As Peter finally got out of the shower, still feeling emotional, he recalled the parting words of a relatively young partner at the firm, who recently took an early retirement: "Sometimes money costs too much."[25] Peter suddenly understood what the partner meant.

Many of Peter's peers in the industry seemed so preoccupied with filling their 1D and 2D accounts that they lost perspective on life. It didn't help that elitism was pervasive in Peter's field. Many of his colleagues were so used to transactional deal-making that they assumed others always wanted something from them, even when that was untrue. Many were also self-conscious of their social class and mostly stayed in silos of their own kind, while appearing distant or arrogant to those on the outside.

Over late-night drinks at firm events, some of Peter's peers often quietly shared a wistful longing for simpler lives and deeper connections with their families and friends. In the depths of their hearts, they knew how money and prestige failed to deliver the desired returns in their 3D accounts. In fact, focusing on their 1D and 2D accounts seemed to reduce even the marginal returns in those as they needed ever more to impress others around them (e.g., second homes, celebrity name-drops, or exotic vacations).

This was not what Peter had signed up for when he joined his firm a decade ago. It was also not what his dad worked so hard for, or would have wanted for his son. Unlike his dad, who climbed his way out of poverty by working at a factory all his life, Peter realized he had a choice.

Peter felt relief wash over him. He could not remember the last time he sensed such clarity, as if a weight lifted after all these years. He realized he was still living out a childhood feeling of trying to make his dad proud, yet repeating the very past he sought to transcend. As Peter got ready and left for work that morning, during his commute, he asked himself three simple questions:

1. Does this satisfy a survival necessity or does it just feed a short-term emotional impulse? (1D)
2. Does this grow my potential or does it just feed my ego's hunger for validation or significance? (2D)
3. Does this nurture my soul? Is it aligned with my sense of meaning, purpose, and values? (3D)

Peter used these questions as a lens to reflect on all aspects of his work and life, including the many associations, boards, and committees he had joined through the years to advance his career.

Upon reflecting on the trade-offs Peter had made across his three accounts, he realized that while the promotion would put a little more in his 1D and 2D accounts, it would not only *not* fill his 3D account but deplete it further. The promotion would leave him with less time and freedom to pursue the simple joys he cherished: hiking in the nearby hills, hosting a relaxing backyard barbecue for friends, camping under the stars, or even just taking his dog for long walks on weekends.

As Peter gained renewed clarity on what mattered to him, he decided to cut back on many of his professional obligations and to rethink his career. Eventually, he decided to retire from the firm and practice his skills in a small town where life was simpler, the pace slower, nature all around, and his mother a short drive away.

At his farewell lunch, Peter smiled with delight as he recalled words his grandmother often repeated when he was young: "When we are happy, we want to be happier. When we are content, it is enough. There is no contenter."

BALANCING OUR ACCOUNTS

Research studies show, and many lives publicly lived validate, once we have enough to meet our basic needs, more money and more accolades do not buy us more happiness. In fact, in excess, they tend to have the opposite effect, as daily news stories on the dark sides of power, riches, and fame remind us. This happens because those with outsized balances in their 1D and 2D accounts mostly get focused on either protecting or growing them. For, 1D fears losing what it has, or that it does not have enough. In parallel, 2D seeks to sustain its stature by comparing itself to others, engaging in an unwinnable game that conceals deeper truths.

Often, that which we desperately want is entangled with what we just as much do not want. For instance, 2D may not want someone's success *and* their sacrifices, or their fame *and* their loss of freedom, or their powerful title *and* its associated lifestyle. At times, 2D tries to feel good by comparing its balances to those who appear to have less. Yet all comparisons—whether with those 2D sees as better or worse off—leave us on a wobbly plane.

No one has it all, regardless of how we define what "all" looks like. We may love our job but not all our colleagues. We may love our city but not everything about it. We may love our relatives and friends but not all of their habits and choices.

When we focus on what we want to have, or what someone else has, we miss out on what we already have, and always will. For, while we do not get to choose everything life serves us, we do get to decide how we perceive its trade-offs. Time takes us all through highs and lows that remind us of this truth. What we decide in our mind, as we ride through life, is our choice.

In facing loss, do we mourn what was or celebrate what it made possible? In gaining more than others, do we grab and stash it away or share it with those in need? In facing those who differ from us, do we focus on what is "wrong" with them or on what may be missing in our own hearts? In the face of a crisis, do we focus on our own survival or on our collective thriving?

The thoughts we choose from moment to moment write the stories of our brightest and darkest days. We learn how every thought itself has trade-offs, and how we can let go of ones that don't serve us to live by ones that nurture and sustain us. We realize, deep within, how true joy does not rest in getting what we want, but in the wisdom of accepting that everything—every single experience—has trade-offs that can teach us something, even if this is difficult to believe in the ecstasy of pleasure or to accept in the depths of despair.

To be content with what we have, and to be at peace with what we traded off for it to have become possible—whether by circumstance or conscious choice—is the secret to enduring happiness, true wealth, and lasting inner success.

We discover contentment not by maximizing or optimizing what we have but by finding deeper joy in our heart where we are, with what we have. As we attain such a way of being, we gain greater harmony, harness resonance, and release resistance at each step of our way. We focus on "filling" our three accounts aligned with our sense of meaning, purpose, and values.

Then, decisions become simpler. When 1D asks, "If I can get more, why shouldn't I take it?" 2D can add, "What will you lose to gain this?" and 3D can ask, "What do you truly seek in your heart?" In this way, as we consciously choose the thoughts, stories, and paths that guide our lives, we not only live with more resonance and resilience, but also gain the power to decide who we become within and, ultimately, in the world.

PLAY, PONDER, PRACTICE:

THREE ACCOUNTS

To reflect on your three accounts, you can explore your current work and life through the questions Peter asked himself on page 163. Beyond those, here are a few more questions to consider as you think about your accounts:

1. How have I filled my 1D, 2D, and 3D accounts?

2. How full does each account feel to me?

3. How might I (re)balance my accounts to attain a holistic sense of contentment across all three?

PART IV

How We Work Together

Jim and Jill at Happy Hill

Hiking in the Norwegian fjords, Jim had just begun to enjoy retired life when the chair of Happy Hill's Board of Directors called late one night, pleading for his help. Happy Hill, one of the world's largest cookie companies, was in crisis. Its CEO had just departed after a whistleblower uncovered improprieties. Its leadership team's morale was plunging. Senior executives were fielding more calls from headhunters offering jobs than from distraught employees demanding answers.

The Board Chair asked Jim if he would consider the CEO role. At first, Jim politely refused. He loved retired life. "Call me if you change your mind," the Chair said as he hung up.

As Jim lay awake later that night, he pondered the opportunity. He always loved a challenge. Rescuing distressed companies was his passion. Beyond that, and perhaps most compelling to him, he had been a loyal Happy Hill customer all his life. He cared about seeing the company thrive. The next day Jim called the Chair to accept the role and booked a plane ticket back to the U.S.

Over the following years, under Jim's leadership, Happy Hill regained its stature as a leader in the snack food industry. Its customers loved the company's variety of colorful, single-wrapped cookies sold through coffee shops, corner bodegas, lunch delis, gas stations, and grocery stores. Made from simple ingredients (flour, sugar, and butter), and without preservatives, they were the closest to home-baked cookies many loyal customers said they could find.

Jim treasured daily notes from delighted customers on how Chocolate Chip Crush had been the highlight of a birthday lunch or how Peanut Butter Jiggle, affectionately known as PBJ, had brightened an afternoon office meeting. Customers often shared how they relished PBJ's grape jelly center melting with the soft-baked cookie, which evoked fond childhood memories of peanut butter and jelly sandwiches.

This was exactly what Meg (Megumi) Walker, Happy Hill's legendary founder, had envisioned when she started the company in her kitchen during the years after World War II. Inspired by a small snack shop her father's family in Tokyo, Japan had run for over five hundred years, Meg aspired to build a similar company in America to last for centuries. After she lost her husband in the war, she hoped the company could help support both her livelihood and her hometown, where ethnic and racial tensions ran high in the war's aftermath.

Jim got out of bed every morning excited about Happy Hill's future. Yet, a few years into his tenure, some members of the company's Board of Directors ceased sharing his enthusiasm. Worried about fast-moving trends toward healthier, allergen-sensitive snacks, they felt Happy Hill needed to innovate faster to stay ahead. To them, the status quo, even if executed with perfection, spelled extinction. When they had recently asked Jim to draft an innovation strategy, they were underwhelmed by his ideas.

At the next Board meeting, these Board members made their case for change. Jim's strengths as a CEO were inward-focused: management, operations, and execution. No doubt, Happy Hill's employees loved him and the warm, collegial culture he had built. Jim had brought attrition to a halt and the leadership team was intensely loyal to him. The company's suppliers and distributors valued Jim's focus on transparency, integrity, and trust. He was deeply respected in the industry, even among Happy Hill's fiercest competitors.

But Happy Hill could not survive without innovating, the Board members argued, and their patience with Jim had run out. After a heated debate, their proposal to replace him prevailed by one vote.

A few months later, after an extensive search, the Board hired Jill as Happy Hill's new CEO. At the company town hall where her appointment was announced, everyone seemed surprised. Jill was a novice at snack foods. Her prior company, Well Water, which she had started a decade earlier, was a pioneer in organic sports drinks. It grew from a small startup to an industry disruptor through continuous innovation in flavors for hydration products for professional and recreational athletes. Six months ago, it was acquired by one of the world's largest beverage companies.

After some months off, Jill was itching for her next challenge. Several Happy Hill board members were inspired by the Well Water story, which she had shared extensively through high profile media coverage, news articles, keynote talks, and a recently published book. They hoped Jill could fill Meg's shoes in defining a new vision and strategy for the company.

A few board members had reservations about Jill's lack of experience and felt that, while she could bring a fresh perspective, Jim's guidance would be invaluable in ensuring stability in internal operations.

Lucky for them, after meeting Jill, Jim agreed to stay on as COO through the transition. Jill seemed to complement his skills and he welcomed the breath of fresh air. A part of him also felt relieved to relinquish external responsibilities. Jim decided to ride this out as his last rodeo.

Jill had also grown up with Happy Hill cookies, but she felt the company had become stodgy and outdated. Three months into her new role, Jill set up a new innovation unit that reported directly to her. She hired its head from her prior company. She pushed for healthier ingredients, such as replacing refined sugar with organic cane sugar and stevia, and adding trendy superfoods such as organic chia seeds, which were high in omega-three fatty acids.

Jill's vision for the innovation unit was to launch two new cookies per year, and to phase out one old product with each launch. She also announced a new branding task force to re-design the company's look and feel. All this was bold, for sure.

Many longstanding Happy Hill employees were startled by the speed of change. They sensed disregard for what the company had built over the last seven decades in the cookie business. Among customers, while some welcomed novelty, others complained. They longed for the familiarity that defined their childhoods—the same colorful wrappers and classic tastes that were part of traditions in families, at office parties, and among friends.

On many evenings, as Jim would get ready to leave the office, employees often quietly pulled him aside to share their concerns. Reflecting on these conversations, often late into the night, Jim sometimes felt as if he no longer recognized his own company. He worried about the effects of Jill's leadership on the team.

Not long into Jill's tenure, tensions boiled over one Monday during the weekly leadership team meeting. The innovation unit presented the new Organic Protein Power (OPP) cookie and proposed it replace Peanut Butter Jiggle (PBJ), which had become more difficult to make due to rising food sensitivities and the need to avoid cross-contamination on the factory floor.

Jill's passion for the OPP cookie was palpable. Her daughter had a peanut allergy, so she personally understood the risks of allergens. Jill's voice trembled as she made an impassioned case. When Jill got into selling mode, she could sell snow in Alaska, her Board champions had once joked, evoking a tired yet true cliché.

This was the first time Jim heard of shelving the long-standing customer favorite. PBJ was the first cookie Meg Walker had made at Happy Hill. It had even made an appearance in a Hollywood classic. Jim sighed as he realized Jill was not even born when that movie was released.

Jill powered through her slides and shared an updated financial model on how the cost of the new OPP cookie, alongside the innovation team's growing budget, would reduce funding for the company's foundation. "The foundation will need to pivot toward outside philanthropic support," Jill said as she wrapped up and asked if there were any questions.

Jim felt deep sadness well up within. Meg had established the foundation not long after she founded Happy Hill. It helped first-time entrepreneurs gain access to the resources and mentorship that Meg wished she had received when she started her company. Jim deeply respected its mission and work.

A few months after becoming CEO, Jim had visited Meg in the hospital just before she died. He had promised the 98-year-old pioneer, a true trailblazer for her times, that he would do everything in his power to sustain her legacy, including the work of her foundation, which meant so much to her.

After Jill's presentation the room was deeply divided. Tension filled the air. Each side had compelling evidence to bolster its case to either drop or keep PBJ. Some cheered for change. Others felt the cookie was the heart and soul of the company, and they were opposed to any changes that affected the foundation.

Emotions ran high and the chatter of side conversations grew louder. Jill wondered, aloud, if she should just call a vote and let the majority decide. In that moment, a thought flashed into Jim's mind.

As he spoke, the room fell silent, and everyone listened. "Why don't we mull this over for a few days?" he said. "I know there is a sense of urgency, but I also sense that there are important questions we need to address."

Jill reluctantly agreed. A deep sigh of relief rippled across the room. At least they now had some time to make the decision before next month's Board meeting.

The battles at Happy Hill are timeless ones: creating space for change versus honoring tradition, embracing innovation versus preserving the establishment, and driving novelty versus ensuring stability. They reflect deeper, universal questions that arise in teams of all sizes, whether families, startups, organizations, communities, or nations: How do we find common ground across diverse or opposing viewpoints? How do we coexist in harmony and unite behind a shared vision? And how do we collaborate to realize our individual and collective dreams together?

Happy Hill's story traces through the next three chapters. It reflects themes from real-world stories across diverse teams and organizations. Here, we define a team as two or more people who interact with each other because of a shared mission (e.g., employees in an organization), a shared intention (e.g., members of a community), or a shared context (e.g., relatives in a family).

As we work together in teams, while some of our interactions are guided by formal contracts or rules, most emerge from informal and unwritten ways of being. In this, three core pillars guide us: **communication** among a team's members as well as across teams (Chapter 10), **leadership** that unites a team behind a shared vision (Chapter 11), and a **culture** that helps all members of a team thrive (Chapter 12).

How We Talk to Each Other

The instant two minds meet, two worlds of thoughts, feelings, and stories collide. Beyond spoken words, we perceive each other's body language, facial expressions, and gestures. We weave what we learn with what we know to guide how we relate to each other. Along the way, we connect with resonance, collide with resistance, or, most likely, engage in a dance with both forces at play.

More than any other human skill, the ability to communicate is vital to our survival as tribal beings. It guides our relationships at home, at work, and in the world. When we meet in resonance, we can experience a sense of belonging and connection, even with those we have just met. When we clash with resistance, we can lose the capacity to understand even those to whom we are closest.

Even though we have more devices, technologies, and platforms to talk to each other than ever before, it is remarkable how often we still fail to engage in genuine, meaningful conversations. We either neglect or avoid chances to connect or, even when we do, engage in shallow exchanges that stay silent on our hearts' deeper truths.

We mostly learn how to talk to each other by observing and absorbing patterns and habits from others around us. Few of us receive a formal education on how to communicate—how to express ourselves clearly and how to listen attentively to another.

Thus, we tend to reflect on our communication skills mostly once they have landed us in trouble. This results in an immense waste of human potential—not only through active conflicts but also through passive aggression, silent rifts, estrangements, and countless hours of rumination on conversations gone awry.

When the stakes are high, such as in a crisis or disaster (e.g., a pandemic), how we communicate can spell the difference between life and death, since it drives what we do to keep others and ourselves safe. Throughout human history, nothing has likely caused more harm and loss than misspoken, misunderstood, or misjudged words. Along the way, we lose countless opportunities for deeper connection, stronger teamwork, and ways to thrive together. But it does not have to be this way, as we explore next.

THE THREE STATES IN CONVERSATION

We begin by looking at how we talk to each other through the lens of the three mindstates. While we tend to lean on all three states in a conversation, we often default to some more than others, based on our own tendencies and the contexts of what we face.

1D CONVERSATION (Me State)

When led by our 1D mind, which tries to keep us safe, we tend to communicate in reactive, self-protective, or impulsive ways. Since the mind's focus in this state is on itself, we can think of 1D communication as the "me" state. This manifests in varied ways.

Some enter "fight" mode marked by reactive, emotional, or intense speech that can come across as being snappy or aggressive. Others may resort to dramatic or exaggerated language, marked by words such as "always" or "never," or they may overreact and jump to conclusions. Some speak in an irritated or tense way, driven by frustration, anger, anxiety, or other forms of inner resistance.

Still others may enter "freeze" mode and dwell in the past, repeating old stories in excruciating detail, as if those tales still define their whole reality. Others may speak with a critical or negative tone, complaining, venting, or airing grievances and gripes on perpetual replay.

Yet others, driven by 1D's urge to escape, enter "flight" mode and avoid having a conversation altogether. When they sense intense emotions being triggered, they may "shut down," put up a wall, or have their guard up. Or they may act in passive aggressive ways, such as making excuses about being too busy, or having no time to talk. Some disengage from any interaction, also referred to as ghosting, focused on their own emotions, while disregarding how their behavior affects others.

Sometimes, a mind in the 1D state may even disassociate from its own emotions, pretending they don't exist or speaking in ways that come across as cold or uncaring. Or, when 1D gets "triggered," it proceeds to blame others for its own reactions. For example, 1D may exclaim, "you make me so angry" or "you push my buttons" while the other person may sometimes have no way of knowing how they "pushed" a "button" that they could not see or touch.

As is likely apparent by now, since 1D sees conversations as zero-sum battles, it is not the best state of mind to lead communication. As a listener, 1D cannot grasp the deeper intentions of others' words or see a situation from their point of view. It also tends to impatiently interrupt and blurt out its thoughts, worried it will forget what it has to say. While 1D's concerns and emotions often do deserve our attention, instead of expressing them led by 1D, we can bring 2D's reason and 3D's compassion to articulate and understand them in calmer ways.

2D CONVERSATION (Me versus You State)

When led by our 2D mind, we can communicate in a more orderly and composed manner, guided by 2D's rational tendencies. While 1D often blurts out words without filters, 2D exerts self-control to think through what to say and what to leave unsaid.

Thus, 2D can share its thoughts logically and support them with concrete examples and data. It is also able to articulate 1D's emotions without getting caught up in their intensity or drama. But while 2D may take pride in its talents, especially when compared to 1D, it harbors its own limitations. Since 2D focuses on validating our sense of self, it tends to default to a "me versus you" mentality, which can inhibit connection and foster a sense of separation, fueled by siloed and binary thinking.

The 2D mind tends to anchor its words and views in its own stories and beliefs, often defending their righteousness, while blind to how its own judgments color them. In the face of a disagreement, rather than patiently understanding the other's position, 2D easily points fingers to assert its innocence, or to claim it is a victim of another's behavior. "I can't help it if you are angry with me," 2D may say, rationalizing away its own responsibility in an interaction, a tendency referred to as gaslighting in the extreme.

Also, driven by what it can tangibly perceive, 2D is easily swayed by—and draws conclusions based on—appearances and first impressions. Thus, 2D may become focused on style over substance or take pride in its cool composure, while forgetting the deeper intention of communication. It may even project a facade of polished perfection that can come across as inauthentic or untrustworthy to others and inhibit a deeper connection.

The 2D mind also has a proclivity for indulging in stereotypes and gossip about others, projecting its own assumptions and stories onto them. Yet 2D's elaborate tales about others, especially absent 3D's insights and wisdom, mostly just showcase its own biases and views, rather than genuine truths about another.

As a listener, 2D can be more attentive than 1D, since it is able to consider the other's perspectives. Yet 2D mostly listens in order to prepare its own counterarguments, explanations, or defenses, rather than to understand the other at a deeper level. Or 2D can become transactional or calculating, focused on what it can gain from an interaction.

While 1D sees a conversation as a battle to survive, 2D tends to treat a dialogue as a competitive duel in which it must not only defend itself—and its beliefs and stories—but also come out on top. Hence, 2D may proceed to undermine another's credibility to justify dismissing their views. Or it may dissect others' spoken words in exquisite detail, while failing to grasp their deeper meaning, which may be left unsaid. Or 2D may declare, "let's agree to disagree" to avoid having its own opinions challenged.

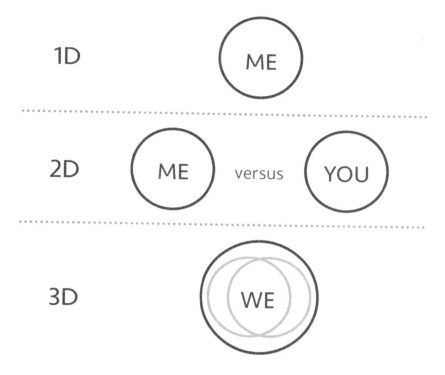

Thus, in communication, although this is difficult for 2D to accept, it is limited without 3D's humanity, kindness, and heart. By learning to recognize when 2D gets in our way, we can gently ask it to step aside to let 3D lead us instead.

3D CONVERSATION (We State)

When led by our 3D mind, which we can also think of as the "we" state, we communicate with the intention of building mutual understanding and connection. We transcend 1D's emotions and 2D's ego to speak and listen guided by 3D's compassion.

We focus our attention on the relationship ("we") rather than on just ourselves ("me") or notions that there are two sides ("me versus you"). This fosters resonance and harmony as we express our truths with patience and positivity. We are open, honest, and authentic in sharing how we feel and what we think.

We also strive to learn about the other without judgment and with humility. We ask thoughtful questions with the intention of knowing another from their perspective, guided by empathy. We seek connection, such as through timeless values that reflect our shared humanity. This builds mutual trust and respect.

We realize how 1D's emotional reactions and 2D's ego-driven judgments grasp just a small part of a much bigger whole. Instead of thinking of a conversation as a battle or duel, 3D sees each interaction as a chance to connect, learn, and grow; and, in the face of a conflict, to forgive, heal, and let go.

This is how 3D guides us to calmly engage in difficult conversations that feel unpleasant to 1D or threatening to 2D, leading both to avoid such discussions. While 1D fears discomfort and 2D seeks control, 3D knows that communication is neither a conflict we must fight nor a competition we must win.

Guided by 3D's intuitive insights and wisdom, we can share our emotions with mutual kindness and compassion, without feeling overwhelmed, agitated, or scared. We can also share our views with humility and without judgment or self-righteousness. We express our feelings and perspectives in service to the relationship rather than to defend or assert ourselves, as 1D and 2D might.

In the 3D state, we become truly compassionate listeners. We stay centered and calm to understand each other as fellow human beings and beyond the literal meaning of spoken words. This reflects what we mean when we say, *little was said yet much was understood*, or when we feel truly seen and heard to experience a deep sense of belonging with another.

Guided by 3D's wisdom, we remember that life is not a duel to fight but a dance in which we are all waltzing along as best as we know. We accept that we all get clumsy or fall out of step sometimes, and recognize that most conflict is born from 1D and 2D not knowing where to turn.

When 3D leads our mind, we help 1D and 2D bring their best to communicate with a united mind. Even when we engage in a conversation with another mind in the 1D or 2D state, we help uplift the interaction in ways that often transform it. To explore how this can happen, let's return to Jim and Jill.

THE ART OF COMMUNICATION

After the tense Monday morning meeting on the fate of the PBJ cookie, Jim returned to his office and settled into his chair to reflect on the challenges at Happy Hill. Decades ago, when he was around Jill's age, and still early in his career, the business world was different. Today, a relentless barrage of new technologies and global forces was reshaping all aspects of work.

Ever-shorter market trends, shrinking product life cycles, and shifting supply chains made it harder to keep up. Many established sources of thought leadership had become obsolete. At times, young social media influencers seemed to know more about trends than long-standing industry experts. Yet both upstarts and stalwarts still struggled to extract meaningful insights from the ever-growing content speeding along the world's cyber highways.

Most leaders and organizations tended to respond reactively, by chasing trends and their competitors' tails. Jim sensed this was what Happy Hill's board had done in hiring Jill, and what she was doing now in pushing for innovation. In pursuing rapid, wholesale change, the company risked throwing out the baby with the bathwater, as Jim often said to his team.

Happy Hill's core values of striving for simplicity, honoring tradition, and supporting local communities were fundamental to its mission. While some of the company's products and practices were admittedly ripe for reinvention, others were the result of decades of expensive, hard-earned, trial-and-error learning.

As Jim reflected on this, he realized Jill lacked the deeper historical context of the company's legacy. This made it easier for her to come in as a radical change agent. But it also made it harder for her to see the value inherent in the status quo.

These days, new seems to spell better, Jim mused. *All new eventually becomes old but not everything grows mold. When it is gold, it retains or even gains value with time.* Jim realized it did not make sense to wholesale discard Happy Hill's crown jewels—its most popular products and best practices—just because they had been around for a long time. This extended to its loyal employees, many of whom had been with the company for decades but were now threatening to quit as they felt disrespected and devalued by recent changes. *If we don't take care of our people, we are nothing,* Jim thought. *They are like our family.* At the same time, Jim also recognized how some employees had become so comfortable in the familiarity and consistency of established processes that they resisted necessary change under the guise of honoring tradition.

Jim began to reflect on his home life. He and his wife came from very different family backgrounds. His was conservative—politically, socially, and economically—and hers liberal on all fronts. He had grown up in rural Alabama and she in downtown Baltimore. When they first met in college, each harbored stereotypes about the other. Through many long, deep and at times difficult conversations, they came to respect and appreciate how each had arrived at their beliefs, based on their unique cultural and life experiences.

Jim pondered whether a similar dynamic existed between the innovation team that reported to Jill and the old guard that reported to him. Rooted in different histories, both held onto their stories and had not gotten to know the other at a deeper level.

Each side had also constructed arguments that rationalized its ways as being better. He sensed that both sides also feared for their own survival and felt threatened by the other. This had pitted them against each other. Each blamed the other for the rift and sought to "win" the civil war that was tearing the company apart.

These tactics were about as effective today as on battlefields through time. Everyone was bearing their toll. Stress had increased, productivity had declined, and customers were less satisfied. Trust and respect had eroded across teams. Work began to feel like a tiring chore to many who had known and missed better days.

As Jim pondered potential solutions, he decided to start by inviting Jill over for dinner so they could get to know each other better and share their perspectives on the company's vision, mission, and values. Jim looked up at his bookshelf and picked up his copy of *United Mind.* He turned to page 183 to reflect on how to approach the conversation. This is what he read:

THE SCIENCE OF INTERACTION

While the art of conversation can seem mysterious, we can distill its essence into practical steps, especially in navigating a challenge, conflict, or negotiation. It is important to acknowledge that the starting point for any meaningful interaction is two individuals or parties who willingly want to meet and talk, with the shared intention of understanding each other. We cannot force others into a conversation they do not want to have. Then resistance tends to dominate. Although, as we transform how we meet others—whether perfect strangers or dear friends—we often experience, in profound ways, how our own ways of being shift their response as resistance melts and resonance takes its place. Once two sides agree to talk, these four steps can serve as helpful guides:

1. CREATE A SAFE SPACE

For any meaningful conversation to take place, both sides need to feel safe (1D), guided by mutual trust and respect. Each side needs to trust that it can honestly share its feelings and views without feeling "attacked" by the other's emotional or judgmental reactions.

To create a safe space, both sides decide on the principles that they will mutually honor, such as: maintaining confidentiality, not interrupting each other, and speaking in a calm tone of voice. These questions can help establish such a space:

1. What helps you feel safe, so you can be vulnerable and share with honesty and authenticity?
2. What helps you feel respected and that your words are heard and honored?
3. What helps you experience trust, so you can be both trusting and trustworthy to help foster connection?

By creating a safe space, we help build resonance and reduce resistance. By setting mutually respected boundaries, we soothe 1D's fear of turmoil. By creating well-defined guidelines, we reduce 2D's need for control.

It is also vital both sides honestly articulate their intentions for engaging in the conversation. This fosters mutual trust, respect, and alignment. When one side, driven by 1D or 2D motives, has predetermined the outcome, or misrepresents its intentions, it can be tougher, if not impossible, to find common ground. Resistance tends to stall the conversation or keeps it from gaining momentum. It may move in circles, wasting time and energy without progress. Or we may discern a lack of sincerity and authenticity, such as words that don't align with actions, roundabout rationalizations, polite deflections, or empty promises. On the other hand, when two sides are aligned in their intentions for coming together, they can always find a path toward greater understanding or connection.

2. SHARE STORIES

Once two sides establish a safe space, both can share their thoughts, feelings, and stories. Guided by 3D, we openly talk about who we are and what matters to us. We speak our truths yet also respect and honor each other's feelings with compassion.

As listeners, we strive to understand each other's sense of meaning, purpose, and values. We suspend our own preconceived notions and ask genuine, open-ended questions to learn about the other as a human being (rather than to confirm our own stories about them). This fosters positive, resonant exchanges in which we often discover new insights and truths. Sometimes, just being able to honestly express our thoughts, feelings, and stories to another fully present, non-reactive, non-judgmental, and compassionate being leads us to our own answers and wisdom.

3. FIND SHARED MEANING, PURPOSE, VALUES

As both sides let their guard down, they feel safe and transcend 1D's fears. As they suspend judgment, they step out of their silos and release 2D's need for control. As both share from the heart, with courage and humility, they begin to find common ground beyond the differences that 1D and 2D tend to see. As we grow our understanding, we naturally discover deeper points of connection rooted in our shared humanity. Though two sides may have vastly different histories or experiences (as far as 1D and 2D can tell), 3D's wisdom reminds us of what we share when it comes to our heart's most fundamental needs and longings.

A documentary filmmaker once shared how she explored this by bringing Israeli and Palestinian women together in a weight loss program. As the women discussed their shared struggles in losing weight, they laughed together and built rapport and camaraderie, which ultimately built new bridges of compassion and trust.

4. WRITE NEW STORIES TOGETHER

As we find shared points of connection, we create space to imagine new possibilities, ones neither side may have considered on its own before. Then we can come together to write new stories, ones that resonate with—and reflect the shared truths and values of—both sides. In this way, two sides can look beyond their differences to envision a future both long to see. This fosters connection and belonging as they realize how they can attain their own, and their shared dreams, together.

THE POWER OF CONNECTION

When Jill came over to Jim's home for dinner later that week, both felt grateful for the chance to get to know each other better. Jim listened with patience and interest as Jill shared her life story.

As the daughter of immigrants who worked long hours at multiple jobs to make ends meet, Jill had drowned herself in books as a child. They were her babysitters, teachers, and friends. After excelling in high school, she received a full scholarship to a top college. Jill shared how Happy Hill cookies had been a part of her birthdays for as long as she could remember. Even after becoming a successful entrepreneur, she would still stop by a corner deli each birthday to treat herself to a Happy Hill cookie.

Jim shared his own journey, from being raised on a humble farm to developing a passion for turning around struggling companies and eventually landing at Happy Hill. Jill listened with attentive curiosity and came to appreciate the depth of Jim's experience and perspectives.

As the hours flew by, and dinner and dessert were long past, Jim and Jill's meandering conversation filled both with deep resonance. They gained renewed respect for each other. Jim sensed Jill's sincerity in trying to help build a great company. He now grasped how her zeal for change had been mistaken as disrespect by some in the old guard. He sensed her heart was in the right place.

Jim shared more about Meg Walker's journey in founding Happy Hill after her husband died in Pearl Harbor. Meg had deeply grieved for him, an American of Scottish descent, who was killed by the Japanese, her own people. As Meg mourned the senselessness of war, she pledged to commit the rest of her life to building bridges of love and understanding in diverse communities.

Jill was amazed to learn about Meg's fierce and indomitable spirit. "I had no idea Meg led such a courageous life," Jill said. She could relate to the legendary founder's struggles and loss. Jill quietly described how she had lost her parents in a car accident when she was in college.

Tears started flowing down Jill's face. "I am so sorry," she said, embarrassed. "I really miss them right now. They would be about your age if they were alive today. They would have been so proud."

Jim's heart filled with compassion as he gained deep admiration for the courage it must have taken Jill to get this far. He responded, "Jill, I can understand how much you must miss them. Please don't apologize. One of my teachers once said, 'tears water the soul.' At Happy Hill we bring our whole humanity to work. It is okay to be vulnerable. We all are. Life has taught me that opening our hearts makes us all stronger, because it gives others permission to be their fully human selves too."

"If only the world had more leaders and mentors like you," Jill said, smiling through sniffles. She now sensed, in the depths of her being, the fierce loyalty and affection many in the company held for Jim's caring compassion as a leader.

Jim continued, "Jill, Happy Hill is a family. Meg always believed this company served a higher purpose: to bring us together through our shared humanity. No matter what happens at work, we all look out for each other. You are now part of this family, and always will be, no matter where else our lives may take us. Trust that you have my full support as you lead the company."

Jill felt a profound sense of peace enter her being. As they parted ways, they decided to meet in the boardroom the next day to review Happy Hill's vision and strategy together.

As Jill drove home, she reflected on how some of her peers seemed to get carried away by a focus on growth and innovation, often at any cost. Many used trendy, mission-focused language that did lip service to serving humanity while prioritizing profits, at times bolstered by short-sighted business practices. *Maybe this is why stress, discontent, anxiety, depression, and addictions seemed so prevalent among them,* Jill wondered. *They are living divided within.*

In private, many fellow CEOs had confided in Jill about the pressures of trying to keep up with their peers. While projecting perfection outside, they often felt hollow within, as if trapped in an unending grind. More was never enough. There was always one more box to check, goal to chase, or feat to attain.

Jill admired the deep contentment that engulfed Jim and the positive effect it had on Happy Hill. She felt blessed to have Jim as a mentor and looked forward to learning from him.

Jill also realized she had not fully appreciated the power of Meg's foundation, which reflected her passions too. Jill's eyes welled up as she reflected on its potential to help aspiring entrepreneurs like her younger self. As ideas gushed through her mind, she decided to save them for her meeting with Jim the next day.

❧　　❧　　❧

When guided by their 3D minds, two beings, no matter who they are, can always find shared threads of connection. The 2D mind may proceed to challenge this by thinking of our worst nemesis or history's darkest figures, convinced there would be no common ground. The 1D mind may fear how this statement threatens its comfort zone of staying away from its foes. Yet beyond the many ways in which our emotions and ego attempt to protect us, we all long for the same truths, even when those longings sometimes tear us apart—whether in our own hearts or from each other.

We all long for the joy that emerges from feeling connected—to our own self, each other, and something that transcends us—however we experience that. We want to know that we matter, and we want to live with a sense of meaning and purpose.

As we understand our own mind and heart better, we grow compassion for why others are as they are and learn to accept them as such. We recognize how most conflict consists of unresolved inner struggles cast onto others or the world. While such projections can be mistaken as shows of might (1D) or validation (2D), our heart's wisdom knows that violence, conflict, hurt, and hate are just misplaced longings for love (3D).

When we talk to each other—and ourselves—led by our 3D mind, we come to see that we each have inner turmoil to resolve, in our own way on our own terms. We judge less and don't take others' words or actions personally. We accept that we are each on our own journey with its own struggles, which others often cannot see. We come to share and care from the heart, often without the need for words. We learn to trust that, when we help another feel safe and whole, they mostly reciprocate. Ultimately, we realize that, when all is said and done, when we talk to each other, we all want the same—to feel heard and understood.

PLAY, PONDER, PRACTICE:

CONVERSATION CANVAS

To explore the themes of this chapter, while teaching students or leading workshops, I have used a simple exercise called the **Conversation Canvas**. If you would like to try it out, the exercise is included in **Appendix D**.

The Canvas allows us to reflect on the inner monologue that runs through our mind as we engage in a dialogue with another person. As we reflect on our own thoughts, and how they align with our words, we can gain insights that transform how we talk to each other.

CHAPTER 11

How We Become Leaders

As communities and nations around the world confront massive parallel economic, social, political, and environmental challenges, the need for good leadership is more urgent than ever. We need leaders who can bring us together to solve these challenges in enduring ways. Such leadership is not a calling for a few to pursue, or for some to wait for until called upon to lead. It is a duty we must each honor, in our own way, to help unite, heal, and better our world.

In a graduate course on *Leading Change in Biotechnology* that I have taught at Johns Hopkins for several years, we explore the mastery of such leadership through the lens of the fast-changing life sciences field. Though the course's insights and lessons hold true for leaders anywhere. Students in the class are mostly full-time working professionals who range in age from their twenties to their seventies and span diverse roles across healthcare organizations, private and public research laboratories, biotechnology and pharmaceutical companies, startups, nonprofits, investment firms, and branches of the military.

We start each semester with a deep dive into the vast range of leadership theories and models developed by the world's leading scholars on how to motivate, influence, and manage others.

These include trait and behavioral theories, change management frameworks, and emotional intelligence skills, to name just a few.

Inevitably, as the semester progresses, a shift occurs. Students evolve from studying concepts and case studies (2D) to reflecting on their own leadership (3D). Their learning transforms from imbibing intellectual knowledge to experiencing inner change. They become more aware of how they think, act, and lead—not just at work but across all dimensions of their lives.

The students come to recognize that while leadership may be bestowed on some by lofty titles, its true power does not reside with them. Ultimately, they arrive at a deeper understanding of what it means to be a leader: to serve as a guiding light to uphold and uplift our shared humanity. They realize we can—and must—each take on the mantle of leadership, regardless of who we are, or where we sit in the hierarchy of an organization, system, or society.

By semester's end, most conclude that leadership is not a talent some are born with, or a rarefied set of skills a few attain, but a way of being we can each learn. They come to see how the work of changing the world begins within. For, we become leaders by leading our minds and hearts first, which gives us the clarity, courage, and confidence to inspire others and help change the world.

THE THREE STATES IN LEADERSHIP

In this chapter, we explore how we can each master the essence of such leadership, as well as, how we can support it in leaders around us. To begin, we look at what happens when each mindstate comes to dominate a leader's ways of doing, thinking, and being.

1D LEADERSHIP

In the 1D state, a leader tends to engage in urgent, rapid action in reaction to outer forces. In the face of a looming crisis, this can be a vital skill to avert greater catastrophe. Yet, when 1D leads a leader's mind, trouble tends to follow.

A 1D leader's worldview is mostly rooted in short-sighted thinking, self-protective (and often self-serving) instincts, and a scarcity mindset. Guided by reactive impulses, such leaders tend to be at the beck and call of their emotional urges and gut instincts, which, to complicate matters, they easily mistake for their intuition.

Such leaders often restlessly move from one thing to the next, unable to prioritize challenges or sustain their attention on any one matter for long. They tend to lead with irrational or unpredictable actions that can confuse, or even mislead, those who follow them.

In facing a complex decision, they easily succumb to tunnel vision, focused on erratic quick fixes, ignoring both relevant details and data (2D) and the greater, holistic big picture (3D). Instead of thinking ahead to prepare and plan, such leaders tend to stay in denial, believing mostly what they see with their own eyes, or often taking action when it is too late, once a crisis has caused avoidable destruction or spiraled out of control.

Even absent a crisis, such leaders mostly focus on their own needs and interests in 1D ways. Easily threatened by dissent or having their trusted "gut" questioned, 1D leaders tend to shun frank, open dialogue with diverse minds. They often demand blind loyalty from those on their team and prefer to rule over others with intense emotions, such as anger or fear. They may use emotionally charged rhetoric such as, "The world is dangerous. Only I can save you." Such leaders also tend to look backwards and talk about preserving the status quo or returning to a past long gone.

Those who tend to follow 1D leaders often get swiftly swayed by their own 1D minds. When such leaders evoke fear, their followers may feel as if the leader "gets" them and their emotions in visceral ways. Yet, when such fear-filled talk lacks 3D's compassion, wisdom, and vision, it becomes a false safety blanket that ultimately leaves such a leader's followers in the cold, as history repeatedly reminds us. Since 1D cannot think beyond itself, a 1D leader's followers often fail to see that, despite what such leaders may proclaim, they rarely serve or save those who follow them.

Ultimately, 1D leaders fail to endure since they harness resistance in all its forms, which becomes depletive, unsustainable, and often self-destructive. Some 1D leaders succumb to impulsive acts, such as ethical, moral, or legal transgressions that eventually catch up with them. Many lack strong teams around them since they tend to attract opportunists who "use" such leaders to satisfy their own needs, and then easily turn against them when that may serve their needs better.

Thus, while 1D leaders can gain positions of power, and may even exert dictatorial or authoritarian control for a while, they eventually run themselves (and their followers) into the ground. Ultimately, such leaders never attain that which they crave most: genuine appreciation, loyalty, respect, and a legacy that lasts, all of which arise from selflessly serving and winning hearts.

2D LEADERSHIP

In the 2D state, a leader tends to operate in more rational ways. In facing a crisis, 2D leaders make decisions guided by logic and data. They lean on experts and metrics to evaluate options and develop solutions. Today, 2D leaders sit atop most of the world's large organizations, establishments, and nations, since they tend to excel at making plans, mastering skills, and rising through ranks of power.

Yet, while such leaders may take pride in their cooler heads, being led by the 2D mind harbors its own limits. These can be tricky to spot because some 2D traps are double-edged and, in other contexts, serve as talents too. To grasp the limits of 2D leadership, let's untangle how the needs of the ego can bungle it.

Since 2D cannot think beyond itself, such leaders become easily beholden to serving their ego—to establish it matters and makes a difference. This need for validation can manifest in varied ways, such as seeking public recognition through titles, awards, or positions of power or prestige that signal success. Yet, as 2D leaders focus on serving their egos, they come to neglect a much greater power which resides in honoring our shared humanity.

Thus, 2D leadership can easily devolve into transactional, calculating, or self-serving ways of being. Often, such leaders become focused on how others can be of use to them, instead of interacting with a selfless spirit of service and connection.

At times, 2D leaders resort to socially acceptable, 3D-sounding rationalizations such as, "I want this position of power so I can serve others" or the pernicious humble-brag, "I am so humbled to receive such high praise." Yet, as 3D knows, we do not need powerful titles or high honors to serve our fellow beings.

Like 1D leaders, 2D leaders tend to attract followers who share their ways of thinking. Thus, such followers value and are easily impressed by 2D aspects of leadership. They often find comfort in the credibility bestowed on their leaders (and, by association, on them) by well-established silos. Yet, this can lead 2D leaders and their followers to come across as elitist to those who don't share their silos, which can foster divisiveness and disunity.

Sometimes, 2D leaders may impose rules on others that they do not follow themselves. For instance, during the Covid-19 pandemic, several leaders declared social or travel restrictions that they themselves proceeded to violate. At other times, 2D leaders may dismiss those who don't share their views as "ill-informed" or "ignorant" while missing the deeper truth that we cannot gain the trust of those we judge.

Guided by 3D's wisdom, we can learn to see beyond a 2D leader's appearances to discern how their walk matches their talk: Do they say one thing but do another? Do they declare an intention (e.g., to increase equal opportunity, protect the environment, or reduce poverty) but then rationalize decisions that further the status quo or do lip service to their words?

Also, 2D leaders tend to be overconfident in their ability to avoid their own ego's sway over them, ignoring the influence that access to immense power or money has on most minds. For example, a political leader may talk about serving the people yet take election funding from organizations that compromise the welfare of the very people the leader promises to serve.

Another example rests in the revolving door between corporations (which serve shareholder profits) and government agencies (which regulate corporations to serve the people's welfare), leading to a corrosion of trust in leaders at both kinds of institutions.

When confronted with such discrepancies, 2D leaders tend to rationalize or dismiss them. Ever concerned about their own reputations, 2D leaders usually hesitate to face the truth or to speak truth to power, especially if doing so may rattle their stature in the very establishments that enabled their rise. Thus, they often focus on promoting or implementing marginal, socially acceptable, or by-the-book solutions that don't rock the boat.

Yet this is exactly how such leaders often fail to address the root causes of challenges or to drive real change. When courageous voices guided by timeless truths stand up to challenge them, 2D leaders often judge or dismiss such voices as being too idealistic or naive about how the system really works, how the game is played, or how the sausage gets made.

As 2D leaders fixate on silos and pedestals of their own making, they become blind to how pride breeds arrogance, narcissism, and a false sense of invincibility. This eventually paves the path to the decline of many 2D leaders, as they fail to honor humanity's shared welfare at the cost of upholding their own ego.

Ironically, insignificance is what a 2D leader fears most, given the ego's hunger for outer validation. At this point, 2D may feel defensive and assert, *I'm not like that. I behave like everyone else around me. No one is perfect. Reality is messy. What is wrong with wanting validation? Don't we all need it?*

Despite what 2D may say, guided by 3D, we can see the holes in its rationalizations. Rather than justifying the ways of 2D leaders, as 2D would love to do, 3D guides us to discover deeper answers by courageously facing the only leader we truly know—ourselves. As we do, we access the essence of true leadership.

3D LEADERSHIP

In the 3D state, a leader thinks, speaks, and acts guided by the power of resonance. To a 3D leader, leadership is selfless service, guided by a deeper universal sense of love for humanity. Such leaders strive to serve a higher purpose: to uplift our shared humanity, whether by changing one life, guiding a community, or serving our collective well-being.

Led by their 3D minds, such leaders unite and bring the best of all three states to their leadership. They harness patience, courage, and calm to transcend 1D's impulsive reactions. They bring a deep sense of humility to rise above 2D's egoic needs. Yet 3D leaders also harness 1D's focus on action and 2D's reason to guide them. Unlike 1D's scarcity thinking and 2D's transactional tendencies, 3D leaders harbor an abundance mindset, which leads them to uncover creative possibilities, discover potential inherent in everyone, and find opportunities everywhere.

The secret to 3D leaders' power rests in the simple fact that they know themselves. They know what they stand for, and why. They have clarity on their sense of meaning, their life's purpose, and the values that guide them. Such leaders have learned to trust their inner voice—and its intuition and wisdom—to light their path. They see everyone as deserving of equal dignity and respect and generously share appreciation and gratitude.

Such leaders are deeply authentic in acts large and small, even absent a witness or judge. This is how they harness the power of a united mind. They are the same person across all dimensions of their work and lives, which helps them reduce friction and resistance and exist in harmony and resonance.

They are widely loved and earn trust with a loyalty that no 1D or 2D force can match. They attain this not through grand titles or talks but by leading by example. They live their words and steadfastly honor values such as kindness, caring, and compassion.

Unlike 1D and 2D leaders, who anchor their leadership in the outer world, 3D leaders' signposts are inner ones regardless of, or sometimes despite, public praise or rebuke. This gives 3D leaders an unshakable sense of inner courage and confidence. While 1D or 2D leaders get easily defensive or insecure in accepting their flaws or weaknesses, 3D leaders openly recognize that we each face challenges in life, just in different forms.

Thus, 3D leaders are open about mistakes they made when misled by their 1D or 2D minds, knowing this is how we all grow and learn. They speak with courage and candor, free of fear and shame, which inspires others to do the same. In guiding others, rather than instilling fear (1D) or exerting control (2D), such leaders abide by the spirit of what they strive to impart. They lead others by inspiring them to trust the leader within themselves.

All this perplexes the 1D and 2D minds, which struggle to grasp the source of 3D's power, convinced it must be more complex than this. Yet 3D can distill it to one word: love. The secret of true power is love. With love in our hearts, we bring kindness and compassion to all our interactions. We can face hard truths and speak truth to power guided by a deep sense of caring and duty to honor all fellow beings. We can weigh the holistic, big picture impact of our actions. Yet we can also see how we may affect a single life, ensuring that we further everyone's welfare.

By now, 2D may be itching for examples of 3D leaders to decode how real humans can be like this. While 2D may consider such exemplary leadership an unrealistic ideal, it is all around us. Such leaders are the ones among us who uphold our shared welfare, restore our faith in humanity, and keep us going. They are often not well-known because they do not seek out lofty titles, magazine covers, or attention.

You can find the most powerful examples of such leadership by reflecting on beings you met in your own life's journey who embodied such 3D qualities and had a profound influence on you. **Appendix E** includes some examples that readers, audiences, and students have shared through the years.

Although 2D prefers to focus on case studies of famous leaders, such curated profiles offer limited insights to guide us. Ultimately, we learn to become leaders not by following in another's footsteps but by knowing the mind that matters most in our leadership journey—our own. To explore how, we return to Happy Hill. (And just so 2D knows, we will also touch on some notable 3D leaders).

LEADING FROM WITHIN

When Jim and Jill returned to work the next day, they met in the boardroom in the afternoon. Each had taken some time to reflect on their own leadership styles. Jill realized that, while she was good at painting a bold vision and sharing it with passion, she was also easily overcome by fear and self-doubt. To cope, she often sustained a restless sense of urgency, always trying to get more done in less time.

Yet Jill could now see how this often became stressful, draining, and even counterproductive. She realized she was easily swayed by her 1D and 2D minds. Jill traced this to her fear for survival and her fierce drive to succeed, which had served her well in overcoming the challenges of her younger years.

Jill now recognized how her relentless drive alienated some colleagues, especially when it drove her to impatiently micromanage them or to enforce unreasonable expectations. She had heard through the company grapevine that some thought of her as being an arrogant know-it-all. She realized that her zeal to prove herself, led her to easily succumb to 2D's need for validation, such as by demonstrating her knowledge or by seeking public recognition. While excelling and standing out had helped Jill escape hardship when she was young, she realized how it now hindered her ability to build a collaborative, unified culture at Happy Hill.

Jill also admitted to herself she could make more time to pause and listen to her intuition's guidance. She felt renewed gratitude for Jim's wise ways and realized there was much she could learn from him. His rooted sense of peace, which she had always longed for in her heart, gave her a profound sense of grounding and stability.

Jim, for his part, reflected on his own leadership, which he had nurtured through the years as a way of being. He thought back to the many leadership theories he had learned over the decades—with names such as authentic, resonant, enlightened, compassionate, servant, purposeful, mindful, values-driven, wise, holistic, or humanistic—which all, described what was, in essence, 3D leadership.

Jim had long been inspired by the life journeys of leaders such as Mahatma Gandhi and Martin Luther King, Jr., who were guided by a higher purpose and fought for causes greater than themselves. While neither held elected office nor commanded an army, both harnessed a power before which their mighty opponents felt humbled and became defenseless.

Gandhi and King fought for timeless truths—equality, justice, and freedom—with steadfast conviction. They challenged the status quo of their times with courage and grace. Their greatest weapon was standing in truth, which inspired millions to join them, stirred by its power in their own hearts.

Along the way, Gandhi and King faced their own personal challenges and inner struggles. *They had their foibles, faults, and vulnerabilities, like we all do*, Jim mused. Nonetheless, he deeply admired both men's selfless commitment to uplifting their fellow beings, guided by universal values such as peace and harmony.

The change both sought began within, in how they led their minds, which gave them the strength to lead in the world. They gained such power by knowing their truths and living by them. As Gandhi once wrote, "All the tendencies present in the outer world are to be found in the world of our body. If we could change ourselves, the tendencies in the world would also change. As a man changes his own nature, so does the attitude of the world change towards him. This is the divine mystery supreme. A wonderful thing it is and the source of our happiness. We need not wait to see what others do."[26]

As Gandhi and King challenged the dogma and laws of their times, they sustained conviction through hardships wrought by opponents who feared the loss of their own power. While doubters mocked them, critics dismissed them, and their opponents jailed them, and ultimately took their lives, their missions survived and prevailed, burning bright to this day in hearts striving for equality, justice, and freedom around the world in peaceful ways.

While Jim's own journey was different from those of Gandhi and King, he strove to abide by the authentic and fearless ways of being that had guided them. Jim's purpose, he had resolved long ago, was to bring joy to others through service. This passion infused everything he did, whether volunteering at the local food bank, brightening someone's day in an elevator ride, or sharing free Happy Hill cookies with excited school groups who visited for factory tours. It also guided his relationships with Happy Hill's employees, partners, and customers.

Jim always kept this quote by King on his desk: "Each of us has the capacity, if only in some little way, to lift the level of humanity to higher heights, and thereby share in a greatness that outlasts the fall of empires. All history in the end bears witness to the fact that greatness—all greatness that lasts—is service."[27]

During a recent financial downturn, when Happy Hill's Board of Directors had asked Jim to prepare worst-case scenarios, he ensured that no one lost their job. When those scenarios turned real, Jim gave up his own salary and searched for creative ways to cut costs. Inspired by Jim's example, many executive team members followed his lead. Several factory floor employees also stopped by his office and quietly volunteered to take pay cuts to save their colleagues' jobs.

When other companies in town laid off workers, Happy Hill's employees rallied to set up volunteer food banks to ensure no one went hungry. To support local families, they also turned an empty Happy Hill warehouse into a child and senior care center staffed fully by volunteers from the company.

As Jim reflected on his journey, he realized that his path to 3D ways of leading was paved with painful lessons that he had learned when he let 1D or 2D take charge. This gave him immense humility and compassion as a mentor. He could see his younger self in Jill. Jim also admitted to himself that, even at his age, there was much he could learn from her. Happy Hill did tend to get too comfortable in the status quo. Jill's passion and fresh perspectives would help drive much-needed change. He saw immense potential in their partnership and, though he had not thought of it this way when she joined the company, Jim was grateful to be on Jill's team.

THE HEART OF LEADERSHIP

After sharing insights from their respective personal reflections, Jim and Jill decided to continue their discussion on Happy Hill's future through the three core pillars of 3D leadership: Vision, Strategy, and Execution.

VISION

Guided by a sense of meaning, purpose, and values, 3D leaders articulate a clear vision that upholds and uplifts humanity's shared well-being and inspires others to join them. Such leaders live by their words so that their vision and values don't just sit on a wall but guide their every action. This is the secret to resonance in any team, whether a family, organization, or nation. When a team struggles to unite around a vision, it easily becomes fragmented or divided. Thus, 3D leaders also strive to align their vision with their team's sense of meaning, purpose, and values. This fosters harmony and resilience in the face of any resistance that may arise.

STRATEGY

Steered by 2D's talents, 3D leaders also develop a clear strategy on how to realize their vision. For, even the boldest, most creative and visionary ideas remain just a dream without plans to make them real. Such leaders gather data and research to identify a path forward and lean on metrics, as needed, to assess progress. Although 3D leaders have clarity on their destination, they remain open to different paths there, knowing that stumbles and detours are part of most journeys. This gives them agility in adjusting their strategies based on what they learn along the way. Such leaders also learn the unique strengths of their team members and tap into them to unlock their individual and shared potential.

EXECUTION

Driven by 1D's focus on action, 3D leaders ensure they execute on their plans to make progress. They try things out to learn, grow, and keep moving ahead, knowing that even the best strategies are pointless if not acted upon. When roadblocks appear, or things don't go as planned, they don't give in to fear (as 1D may) or blame external factors (as 2D might). Instead, they adjust their plans to keep moving ahead and attain their vision. In this way, 3D leaders lead with a united mind, drawing on the best of all three states.

❧　　❧　　❧

As Jim and Jill reflected on these pillars, they decided to complete a **3x3 Matrix** exercise, which they had received at a recent workshop on teamwork. (In case you would like to try it out, the exercise is included at the end of this chapter.)

TABLE 4: 3 X 3 MATRIX			
	3D VISION Where we want to go together	**2D STRATEGY** How we plan to travel together	**1D EXECUTION** What we will do to get there
Resonance: how to best move forward	**1)** What is our shared vision? What shared values will guide us along the way?	**4)** How do we plan to achieve our shared vision and measure progress?	**7)** What actions will we each take to attain results and reach our destination?
Alignment: how to ensure harmony on the journey	**2)** How do we align our personal vision and values with our shared ones?	**5)** How do we align our personal plans and metrics with our shared journey?	**8)** How do we align our personal tasks and results with our shared work?
Resistance: how to overcome bumps, roadblocks, derailment	**3)** What differences may we encounter? How will we transcend them?	**6)** What trade-offs might we each need to make? How will we reach consensus?	**9)** What conflicts or clashes may arise? How will we resolve them?

The questions in the **3x3 Matrix**, which are shown in **Table 4**, helped Jim and Jill explore how to align around the three pillars of leadership by harnessing resonance and transcending resistance. After Jim and Jill reflected on the questions individually, they discussed their responses.

They explored their unique strengths and how they could best support each other. They also agreed to slow the pace of innovation and to invest in building a more cohesive culture. Jill also decided that Meg's foundation would have to be an integral part of any decisions made at Happy Hill.

As they wrapped up, Jill said, "Jim, I'm so glad we did this. I have much more clarity now on how we can lead together. In hindsight, I see how the clashes between our teams arose. Both acted based on several mistaken assumptions about the other. I am so grateful for your wise guidance. Thank you for being you."

Jim responded, "Jill, I've learned a lot too. I think we can lead change in a way that honors both the old and new. I really appreciate the passion you bring to your work, including how we engaged in this exercise. In fact, I think I am going to complete the Matrix with my wife tonight," Jim added as he wondered if it could help them resolve friction around a big home renovation project they had recently begun.

As they parted ways, Jim thought to himself, *knowing yourself really is the greatest power. A wise mind always finds solutions guided by insights and truths. I am so glad I trusted my intuition in staying at Happy Hill. This has been my most rewarding career chapter yet.*

TRUSTING OUR INNER LEADER

When Jill went home that evening and rolled into bed, she could not fall asleep. The day's discussions swirled through her mind and whispers of doubt appeared: *How do I convince the Board of Directors to be on board with the new vision Jim and I share? They hired me to lead rapid change and grow profits.*

Jill also thought of her team: *How do I show up as a leader for them? Does being authentic mean that I reveal all my thoughts and feelings, including my fears and doubts? How will I gain their respect?*

As such thoughts flowed through her mind, it suddenly dawned on Jill that they were mostly created by 1D and 2D challenging her 3D mind. She chuckled, relieved. *Of course, 1D and 2D will worry and resist,* she thought. She recalled what a leadership coach, with whom she had done some work, once shared:

As 3D begins to confidently lead our mind, it is common, almost expected, that 1D and 2D resist with fear and doubt. They may feel scared of—or threatened by—an unfamiliar, new way of being that relies on them less.

Jill's coach had called such thoughts and feelings "saboteurs" since they stifled 3D's resonance with myriad forms of resistance, such as inner roadblocks and limiting thoughts. To surmount these tendencies, we learn to recognize our saboteurs and when they tend to show up. For instance, Jill often felt nervous before speaking to her Board of Directors. Thoughts of imaginary stutters or others' critical judgments would fill her mind. Once she became aware of this, it reduced the power such sabotaging thoughts had over her. When 1D or 2D raised concerns, she acknowledged the presence of such thoughts but did not let them take charge of her mind. With time, Jill noticed how her saboteurs seemed to lose strength and slowly disappeared.

After Jill's recent discussions with Jim, she trusted she had his unwavering support. This gave her immense peace of mind. She reflected on her sense of meaning, purpose, and values and how they could guide her in leading change at Happy Hill.

Jill also thought about the leaders she admired most. They were genuine, thoughtful, and transparent about how they made decisions. They welcomed diverse perspectives, knowing how such views enriched their own. They also sustained an inner clarity and calm that gave others confidence in them.

Beyond this, Jill realized they all shared one quality: they were authentic to their core. They cared deeply about helping others grow and connect to their own heart's truths. Their lives were open books, which engendered trust and respect among those who spent time with them, whether as professional colleagues or close friends. Jill recalled an article she had recently read on how "authenticity, or the feeling of being true to oneself, is key to both well-being and employee engagement."[28]

When we conceal our true selves or project a facade, we come to feel divided within and create inner resistance that wears on our physical and mental health. When we are open and authentic, we harness a united mind with resonance, which energizes and empowers us. We feel whole and at ease without the need for a mask or shield. We grow compassion for ourselves and others, knowing everyone is perfectly imperfect in their own unique way.

As she rolled over in bed, Jill wondered, *why do so many 1D/2D leaders continue to rise into positions of power in the world today? And why do so many followers continue to enable their rise?* Moments later, the answers flowed into her mind.

When we are led by our own fears or a fixed sense of self, we are likely to follow 1D or 2D leaders who seem to "get" or reflect us. When we are guided by deeper truths rooted in our shared humanity, we recognize 3D leaders through that lens. Thus, fostering great leadership in the world begins by nurturing it in our hearts. We refuse to capitulate to fear. We see the absurdity of taking our ego too seriously. We live and lead with the lightness of being that sustains when we interact not to gain or transact but to give and serve from the heart. As 3D leads our mind, we begin to see and recognize 3D leaders all around us, whether they are baking cookies, building companies, or bringing joy to communities.

PLAY, PONDER, PRACTICE:

3 x 3 MATRIX

The **3 x 3 Matrix** can help you reflect on a challenge you face with another person or team. It has been used in varied contexts, including by startup co-founders, community leaders, and couples, among others, to foster insights on how to best work and lead together.

1. To complete the exercise, each person or party should take some time to respond to the questions in the Matrix provided in **Table 4** on page 201. It helps to approach the questions in the numerical sequence listed in the Matrix.

2. Then, get together with the other person or party to share and discuss your responses to the questions.

3. Use the discussion around each question in the Matrix as a starting point to explore how to grow resonance, foster alignment, and reduce resistance in collaborating and working together.

CHAPTER 12

How We Nurture Culture

From playgrounds to boardrooms and dinner tables to town halls, culture reflects how we come together. Though intangible and seemingly elusive, culture is one of the most vital forces that guides how the members of any team interact.

While companies often discuss their cultures in annual reports, and countries describe theirs in travel brochures, that is not where culture resides. Beyond what a culture's members say, it reflects the deeper—mostly unwritten and unspoken—customs and norms that drive what they actually do.

In a team of any size, whether a family or nation, culture guides how we express ourselves, make decisions, and face change. It defines what we celebrate, what we refuse to tolerate, and how we treat each other: *Do we trust and respect each member? Do all members feel safe to speak their truths and that their voice matters?*

In the face of a challenge or crisis, culture decides whether a team breaks down or breaks through. Research shows, and many real-world examples validate, that teams and organizations with healthy, thriving cultures harbor more resilience and attain greater success. They experience higher productivity, performance, and innovation. And their members benefit from increased well-being and satisfaction, as well as, reduced burnout and turnover.[29]

When a team does not get culture right, it can pay a high price. Among startups, more fail due to conflicts in their teams and cultures than due to challenges with their underlying products and services. In corporate mergers and acquisitions, culture clashes tend to be among the leading causes of failure in realizing the vision that motivated such unions in the first place.

In an unhealthy or a toxic culture, everyone suffers. For example, in healthcare, caregivers experience higher burnout, which tends to increase error rates and lead to worse health outcomes for patients. In customer service, call center workers feel disempowered to meet customers' needs, which lowers both worker and customer satisfaction. Across industries, when frontline employees are overworked and undervalued, they experience higher stress just to survive, which diminishes their own, their organization's and society's overall capacity to thrive.

A healthy culture, on the other hand, takes care of not just its members and those they serve, but also of its greater community. This motivates and empowers everyone touched by it and fosters collaboration and connection. In the face of challenges, such cultures produce more creative, resilient, and enduring solutions. Thus, building any team begins with getting culture right.

THE THREE STATES IN CULTURE

While creating a thriving culture may seem like a mysterious art, like communication and leadership, we can grasp its essence through the lens of the three states. For, a culture is simply a reflection of the mindstates of its members. Here, we will examine culture through the lens of an organization such as Happy Hill. Although the concepts of this chapter apply to other cultural contexts too.

1D CULTURE

When a culture is led by 1D's ways, its members tend to focus on self-preservation and protecting the status quo. Organizations with such cultures mostly operate through reactive actions focused on short-term results, such as increasing profits, or playing catch up with competitors.

Leaders of such cultures tend to direct their attention to their own needs and interests, motivated by the currencies of their 1D accounts. They also tend to rule by fear, fostering risk-averse, high-pressure environments that often neglect or sacrifice the welfare of their own employees and customers.

In a 1D culture, a perpetual sense of urgency, or even panic, is often the daily routine. Such cultures can feel like war zones focused on fighting battles or putting out fires. High discontent, burnout, and turnover tend to rule. The prevailing mindsets in such cultures tend to be rigid and closed-minded, marked by words such as, *this is the only way to do it*, or *this is how we have always done things*.

Challenges are typically tackled with avoidance, short-cuts, or quick fixes. Missteps, and even wrongdoing, may be faced by closing one's eyes or looking the other way. Hence gossip, tattling, paranoia, and secrecy often abound. Concerns often fester until they can no longer be ignored.

Driven by its reactive ways, a 1D culture mostly changes when it is forced to (e.g., through whistleblowers, lawsuits, or shareholder demands), and only as much as it must to survive another day. Sometimes, a 1D culture can appear to "get away" with its ways in the short run because it "succeeds" at generating financial profits.

Yet, absent an alignment with timeless truths—such as integrity, transparency, and trust—a 1D culture remains inherently fragile. In the face of a crisis, it tends to implode or explode, laying bare everything it had sought to hide. Meanwhile, its leaders often swiftly shift from seeking media coverage to running for cover, leaving others to clean up the mess. Hence, no matter what 1D cultures may look like, they do not create long-term value and harbor the seeds of their own demise, which ultimately renders all their "success" meaningless.

2D CULTURE

When a culture is led by 2D's ways, it focuses on productivity, guided by strategic plans and metrics to measure progress. Organizations with 2D cultures tend to rely on structures and hierarchies supported by rules and guidelines to maintain a sense of order and control. They motivate performance with both 1D rewards and 2D awards, such as bonuses and promotions. Many aspects of a 2D culture are valuable for helping teams succeed. Yet such cultures also harbor their own limits.

For instance, hierarchical structures can devolve into complex, siloed bureaucracies, especially in large organizations or systems. This can lead to cultures where internal procedures come to rule over the higher mission they are meant to serve. Often, such cultures experience inefficiencies and wastefulness. Or activities, such as attending meetings or meeting metrics, stifle autonomy, productivity, and creativity.

A 2D culture can also foster transactional behaviors as its members often get focused on mastering the rules of the game, however defined, to rise or reach the top. This can create competitive environments in which collaborative teamwork and novel ideas become rare, as members operate in isolated silos defined by hierarchies or ranks.

In the face of a challenge or crisis, a 2D culture tends to place blame on external factors, driven by the ego's tendencies. Leaders of such cultures often focus on protecting their own image and reputation. Ethical or moral transgressions may be rationalized with statements such as, *this is how the system works*, or *this is the only way to survive or win*. Over time, 2D cultures can develop fissures driven by actions that neglect 3D's wisdom and resonance, which make up the invisible glue of all thriving cultures.

3D CULTURE

When a culture is led by 3D's ways, its leaders and members keep their organization's vision, mission, and values at the center of all decisions and actions. Such a culture fosters trust, openness, transparency, and integrity, and nurtures resonance and belonging.

The leaders of a 3D culture are guided by holistic, long-term, big picture thinking. They strive to support not just their employees and customers but also their greater community—and the planet— to thrive in sustainable ways. They foster collaboration and value diversity of thought, experience, and background, recognizing how it enriches everyone. In making decisions, they ask not, *what's in it for me (1D)?* Or, *will this grow the business (2D)?* But, *does our work create an enduring, positive impact on all touched by it (3D)?*

In the face of a challenge or crisis, 3D cultures are adaptive and resilient. While 1D cultures resist change, and 2D cultures guide incremental change, 3D cultures lead transformation. Leaders of such cultures are proactive rather than reactive, and they focus on how any change—planned or unexpected—can foster valuable learning and growth.

In such cultures, rules serve as guidelines to be followed with wisdom and judgment rather than as strict, rigid policies to be blindly obeyed. This empowers all employees or members to solve challenges in creative ways and to lead their own work with courage and confidence.

A 3D culture views incentives, such as bonuses and promotions, as means in service to a higher purpose rather than as ends. In such cultures, everyone feels inspired and loves to come to work. This builds camaraderie, loyalty, and trust among a team's members, as they feel cared for and supported. To explore how such a culture comes to be, we return to Happy Hill.

When Jim and Jill met again a few days later, they had both spent some time reflecting on what Happy Hill's culture meant to each of them. Jim was deeply inspired by how Meg had infused elements of both her Japanese heritage and American traditions into the company.

In Japan, like in many older cultures around the world, companies were often founded to last for generations. They were family endeavors guided by collectivist principles that focused on the organization's mission over the role of any one individual. Although their products could be as simple as tea or cookies, the intention of such companies was often to serve a higher purpose, such as feeding pilgrims and travelers visiting a sacred site, or supporting a local town or community.

In America, where culture was guided by more individualistic principles, companies were often built around iconic founders or leaders whose personas became branded into the cultures of their organizations. Silicon Valley epitomized this trend with its legends of garage entrepreneurs turned global titans, many of whom became household names around the world. As a Japanese American, Meg strove to integrate elements of the best of both cultures into Happy Hill.

As Jim and Jill chatted, they revisited the tensions between the innovation unit Jill had created and the old guard Jim led. The innovation unit consisted of star players who saw success as personal and focused on rapidly launching new products. This was how they had run innovation at Well Water, Jill's prior company, which had primed it for an acquisition by an industry leader.

Happy Hill's old guard, in contrast, sought to honor the values that Meg had instilled in the company—respect for tradition, taking care of the community, and ensuring stability—to serve a higher purpose.

"Happy Hill needs to change with the times, but I am realizing we cannot drive change just to look innovative," Jill said, reflecting on the charge she had given the innovation team.

"I agree," Jim said. "That is what longtime Happy Hill employees want too—meaningful change that lasts. They fear growing so fast that it weakens our ability to sustain through hard times."

"Maybe, instead of chasing trends to replace existing products, the innovation team can create prototypes based on input from Happy Hill's employees and customers?" Jill wondered. "This will give everyone here a sense of ownership in new products and likely result in better ideas too."

"That is a great thought," Jim said. "It will help all team members feel like leaders in driving innovation rather than like helpless bystanders who have change thrust upon them."

Jim got up to refill his coffee mug in the kitchen down the hallway. As Jill waited for Jim, she realized that, while he seemed old-fashioned (he still used a flip phone outside work!), he harbored deep practical wisdom which she longed to attain. When Jill had first joined the company, she had been dismissive of Jim's slower and quieter ways. Now she came to appreciate their virtues.

When Jim returned with fresh coffee, Jill wondered aloud how they would get others on board: "I love that we are aligned, but not everyone thinks like us. People get set in their ways and hold on to their beliefs. How will we change a whole culture?"

Jim settled into his chair and slowly spoke, "We often think of culture as a unique, sacrosanct aspect of our identity, whether as individuals or as teams. Yet a thriving culture, as the rise and fall of civilizations reminds us, evolves like everything in nature. When a culture is resilient, it withstands change, like a tree swaying through storms. When rigid or fixed, desperate to preserve an untenable status quo, it breaks rather than bends with the wind."

Jill appreciated Jim's perspective, but was overcome by more questions: "Even if Happy Hill evolves, how do we sustain in the greater world out there? How do we remain 3D in the face of what often feel like overpowering 1D and 2D forces?"

Jim took a deep breath and then said, "I have thought about that too. This is what I have come to believe. While our world can seem full of turmoil, as leaders, we do not act in reaction to 1D or 2D's chatter of the moment. Rather, we honor timeless truths, such as kindness and harmony, which reflect our shared humanity. We sustain courage and trust resonance to prevail over any resistance that arises, whether within or outside. This is how we uplift each other and help create thriving cultures. The essence of this rests on three pillars: (1) start at the top, (2) speak a shared language, and (3) create a unifying ethos. Let's briefly explore each."

START AT THE TOP

For any culture to permeate a team, it helps to start at the top. A thriving culture is guided by leaders who foster belonging among all members of their team. They instill a clear sense of vision, mission, and values, and lead by example, inspiring others to follow them.

In this way, everyone on the team knows what matters and, equally important, what does not. This prevents slippery rationalizations, whether in making decisions, hiring new members, pursuing partnerships, or navigating conflicts. While starting at the top may sound straightforward, we can tease out its impact by studying what happens to a culture when such leadership is missing.

For example, sometimes leaders atop organizations declare bold intentions focused on diversity or social or environmental responsibility. They may create task forces or initiatives to show something is being done, to appease critics, or to appear current with social trends. Yet, when such actions fail to drive real change, such leaders can lose the trust and respect of their own employees and customers who see through the shallow impact of their words.

Another example rests in organizations that abide by the letter of the law at the cost of its spirit. For instance, most technology and software companies offer lengthy privacy contracts that consumers must agree to before using their products and services. Yet such documents are full of complex and esoteric legalese, leading most users to click "I Agree" without really understanding to what they have just consented. While their declared intent is to inform users, such contracts serve the interests of the company. This leads users to give away troves of personal data they might not so willingly provide if they grasped how exactly companies used (and profited from) their private information.

A final example rests in corporations that neglect or dismiss the harmful effects of their products until whistleblowers, lawsuits, or regulations force corrective action. Recent high-profile case studies on this span most industries from automobiles and airplanes to industrial manufacturing and technology. The cultures of such organizations tend to be driven by a focus on short-term results, even if enabled by short-cuts or negligence. Sometimes, such cultures can even make their members believe that they are doing the right thing by doing the wrong thing.

A thriving culture, in contrast, is led by leaders who keep the long-term big picture in mind in every decision. In such cultures, integrity and transparency permeate all levels of an organization. Leaders encourage open dialogue and dissent and avoid the herd mentality or blind obedience to orders from above. Speaking truth to power is valued, and failure is seen as learning.

Even among professionals in fields built on 2D expertise (e.g., pilots, surgeons, or police officers), where failure can spell the difference between life and death, a 3D way of leading often saves the day. It allows a pilot to safely land a plane on the Hudson River, a surgeon to navigate unforeseen complications, and a police officer to de-escalate a crisis, guiding each to honor the highest calling and deepest spirit of their work.

SPEAK A SHARED LANGUAGE

Another vital pillar of a thriving culture is having a shared language that helps its members communicate in simple yet effective ways. Several readers have shared how they started using the terms 1D, 2D, and 3D in team meetings, performance reviews, or brainstorming sessions. Using such new, neutral terms, they said, helped them more candidly talk about their own and others' minds. They could name someone's thoughts or actions as 1D, 2D, or 3D, without seeming to label or judge the person. This reduced emotional (1D) and egoic (2D) reactions, as well as, resistance brought on by team members feeling guarded or defensive. It also fostered resonance, openness, and a spirit of learning.

A shared language that is claimed by no one and serves all, helps to shatter silos and increase collaboration as diverse members can interact with a beginner's mind. For example, in a brainstorming session, guiding 3D principles, such as "there are no bad ideas," allow everyone to give their imagination free rein without fearing critical or judgmental reactions that stifle creativity.

A startup CEO, Grace, once shared how the three states helped her see which mindstates dominated across her company. She realized that its sales team was driven by execution (1D), its technical team focused on specifications (2D), and its founders guided by visionary ideas (3D). Grace often struggled to communicate across teams. When she shared the founders' vision, some on the sales team would say, "That sounds nice, but tell us what to do." Or some on the technical team would say, "Execution means nothing without metrics." As Grace shared the concept of the three mindstates across teams, she noticed how interactions shifted.

Each team became more patient with others' default tendencies and gained new appreciation for the complementary nature of their thinking styles. Instead of judging others' comments or questions as naive or simplistic, members across teams came to see them as valuable ways to refine their own thinking, to uncover blind spots, and to discover new ideas and solutions at the intersections of silos. Members across teams sensed shifts in their own and others' minds as resonance grew. In meetings, they would build on each other's ideas with comments such as, "that's a valid 1D concern" or "that's a valuable 2D perspective," or "I wonder what 3D would say?"

With time, trust and respect grew. Each voice felt valued, and teamwork flourished. Grace also noticed how thinking patterns within teams shifted. For instance, the sales team engaged in more big picture thinking. Instead of focusing on individual targets, it more deeply integrated the company's mission into its metrics.

In solving our greatest challenges, while expertise is vital, no one silo has all the answers. Solutions that truly address a challenge tend to integrate 1D, 2D, and 3D approaches in holistic ways. To explore how this happens, we return to Happy Hill.

CREATE A UNIFYING ETHOS

As Jill drove home that evening, she reflected on her conversations with Jim. She realized that, in a rush to show Happy Hill's board how serious she was about innovation, she had focused on short-term actions without fully grasping the company's vision, mission, and values.

Her obsession with metrics and dashboards had received significant internal pushback. She now saw how she likely took it too far, creating more work without clarifying why it made a difference.

Also, the innovation team spoke its own siloed language of Silicon Valley buzzwords that perplexed and seemed condescending to many on the old guard. Jill now saw how such lingo was just another way to express the core principles already ingrained in the company. Jill also realized she relied too much on outside consultants and could spend more time with Happy Hill's employees and customers. This was so obvious in hindsight, Jill wondered how she had missed it. She also decided to sustain, and even increase, support for Meg's foundation, recognizing how its work was integral to the company.

Over the days that followed, during long evening walks through her neighborhood, on bike rides through wooded trails, and even while washing dishes, Jill contemplated how she could instill a more unifying ethos and culture at Happy Hill.

One day, as she passed a construction site on her street, she recalled a story she had once heard about three workers who were paving a country road:

A curious little boy on his way home from school stopped to ask the workers, "What are you doing?"

"Can't you see? We're pouring tar," the first worker said.

"Actually, we're paving over the dirt path to your school," the second worker added.

Then the third worker spoke, "We're making sure you can get to school safely every day to obtain a great education."

Jill realized this story reflected how she wanted to transform Happy Hill—to help every employee think like the third worker and know how their daily work made a real difference in the world.

A week later, a few days before the upcoming board meeting, Jill re-convened her leadership team to share her newly crystallized ideas. She talked about how she had realized that Happy Hill's classic cookie lines were its heart and soul. No wonder customers were so loyal to them. More than being sweet snacks, the cookies held memories and stories, and Jill had come to respect the sanctity of that.

Since Happy Hill's cookies were already made with all-natural ingredients and without preservatives, they aligned with her vision of providing natural, whole foods. A few tweaks in ingredients would suffice. They were treats after all, not a breakfast or meal. PBJ was the crown jewel of the company and would have to stay. They would invest in new manufacturing equipment to avoid allergen cross contamination.

Jill also shared that the innovation team would no longer work in a silo but be integrated across all departments at the company. She asked its leaders to design creative ways to encourage participation from every Happy Hill employee, from the front desk to the factory floor. Jill wanted everyone to feel a sense of ownership in any new cookies to be launched.

Finally, Jill shared how she had ventured into the company's dusty basement archives over the weekend to find Meg's old journals, which Jim had once mentioned in passing. Jill's voice began to tremble as she shared how she gained renewed respect for Meg's foresight in building the company. Then she read Meg's last journal entry, from just before she died, aloud:

"When I was young, I was sad and angry about the war that took so much from me. One day, when I missed my husband so deeply I could not stop crying, I resolved that instead of continuing to fight against the world in which I was, I would focus on building the one I wanted to see. This is how Happy Hill was born.

"The kind souls who helped me rebuild my life opened their homes—and hearts—to me. They showed me the power of love. I realized love lives not just in the people we cherish and lose, but in every being we meet. I knew I could never repay their generosity, but I realized I could pay it forward.

"To create a better world, we must each give more than we take—from each other, our communities, and our planet. We must replant what we harvest and replenish what we use. We must sow seeds of peace in the soils of war and cherish all life. This wisdom is as old as this land's natives who, for millennia, honored its sacred nature before the rest of us arrived to call America home.

"Profits are not made to enrich a few. Rather, they bestow a great responsibility—to uplift others, nurture communities, and share with compassion. Being true to this is the truest meaning of wealth that I have come to know.

"Many leaders today focus on creating value for their shareholders (and themselves) but we each ultimately have only one stakeholder—our awakened conscience. When we serve its truths from the heart, we enrich not just our own lives but everyone around us. The return on investment of such wealth far exceeds the riches my peers hoard in vaults. I don't say this to judge. My end is near, and I have no fear.

"I say this because I see how we have created most of the problems we face today. Wars are fought by men, not bombs. I lost loved ones on both sides of World War II. Every foe is someone's family, someone's friend. This is what the pain of loss taught me.

"When I die, everything to my name will go to my foundation to help those in need—whether in inner cities, rural small towns, or refugee communities—follow their dreams to build a better world. At Happy Hill, it was always about much more than just cookies."

As Jill finished reading, quiet engulfed the room. Everyone felt the pettiness of the battle that had ensued over cookie lines. Jill shared how she had come to realize it was both her duty and honor to keep the spirit of Meg's dream alive. As Jill learned of Meg's hardships in starting Happy Hill, she realized how her own path was made possible because of courageous sacrifices pioneers like Meg had made.

"Meg's words have given me precious new guidance on how to not only build a sustainable business but also live a meaningful life," Jill said. She added how she had written off many of her own dreams as being too big or idealistic. Meg's words reminded Jill that such idealism was not only realistic but the very lifeblood of true change.

As Jill continued her presentation, she discussed how the company could source more sustainable ingredients from fair trade suppliers who shared Happy Hill's values. She further pledged that every employee would share in the company's profits. Jill also decided to include entrepreneurs supported by Meg's foundation in the company's operations through roles across all departments and seats on the company's board. She further announced plans to create a new learning academy for her CEO peers to help them learn how to build 3D organizations guided by 3D leaders and 3D cultures.

"If we want to be a trailblazer, we cannot just look like one. We have to make the hard decisions that make us one," Jill said with fierce conviction. "If we lose employees, suppliers, or even board members who are not on board with this vision, or are still focused on shareholder value, we are not only okay with their resignations, we welcome them. We cannot afford to be a cookie-cutter cookie company."

When Jill received a standing ovation from her team that morning, and from the Board of Directors days later, she looked at Jim, filled with gratitude. Jim wiped tears from his eyes both times. Meg had shared cookies as an act of love to light in hearts—old and young alike—the spark of believing in and following a dream. As Jim watched Jill, he sensed Meg's spirit flow into her, and through her into the board room, across the company, and into the world.

Over the months that followed, Happy Hill's culture became more relaxed and playful. Excitement and pride rippled across the company. Laughter filled the halls. For the first time in a long time, Jim saw factory floor workers joke around while they worked. Teams were encouraged to participate in shared experiences that built solidarity and allowed members across departments to get to know each other better.

Jill also asked each employee to write a personal credo—a simple statement on how they aspired to live and lead at the company and in the world. She invited a few members to share their credos at the company-wide town hall each month. Most such readings left others in tears as they realized how they all shared the same basic hopes and dreams.

As time passed, Jim sensed how Jill followed not only in Meg's footsteps but also in her heart's song. It was as if Meg was smiling down on Happy Hill. Jim realized he could not have asked for a more fulfilling last rodeo. Jill's transformation had changed him too. He was grateful for her fierce courage and thoughtfulness, which challenged him to learn and evolve, even in his sunset years. *Life really is the best school and everyone we meet is our teacher*, he mused. *We must just show up and be present to receive the lesson.*

A few months later, Jim finally walked out the door one last time. He crossed the parking lot at dusk with a skip in his step, and a slight waltz if you looked closely. He knew his job was finally done.

PLAY, PONDER, PRACTICE:

PERSONAL CREDO

If you would like to try writing your own **Personal Credo**, the exercise is below. It is the final assignment of the graduate leadership course I have taught. Through the years, many students have said that this was among their most valuable assignments in the class.

A Personal Credo reflects how you strive to lead your life and show up in the world. It embodies your sense of meaning, purpose, and values. It can serve both as an anchor during challenging times and as a daily guide.

To write your credo, find a few hours of quiet time alone. Take a pen and paper and write down the core principles that define who you are and how you aspire to be in the world. Write with pen and paper. This will help you think deliberately, and crossed-out words will linger, to be revisited. Keep it short, around 250-450 words. Don't overthink it. Write from the heart.

Remember, these words are not goals but guideposts. Rather than telling you where to go, they guide how you travel your paths. Consider these questions to help guide your reflection:

1. What matters most to you? What gives you a sense of meaning and purpose? What values guide you?

2. What do you know to be true deep in your heart? How do these truths shape your life and dreams?

3. How do you hope to serve the world? How do you aspire to be? How will you work and lead?

Once you have written your Credo, you can share it with others or keep it as a personal guide to light your path.

PART V

How We Change Our World

Arun's Labor of Love

Arun grabbed his favorite Happy Hill cookie from the cafeteria at his large, urban teaching hospital and rushed through its windowless corridors. He glanced at his watch. He had just seen his last patient for the day and was relieved to see he had some time before the start of class at the other end of campus.

By the time Arun reached the classroom, put down his bag, and sank into his seat, he looked forward to shifting his attention to the room. He had recently been invited to take part in a new healthcare transformation incubator class at his hospital designed to help physicians improve the system. It brought together entrepreneurs, innovators, and hospital leaders to explore creative ways to lead change.

As Arun saw patients through the years, he often had ideas for how to improve the practice of medicine, whether on the operating table or at the patient bedside. Sometimes, he would share his insights with colleagues or at department meetings. His research had resulted in a stellar list of publications in leading academic journals, and he had recently been promoted to chair his department. Yet the urgency of treating patients, and the responsibilities of his new role, consumed any time Arun might devote to advancing his ideas. This is why he was so excited about the new class. It offered the perfect laboratory to explore how he could drive change in his department, at his hospital, and in the greater healthcare system.

Arun loved being a doctor. He had followed in the footsteps of his parents, first-generation immigrants from India, who had arrived in a small town in Oklahoma in the 1960s. Growing up, Arun was inspired by the sense of satisfaction and gratification he sensed in their work as they helped patients heal and lead healthier lives.

Arun's father was a cardiologist and his mother a family physician. In the small town where they practiced, their patients became their second family. Arun's parents often attended their patients' birthdays, weddings, and funerals. Arun admired the spirit of caring that infused his parents' work and he knew, from an early age, that medicine was his calling.

Although, today, healthcare was no longer what it used to be. Arun had risen through the ranks at one of the world's best hospitals. He worked long hours yet had less and less time with patients. He shuffled between three facilities in his hospital system, each with its own culture. Health insurance had become so complex that his staff played constant catch up to ensure reimbursements for care. Electronic health records consumed precious time and often felt like a tedious distraction during patient visits.

On many evenings, as Arun walked home, he wondered how the healthcare system had become so sick. Many caregivers felt stressed, overworked, and burnt out, perpetually strapped for time to take care of themselves. *Who heals the healers?* Arun often pondered, repeating a common refrain. He wondered how healthcare could foster more well-being, not just for patients, but also for the physicians, nurses, and staff who worked tirelessly, day in and day out.

A month earlier, the hospital's CEO had invited Arun to lead an Innovation Task Force to re-imagine healthcare, starting with his hospital. Arun was honored by the appointment. Yet he also struggled to squash a nagging doubt whether this was just another initiative to appease the hospital's Board of Trustees or if it would truly make a difference. Thus, the timing of this class could not have been better. Arun hoped it might give him some insights for the next Board of Trustees meeting in a few weeks where the CEO had asked Arun to present his preliminary vision and ideas.

As the instructors for the class launched the first session, they asked everyone in the room to begin with a fast-paced teamwork exercise using ropes and balls.

Arun and his peers formed small teams and jumped into action. The clock counted down as they rushed to the whiteboard and mapped out steps to solve the challenge. They tried different solutions, returned to the drawing board to tweak them, and completed the exercise just as the buzzer went off.

Arun loved the energy in the room as teams engaged in friendly competition. He could not recall the last time he and his colleagues had so much fun together. It was refreshing to interact with them in playful ways that generated laughter and jokes.

Arun soaked in the rest of the class' teachings on teamwork, leadership, and how our state of mind guides change. As the class ended, Arun was pumped for the next session. *This is exactly what I needed*, he thought, as he walked back to the hospital.

❧ ❧ ❧

The following Friday, Arun returned to the class excited. He had looked forward to it all week. The instructors began the session with a new team-building exercise.

This time, the teams solved the challenge in just a few minutes. The instructors were taken aback. They had planned for much more time. One of them had led this exercise with dozens of groups across diverse settings and never seen it completed so fast. "Wow! How?" he asked, stunned. "How did you finish so fast?" The response from one participant generated nodding agreement across the room.

"Today, our default was to not use our default state of mind," she said. "We remembered what one of you said last time about how our ways of thinking drive our actions. When we got here today, we decided to be more open-minded and creative with the activity. That led us to explore more novel and counterintuitive solutions."

As her words sank in, light bulbs went off in Arun's head. He suddenly realized, with more clarity than ever before, how to help heal healthcare. Arun's epiphanies that day, and over the weeks that followed, reveal valuable insights that we can each learn from and apply across the varied contexts of our lives.

In the next three chapters, we explore the three mindstates through the lens of an organization, which we define as a context in which diverse teams come together to realize a shared vision and mission. Here, an organization can stand for a single entity, such as a non-profit, a corporation, a government agency, or a system focused on a sector, such as healthcare, education, or defense. It can also stand for a movement, a community, or an alliance of organizations or nations united by a shared cause.

Typically, an organization, as defined here, is too large for all of its members to know each other. Hence, we explore how to create environments and ecosystems that empower everyone in them to **innovate** (Chapter 13), **create** (Chapter 14), and **succeed** (Chapter 15) together.

How We Innovate

On Monday morning, as Arun walked to the operating room at his hospital to prepare for his first surgery of the day, thoughts of the incubator class still swirled through his mind. He was amazed by how a simple shift in thinking had transformed how teams solved the exercise during the second session. Arun realized the experience gave him a whole new outlook for how he looked at everything.

This is how innovation happens, he mused as he got into scrubs. *A collective shift in how minds think transforms how they act.* As epiphanies flowed through Arun's mind, he realized it was time to focus. He donned his protective gown and gloves and slipped into the operating room. While we will leave Arun to perform surgery for now, let's continue this exploration.

Until less than a century ago, most medical treatments were developed through trial-and-error experiments. While some helped heal patients, others eventually proved ineffective or, worse, caused harm. Today, innovative solutions, such as novel therapies or vaccines, undergo rigorous clinical trials that establish their safety and effectiveness. Thus, modern medicine is guided by research-driven, evidence-based, peer-reviewed data, which is how it should be.

We would not want to be Arun's patient if, while we were lying on his operating table, he mused, *Ooh, I just had a great idea! Maybe I can riff on this surgical procedure today and try something new. I wonder what happens if I cut here instead? Let's find out!*

When our life is at stake, we want to be in the hands of someone who is guided by deep expertise and experience to ensure the best outcomes, not someone driven by the whims of their creative epiphanies. Thus, the healthcare system is 2D by design, which works well—for the most part.

THE ART OF INNOVATION

When Arun and his peers solved the incubator class team challenge the first time, they devised methodical steps and assigned clear roles. The second time, they were conscious of 2D's limits and tapped into their 3D minds to find more creative solutions.

As Arun wrapped up his surgeries for the day, he reflected on healthcare's tendency to approach change in 1D and 2D ways. Since healthcare's core mission was to save lives, its 1D ways made sense. When a patient was critically ill, a sense of urgency could spell the difference between life and death. Yet, in treating chronic or complex conditions, 1D and 2D approaches often had limited effectiveness. And, in driving innovation, they sometimes resulted in painstakingly slow change.

How ironic, Arun thought, *that we pursue innovation in such conventional ways.* Even the word seemed cliché these days. In recent years, most health systems had launched innovation centers under varied names such as incubators, hubs, accelerators, labs, or greenhouses. Arun's hospital had also hired consultants to teach its leaders innovation methods such as design thinking, lean startup, agile development, and patient-centered design, to name just a few.[30]

Despite all these investments in innovation—not just at Arun's hospital but also by companies, government agencies, and nonprofit organizations across the healthcare field—they did not always produce the intended results. At his hospital, Arun often questioned the focus on patentable inventions. Its technology transfer office tended to prefer discoveries with "sizzle," since they more easily attracted media attention and investor funding.

Yet many important advancements, while at times devoid of the aura of novelty bestowed on breakthrough science, were not just effective but also often more accessible and affordable. During the Covid-19 pandemic, beyond the cutting-edge vaccines that science delivered, time-tested practices such as washing hands, wearing masks, and social distancing played invaluable roles in reducing infections.

Over the following weeks, Arun often discussed thoughts such as these with the guest speakers who visited the incubator class. The speakers included a diverse spectrum of healthcare innovators, investors, and entrepreneurs. Several shared Arun's views on how healthcare had become straddled with inefficiencies and often succumbed to short-sighted or suboptimal solutions.

Arun pondered how some of these speakers seemed to embody "3D-ness" (a word he coined). *They have a holistic perspective, speak openly from the heart, and trust their intuition. They are incisive in seeing through the complexity that bogs down modern healthcare. Why don't we teach such ways of thinking to our students?*

The healthcare system in which they operated today was not what Arun and his classmates had envisioned when they first donned white coats in medical school. Many, including Arun, had idealistic visions of being healers in a healthy system that cared about everyone's well-being. *How do we change the system from the inside out?* Arun often asked himself.

One Sunday afternoon, a week before his presentation to the hospital's Board of Trustees, Arun sat in his home office and watched the autumn leaves fall outside. As he began to create an outline for his presentation, he thought back to his most recent charity medical visit to India. There, in remote villages among the poorest of the poor, caregivers demonstrated incredible ingenuity as they made the most of the scarce resources they had.

Arun realized such ways of thinking could be learned by any mind. Transforming the healthcare system started with changing the minds in it. Even beyond his own field, in today's fast-moving world, everyone could benefit from learning to think more like an innovator. *But, Arun wondered, how do we teach an entire system to think in whole new ways?*

THE THREE STATES IN INNOVATION

To explore Arun's question, we return to the three states and look at innovation through their lens. Since we've been through this a few times by now, here we focus on insights that build on prior chapters.

1D INNOVATION

In the 1D state, as is likely apparent by now, we tend not to be very innovative. Since the 1D mind likes to play it safe and protect the status quo, its motives for change are mostly driven by defensive reactions to outer forces that demand action.

Even when we generate a creative 3D idea, if 1D rules over our mind, it can stifle our idea's potential in myriad ways. Scared of change, 1D may focus our attention on what can go wrong or why an idea won't work. Afraid of failure, it can lead us to abandon an idea prematurely. Or, driven by its protective instincts, 1D can drive us to guard our idea so closely it never sees the light of day.

The 1D mind can also limit innovation in other ways. Arun realized that the practice of defensive medicine was often driven by 1D tendencies. It led some providers to perform excessive, unnecessary, or even risky tests or procedures out of fear of malpractice lawsuits and, at times, to boost revenues. Health innovations that spelled the end of a profitable test or procedure could sometimes be met with resistance at first. At times, this was justified with rationalizations such as, *we need to make sure everything has been ruled out, we must exhaust all possible options,* or, *this is how the system works.* In these ways, 1D often helped perpetuate marginally effective yet expensive solutions for managing patient health.

2D INNOVATION

In the 2D state, we are inclined to innovate through incremental improvements supported by careful research, data, and analyses.

Guided by what it can see and measure, 2D views innovation as evolving from an existing reality rather than as embodying a whole new vision. Thus, 2D can help us methodically implement change but is unlikely to reimagine a system.

The 2D mind's comfort zone for leading change is often through committees, task forces, or innovation centers. It tends to view such visible efforts as signs of innovation, even though they are just means to fostering it. Also, captivated by novelty, 2D is drawn to change that looks or sounds impressive, even if it has limited impact. Finally, 2D tends to get caught up in details and minutiae, which can constrain the free flow of ideas and lead to siloed, binary, and circular thinking.

The 2D mind's ways help to explain why large organizations, despite having access to abundant resources and expertise, are often out-innovated by small, scrappy startups. An upstart entrepreneur starts with a blank slate and can be nimble and creative. A stalwart organization has an established brand and reputation to maintain and becomes easily entrenched in established processes and systems.

For example, gatekeepers in large organizations who oversee the allocation of resources (e.g., grants, awards, or budgets) tend to follow set guidelines to ensure fair decisions based on objective, preset criteria. Yet often such careful processes reward conformity or harbor a bias toward familiarity. Thus they can filter out radical voices or breakthrough ideas that tend to emerge from defying convention, shattering silos, or breaking rules.

Hence, large establishments often transform only upon facing the threat of obsolescence. Or they follow in the footsteps of pioneers who have charted a new path. Yet such risk-averse approaches toward innovation turn them into laggards as they play a game of perpetual catch up on playing fields created by other trailblazers.

3D INNOVATION

In the 3D state, innovation is true to the spirit of the word, guided by creative, intuitive insights and epiphanies that reveal new ways of seeing and solving challenges.

Innovators led by their 3D minds look beyond the world that is to imagine what else may be possible. They focus on leading transformation that endures (3D) rather than on seeking reactive (1D) or tactical (2D) solutions. They strive to understand and tackle challenges at their faucet-like origins, rather than with mop-like quick fixes. They are adaptive and resilient and see risk and failure as vital to learning and progress.

In this way, such innovators become trailblazers who chart paths that others follow. Once they define a new reality, others often scratch their heads over how the old ways, which appear archaic in hindsight, were once accepted as normal.

For instance, Rosa Parks engaged in a simple yet radical act of sitting in the front of a bus at a time when that space was forbidden to her race. Today, such segregation in American public transportation is unimaginable. Yet in many other realms of society, 3D pioneers continue to courageously take a stand for justice, equality, and freedom in equally compelling ways.

As Arun reflected on all this, his mind turned to the daunting task of transforming the $4.1 trillion U.S. healthcare system, close to 20 percent of the country's GDP.[31] It had all the elements of a complex challenge. Just listing them seemed overwhelming:

1. Multiple stakeholders (e.g., patients, physicians, private and public payers),
2. with often clashing incentives (e.g., lowering costs versus growing revenues),
3. in service to a non-profit mission (e.g., improving health),
4. with for-profit entities (e.g., pharmaceutical, insurance, and care management companies),
5. across multiple settings (e.g., hospitals, long-term care facilities, and in-home care),
6. with vast data flows (e.g., electronic medical records and patient-reported data),

7. governed by regulatory oversight (e.g., to approve therapies and decide reimbursement),
8. to serve diverse patient populations (e.g., to provide equitable access to high quality, affordable care).

The system often failed in basic ways, such as through needless medical errors, bloated costs, redundant procedures, or lack of coordination among a patient's caregivers to ensure holistic care. In treating chronic conditions, it tended to rely on narrow, expensive, or short-term fixes, such as pills and procedures. Yet sometimes, more affordable and enduring solutions—such as lifestyle changes guided by a healthy diet, regular exercise, or stress reduction—could be just as, if not more, effective.

Arun wondered how healthcare could learn from other fields on how to better serve patients. He recalled a recent visit to Walt Disney World where he was impressed by how Disney made every part of the ride experience—even waiting in lines—engaging and interesting. Arun pondered how healthcare system interactions could be made more joyful for patients, like going on a Disney ride.

Then a question flashed into Arun's mind: *If the healthcare system came to me for a patient visit, how would I "treat" it?* Arun realized that transforming healthcare, like reinventing the patient experience, began with a shift in how he looked at it.

❊   ❊   ❊

To look at our world anew to discover new possibilities, we can learn to tap into three simple shifts in thinking guided by our 3D mind: (1) zoom out, (2) zoom in, and (3) see the whole picture. Here we briefly explore each.

ZOOM OUT

When we invented telescopes to view the skies, and microscopes to probe our cells, we gained the power to look beyond what our eyes can see. In the same way, as 3D leads our mind, we gain insights beyond what 1D and 2D can perceive. Like riding a helicopter over a city, zooming out of a challenge transforms our perspective to reveal new patterns and vantage points. Zooming out is deceptively simple. We return to basic questions, the kind children are experts at asking, guided by curiosity, innocence, and wonder: *Why are things this way? Do they have to be this way? And why can't we do this another way?* Sometimes, just by asking "And why?" in response to each answer, we begin to discover new insights.

For example, by zooming out, we can see how 1D and 2D enable some of the marginally effective yet expensive solutions that populate modern healthcare. When a patient is seriously ill (e.g., with an acute infection), urgently treating symptoms is often the best approach, guided by 1D. Yet, when an ailment's underlying causes are multifactorial, such narrow solutions often fail to heal patients in holistic ways.

While 2D can help us identify symptoms and target treatments against them, it can lead patients to be handed off from one siloed specialist to another, each focused on a different part of the body in isolation. Sometimes, 2D also gets overconfident in healthcare's ability to "fix" us while ignoring its limitations in reaching deeper emotional and psychological aspects of well-being that rest beyond medicine's physical reach.

Led by 3D, we can zoom out further to take a holistic look at the whole patient and to grasp the context of their lives, such as challenges or stressors that might be causing or worsening their symptoms. Arun's colleagues in primary care often shared how, when they took time to listen to what was going on in their patients' lives, they often gained valuable insights on their health (e.g., high blood pressure or insomnia caused by stress due to a job loss, family tragedy, or traumatic event).

Guided by such insights, we can explore more sustainable solutions, such as changes in thinking patterns or lifestyle habits. This fosters holistic healing and reduces a patient's risk of landing in crises that necessitate 1D or 2D treatments in the first place.

ZOOM IN

As we zoom out, we gain new perspectives to help us see where to zoom in to solve a challenge at its root cause. Like zooming out, we can zoom in with simple questions such as: *What is really going on here? What is the deeper story? What rests beyond what I can see?* Led by 3D, we ask questions free of judgment to grow our understanding. We learn deeper truths guided by patience, humility, and compassion. We avoid projecting our own stories onto others or offering solutions based on the little we know.

Several innovation methods that have become popular in recent years, such as human-centered or patient-centered design, encourage innovators to spend time with patients in the contexts of their daily lives to grasp the nuances of how they move through their days. This enables the creation of solutions that are designed with deep empathy and sensitivity to patients' needs.

For instance, engineers developing a better walker might join a patient on a visit to the grocery store, or for a walk in their neighborhood, to learn how to best support patients in those settings. Such in-the-trenches product development is guided by practical insights and informed by the realities of a patient's life. This is in contrast to products that are designed in a laboratory far removed from their real-world use.

❧   ❧   ❧

The next morning, as Arun inhaled the brisk fall air while walking to the hospital, he thought back to the Prince and Sage we met in the Prologue. Reflecting on the Prince's agony, Arun wondered how modern medicine might have treated him if the King and Queen had brought the Prince to his hospital.

Arun zoomed out to consider the prevalent use of psychiatric medications today, prescribed to over one in six American adults (15.8% of the population) in 2019.[32] He wondered, *how have we become a society where so many minds of all ages need chemicals, often with notable side effects, just to feel "normal" or well?*

This topic was so sensitive Arun rarely discussed it, even with his peers. Many of his psychiatry colleagues relied on biochemical theories of mental disorders; yet the mechanisms of action of many medications remained poorly understood. When a pill ceased being effective, they usually tweaked doses, tried other drugs, or treated the side effects of one drug with another, which presented its own challenges. For instance, potent opioid painkillers, which were created to ease physical pain, had become a major source of addiction in America in recent years, causing substantial suffering and loss of life. *How ironic,* Arun thought. *Our painkillers are causing pain and killing patients. How did modern healthcare lead to this?*

As Arun walked through a local park on his way to the hospital, he saw a little girl point at a bench and say to her mother, "Look, it's a bird."

"It's a sparrow," her mother replied.

"No, it's a bird," the girl said more emphatically.

"Yes, we call this kind of bird a sparrow," the mother patiently replied.

"So it is a bird," the girl said. "Does it know we call it a sparrow?"

As Arun overheard their debate, it suddenly dawned on him that all medical diagnoses were simply labels created by the 2D mind to name what was going on in a patient's body. Yet such labels could not capture deeper truths about a patient's inner being, such as what was going on in their heart.

Arun recalled a recent statistic he had read on how as "many as seventy percent of primary care visits are driven by patients' psychological problems, such as anxiety, panic, depression, and stress."[33] Yet often such visits led patients to walk out with a prescription for an acute symptom rather than a holistic solution for how to heal its underlying causes.

Arun reflected on his own past. *We each face struggles that can cause emotional and psychological suffering,* he thought. When a mind seems overpowered by such 1D turbulence, a 2D label that defines that mind's state as a specific mental *dis*order can help it make sense of (and gain some distance from) what is going on. But when such a "diagnosis" then leads to a focus on narrow 2D solutions, those can hinder a mind from identifying and transcending its deeper causes of suffering.

Or, when such a label then seems to define the person, it can make them feel judged. *Maybe this is why there is still stigma around struggles of the mind?* Arun wondered. He had experienced this first-hand in medical school when he felt depressed but did not openly talk about it, worried about being perceived as weak or incompetent. Now he knew better. *Every mind experiences all kinds of weather. There is nothing wrong with storms and dark clouds. Talking about the state of our mind should be as natural as discussing the day's forecast,* Arun mused.

As Arun zoomed into the stories of patients, peers, family, and friends whose struggles he intimately knew, he realized many had experienced mental distress when they confronted a stressful or traumatic life-changing event—such as the loss of a job, marriage, or home, the illness or death of a loved one, or an adverse childhood experience—and struggled to process and make peace with it.

Since 2D cannot make sense of 1D's intense emotions, it proceeds to label their lack of order as a dis-order, Arun pondered. Yet missing in medicine's pill and procedure-based ways were insights to help patients access their heart's wisdom and truths. Such insights could help patients feel whole and heal from within, guided by compassion, connection, and love.

Arun reflected on how practices such as psychotherapy (e.g., cognitive or dialectical behavioral therapy), mindfulness (e.g., meditation or yoga), creative expression (e.g., journaling, painting, music, or dance), or pet therapy (e.g., spending time with animals such as dogs or horses) could help patients tap into their 3D minds. *True well-being,* he realized, *rests in ensuring we nurture all three states of mind.*

As we nurture our 1D mind, we cease to fear or resist its emotions, whatever they may be. This helps us soothe and calm 1D's stress response. Guided by patience and compassion, we gain space to explore and learn from past difficult experiences. We recognize and release stories that no longer serve us. And we access a deeply resonant inner peace that heals us in holistic ways.

As we nurture our 2D mind, we release the ego's need for control. We humbly accept 2D's limits and do not expect outer tools to fully "fix" us, which opens us to deeper sources of inner healing. We accept that there is more to being human than 2D can know and that even science is humbled by nature's mysteries in decoding the essence of life.

As we nurture our 3D mind, we learn to trust our inner wisdom, intuition, and truths. We harness the relaxation response to experience resonance and well-being. We reconnect to our deepest essence, which rests beyond our body and brain, and attain a way of being that arises from the heart. We connect to our sense of meaning, purpose, and values, and live aligned with them. Ultimately, we unite all three states of mind in harmony so they work together as a team.

Arun reflected on the transformation of the Prince we met in the Prologue. He realized the Sage helped the Prince understand, nurture, and befriend his three states of mind. When the Prince grappled with existential questions that caused him inner turmoil and resistance, the Sage guided the Prince into his own heart, where its truths had a healing effect on him.

While medicine has made incredible leaps since the days of the Prince, for which Arun was deeply grateful each time he helped save a patient's life, he also realized there was much modern healthcare could learn from timeless wisdom on the essence of being human.

As we zoom out, like Arun, we come to see how most complex challenges we face today cannot be solved by a single silo or way of thinking. As we zoom into the essence of any challenge, we discover how what heals and sustains us—across all dimensions of life—is universal. We all want to sense connection, belonging, and love, with each other, with something greater than ourselves, and within our own hearts. Ultimately, we realize that the answers we seek emerge when we see the whole picture.

SEE THE WHOLE PICTURE

As Arun entered the hospital's lobby, he thought about how deeper healing—whether for a patient, the healthcare system, or the planet—is inherently holistic. Neglecting 3D-ness in healthcare was like providing care without caring.

How can we bring more humanity into healthcare? Arun wondered. *If we do our jobs right, patients' use of our services (and revenues) should decline,* he mused, as he pondered the healthcare system through the lens of the three states.

1. A **1D healthcare system** can be thought of as sick care, since it focuses on fast, short-term actions to ensure patient survival. It tends to be driven by volume-based, fee-for-service business models. Its leaders mostly focus on short-term metrics (such as profits) to ensure their own, and their organization's, survival. In such a system, stress and burnout can run rampant among caregivers, often leading to worse outcomes for patients.

2. A **2D healthcare system** can be thought of as symptom care, since it is guided by our knowledge of symptoms and diseases. It delivers treatments based on set guidelines and measurable markers to manage patient health. While many aspects of such a system serve us well, it can sometimes lead patients and caregivers to feel like nameless data points in mazes of silos that cater to metrics over humans, despite having scorecards for patient satisfaction too.

3. A **3D healthcare system** is true to the spirit of caring for health. Instead of treating symptoms in silos, it cares for the whole patient in body, mind, and spirit. It takes care of its caregivers too, knowing how their well-being is vital to ensuring everyone's welfare. In a 3D system, patients feel cared for and empowered to take ownership of their health. Caregivers offer treatments as best serve patients, and metrics are in service to care, not the other way around. Financial incentives are aligned through risk-shared payments based on health outcomes rather than procedure volumes. Such a system embodies value-driven care to deliver better care at lower cost.

As we see the whole picture, we discover deeper insights that offer clarity on holistic solutions. A poignant example of this appears in surgeon and author Atul Gawande's exploration of end-of-life care in his book, *Being Mortal*.[34] Gawande discusses medicine's tendency to offer all the latest treatments to patients at the end of life—no matter their costs—driven by efforts to exhaust all possible options in fighting death. Yet, as Gawande describes, the simple act of asking a patient what is important to them, and what they want at the end of their life, can have transformative effects.

Unlike their clinical caregivers, patients have deeper knowledge on what matters to them and can make more holistic decisions on their life's trade-offs. Such a simple yet thoughtful approach leads to better care, higher patient satisfaction, reduced suffering, and lower costs. At times, patients even outlive their predicted survival odds, perhaps driven by an inner shift from resistance and stress (1D) to a more resonant state of inner peace and surrender (3D).

As we keep the whole picture in mind, our perspective shifts in profound ways. For instance, instead of doing more, we may realize how, sometimes, it is better to do less: to change a simple tendency (e.g., an unhealthy habit), to give more of what costs nothing (e.g., kindness and compassion), or to forego a cutting-edge solution in service to deeper well-being (e.g., quality of life). Though such 3D ways may take more thoughtfulness than prescribing a pill or procedure, they not only save resources over time but also return healthcare to honoring the true meaning of health.

That evening, when Arun went home, he sat on his couch to unwind and turned on the television. As he watched the news, a sense of restlessness overtook his mind. *The world has so many massive problems. What difference can one caregiver make?* he thought. *Is it even worth trying to change the system? Is it worth risking my reputation? Maybe I should just put down my head and continue with business as usual.*

Arun turned off the news and closed his eyes. He recalled the simple meditation practice that he had cultivated in recent years and began to take deep breaths to still his mind. Arun realized the news could feel like a perpetual fear machine that fed 1D's endless worries and anxieties. He found his meditation practice helped him re-center his thoughts. These days, Arun practiced it whenever he sensed his mind running away from him.

This had made Arun more conscious of how stress impaired his ability to think clearly. Before performing surgery, seeing a patient, or even attending a meeting or brainstorming session, Arun would briefly close his eyes, take a few deep breaths, and re-center himself to enter his 3D mind.

As Arun sat still on his couch, he recalled wisdom by Mahatma Gandhi that his grandfather had shared when Arun was young. In his non-violent movement for India's freedom from British rule, Gandhi steadfastly honored a simple principle: to conquer any challenge in the world, begin at the smallest level—within yourself. Mirabehn, a close associate of Gandhi, described it as follows upon his death: "[He] was full of love and gentleness, but in his fight with evil he was relentless. [He] could fight the evil without because he had mastered the evil within."[35]

Gandhi himself once said, "It does not require the training of an army; it needs no jiu-jitsu. Control over the mind is alone necessary, and when that is attained, man is free like the king of the forest and his very glance withers the enemy."[36]

Arun had long been inspired by how Gandhi courageously stood in his truth to take on the British Empire. Arun realized that the challenge of changing his hospital, or even the healthcare system, was much less daunting. He also realized that he did not need to wait for any external factors to start leading change.

He would begin where he could, with the countless little decisions he made every day, each of which offered a choice between fostering resonance or perpetuating resistance. Arun realized that this way of thinking, being, and doing would return him to the essence of why he had entered healthcare in the first place—to be a healer in a healthy system that helped patients feel whole.

PLAY, PONDER, PRACTICE:

ZOOM IN ZOOM OUT

The next time you face a challenge or want to explore potential ideas, consider asking yourself these simple questions to apply the concepts of this chapter:

ZOOM OUT

What is the impact of this on a global, societal, or organizational level? What are its long-term effects? What greater, universal patterns can I discern?

e.g., How would this change the healthcare system if everyone behaved this way?

ZOOM IN

What is the specific impact of this on the life of one person? What are its short-term effects? What subtle nuances can I uncover and examine?

e.g., How would this change the life of a single patient in the context of their specific circumstances?

WHOLE PICTURE

How does the larger, long-term impact of this align with its localized, short-term effects?

e.g., Does a solution have a positive impact upon both zooming in and out? Are there long-term trade-offs for short-term benefits?

Examples of the latter include: short-term symptom relief at the cost of long-term side effects, or narrow solutions that miss (or potentially worsen) deeper, intangible elements of a challenge.

CHAPTER 14

How We Create

The future is a blueprint of our deepest aspirations. Everything we have created began as a dream or an idea in a mind. Yet while everyone dreams, some do what it takes to make their visions come to life. With passion and perseverance, they create a new reality. Along the way, they face setbacks and failure. But where others give up, they keep going—and end up changing the world.

Today, learning such ways of being, thinking, and doing is invaluable for each of us, no matter who we are. If we think of innovation (as discussed in the prior chapter) as the art of seeing the world anew, we can think of creativity (as we will discuss next) as generating new ideas and sharing them with the world to create the future we wish to see.

In this chapter, we will focus on harnessing creative thinking, which we define as follows: bringing an idea—no matter how small or large—to life in service to a higher purpose or mission that uplifts our shared humanity.

Thus, the intention behind being creative is not to amass personal wealth (1D), or to gain recognition or fame (2D), but to harness our deepest passions and highest potential to serve our fellow beings (3D).

THE THREE STATES IN CREATIVITY

To become more creative, we bring our ideas to life guided by the best of all three minds. To explore how, let's briefly look at creativity through their lens.

1D CREATIVITY

Although 1D is not likely to help us generate creative ideas, it plays an invaluable role in helping us take actions to make them real. To harness creativity, we can turn 1D's focus on taking action into a vital strength. Instead of pondering or perfecting an idea in our head, we get our hands dirty. We experiment and try things out. We play and observe with the simple curiosity of a child's mind.

In parallel, we guard against 1D's resistance, such as fear of change or failure. This empowers us to step outside our comfort zone. And we sustain courage and resilience as we confront the inevitable highs and lows inherent in any journey to create change in the world.

2D CREATIVITY

The 2D mind also plays a vital role in harnessing creativity. It allows us to gather data to inform our ideas, to design plans to make them real, and to assess progress along the way. It leads us to be curious, resourceful, and scrappy, and to make the most of what we have. Furthermore, many creative ideas are born in minds that develop deep expertise in a niche first, which gives them an inner playground in which to explore and find new insights.

As with 1D, we also guard against 2D's resistance. We lean on analysis when it serves us and avoid siloed, binary, or circular thinking. We also avoid being led by 2D's tendency toward judgment or its need for validation. For instance, when a creator's sense of self becomes intertwined with their work, they may see its highs and lows as reflections of their own identity. This can foster hubris and vanity or humiliation and shame, depending on how things go. To avoid 2D's drama, we focus on the higher purpose behind why we create, beyond how it serves our ego's needs.

3D CREATIVITY

Led by our 3D mind, we generate bold, creative ideas, unrestrained by 1D fears or 2D analyses. Like an adventurous explorer, we meet the world with awe and wonder to find inspiration everywhere, even in the mundane. We sustain clarity on the intentions behind our work and are guided by our deeper sense of meaning, purpose, and values.

We create as an act of service, whether by inspiring with a vision, fostering healing, nurturing learning, or building a better future. This evokes deep resonance, which sustains us through highs and lows and inspires others to join us. Also, instead of focusing on a specific destination, we give our best at every step, trusting our intuition to guide us, as we fail faster, better, and forward, into success.

FAIL FASTER, BETTER, FORWARD

A few days before his presentation to the Board of Trustees, as Arun sat in the last session of the incubator class, he closely listened to that day's guest speaker as she shared stories from her years of investing in healthcare startups.

"As an investor, you gain comfort with risk yet avoid being reckless," she said. "The secret to this is how you view failure. Though we tend to focus on success, being an investor really makes you an expert at failure, because you see a lot more of it than success. If you remember just one thing from today, let it be this: the difference between those who succeed and those who fail is that those who succeed fail more."

This hit Arun like a lightning bolt. In his world, failure was not only feared but to be avoided at all costs, since it could spell the difference between life and death. Among entrepreneurs and creatives, in contrast, failure was seen—and even celebrated—as integral to attaining success. To reimagine healthcare, Arun realized, he and his peers would need to step outside their comfort zone and to rethink their attitudes toward failure and success. *How do we learn to succeed at failure?* Arun wondered.

"We often try to learn about success from those who we think have attained it," the speaker continued. "Yet pioneers do not follow in others' footsteps. They create their own paths through the unknown. Along the way, failure is their best friend and teacher. They don't let fear or doubt overtake their mind. They know that the only failure in failing is not learning from it."

This way of thinking is such a great life skill, Arun thought. *Why don't we teach this in schools and workplaces everywhere? If we all learn to fail better, we would set ourselves up for so much more success.* The speaker shared two stories that stuck in Arun's mind.

The first was of an investor who turned down almost every business plan that crossed his desk. Since most startups fail, this made him mostly right, as he often proclaimed with pride. Yet this eventually spelled the end of his career since he barely made any investments.

The second was of an entrepreneur who was so devastated by the failure of his first startup that he spent years stuck in shame, worrying about what others thought of him. He would generate ideas and develop detailed plans but avoid taking actions to try them out, terrified of failing again.

Then the speaker shared the essence of how we can learn to fail our way to success:

1. We learn to **fail faster** as we train our 1D mind to avoid getting stuck in resistance or giving fear free rein. When we stumble, we get up, dust off, and try again. As we sustain courage to learn and grow, we experience how failure accelerates success.

2. We learn to **fail better** by using our 2D mind to reflect on—and learn from—each time we try something out. We stay humble and curious, and avoid judgment and analysis paralysis to grow from what we learn. As we try something new with each attempt, we experience how failure transforms into success.

3. We learn to **fail forward** by trusting our 3D mind to guide us, driven by a clear sense of vision and mission. We harness resonance to embrace each setback as a stepping-stone that takes us closer to realizing our dream. As we sustain a united mind, we directly experience how failure is the secret to success.

As we learn to fail faster, better, and forward, we become more aware of when resistance rears its head and how to rise above it. This has transformative effects. For instance, when someone else rejects or dismisses our idea, while 1D may find that unpleasant or even painful, 3D focuses on what the experience can teach us. Instead of assuming something is wrong with our idea (or with us), we view each "no" as an opportunity to learn and grow.

Guided by 3D, we are less likely to be swayed by the judgments of others. We release 1D's emotional reactions, such as feeling dejected, and 2D's egoic responses, such as sensing humiliation. Instead, we sustain clarity on what best serves our idea and how we can advance it.

As Arun reflected on this way of thinking about failure, he thought about the hardships his parents endured when they immigrated halfway around the world to build a new life in a new country. Starting from scratch, they gained comfort in taking bold risks—ones that might have daunted others—because they had risked almost everything in moving across continents. Thus, small stumbles or setbacks rarely fazed them.

This is how perceived disadvantages can become an edge in attaining success, Arun thought. He also now saw how subtle forms of resistance had held back many of his own ideas. For instance, when Arun or his peers had a new idea, they would often endlessly analyze its merits, seek ever more validating data, or rely on the approval of committees to move ahead.

As Arun wondered how to value failure more, he realized that, in his own life, almost every setback had turned out to be a blessing in disguise. Many of his role models and heroes, including star athletes, scientists, and entrepreneurs, also often talked about how their paths to success were paved with struggle, rejection, and failure.

But then a question crept into Arun's mind. He raised his hand to ask the speaker, "Sometimes, despite trying our best and doing everything we can to learn from failure, we still don't attain success," he said. "How do you explain that?"

The speaker took a deep breath and, after a long pause, said, "I have asked myself that too. Here is what I have come to believe. Our life is a book that we write from our first breath to our last. Any story of 'failure' or 'success' is just our perspective of what happened in a given chapter, informed by what we have read so far. Yet we cannot see beyond today's page to know how life's twists and turns will unfold. All we can do is give each sentence our best and trust that our story will continue in ways we cannot know.

"There is another truth I have come to know. With the benefit of hindsight, failures often become stepping stones to success. Everything we experience carries wisdom to help us learn and grow. As we pause to learn its truths, we rewrite not only our story but also our very definitions of failure and success."

As Arun walked out of the last class, he was struck by how it had transformed him and his classmates. During the first session, they interacted in formal ways, focused on what they would gain from investing their precious time in this program. During the last session, as they went around the room to share personal reflections on their time together, many eyes filled with tears as they shared how they felt deeply reconnected to their calling as healers.

Arun also reflected on how, through the course of the class, everyone became less uptight and more playful and carefree. They focused less on outcomes and became more willing to play with ideas, even if seemingly crazy, trusting the journey to guide them forward.

Arun also loved the goofy and silly sides he saw in many of his colleagues for the first time. It was as if they were back to being children, unafraid of being wrong, and simply immersed in the effortless ease and joy of play.

THE JOY OF PLAY

Play is one of the most powerful antidotes to failure. It carries a joyful and positive energy that evokes resonance. Being playful, creative, and curious comes to us naturally as children as we explore the world with a sense of awe and wonder. As we graduate from playgrounds to classrooms, and eventually to meeting rooms, it can often feel as if 3D's carefree ways get 2D'd out of us, driven by adulthood customs and formalities.

By consciously keeping a sense of play alive, we continue to look at the world with a child-like simplicity that emerges from the 3D state. We release 1D's rigid and 2D's controlling ways and become fully immersed in the joy of the present moment.

As play liberates us from structured ways of thinking, we experience lightness and laughter, which makes us feel alive. We take ourselves less seriously and naturally come to fail faster, better, and forward as every experience becomes a teacher.

By being playful, whether as an inventor, artist, entrepreneur, or explorer, we experience 3D's sense of deep presence in the moment. We lose track of time and place and our sense of self. Our mind expands, our imagination grows, and we learn to dream like a child again. Often, we have insights and epiphanies that guide our creativity, sometimes as if by magic. Many remarkable inventions can be attributed to such moments. Here is one such story.

In the late 1940s, Norman Joseph Woodland, a young engineering lecturer who taught in Philadelphia, heard about a retailer's struggles with inventory tracking. Woodland started pondering the problem and was still thinking about it when he traveled to Florida one winter to spend some time by the beach.

Woodland puzzled over how to label products, especially since "the only code he was familiar with was Morse, which he had learned in the Boy Scouts. One calm January morning as he sat ensconced in the beach chair, the surf drumming in his ears, he was hit by a solution as hard as Newton's apple."[37]

Woodland described it as follows: "What I am going to tell you sounds like a fairy tale... I remember I was thinking about dots and dashes when I poked my four fingers into the sand and for whatever reason—I didn't know—I pulled my hand toward me and drew four lines. I said 'Golly! Now I have four lines and they could be wide lines and narrow lines, instead of dots and dashes.'"[38]

And this is how the barcode, which labels most products around the world today (including the paperback version of this book), was born. Though it did undergo several evolutions since that fateful beach day.

When we contemplate a challenge with curious wonder, we discover how the dots—or dots and dashes—connect in sometimes surprising ways. We begin to see beyond what is visible to the eye. There is a quote attributed to Michelangelo, one of the greatest artists of the Italian Renaissance, that captures the spirit of this. When asked how he created one of his most famous marble statues, Michelangelo is said to have remarked, "I saw the angel in the marble and carved until I set him free."[39]

Building on this, as we chisel away all thoughts and stories of resistance that conceal our creative potential, we discover the essence of resonance that remains, like a beautiful statue. Work that emerges from such an inner space is often infused with a deep sense of elegance and grace that humbles even its creator, who may feel as if a greater force is working through them in powerful and mysterious ways. Such creations also tend to deeply resonate with other hearts, which discover their own truths reflected in them.

Thus, regardless of what work we do, we can each benefit from having more creativity and play in our lives. Once, after a workshop I had given, a physician asked, "It sounds like you are saying that my hobbies—the time I like spending in my garage, which my wife thinks is a total waste of time—is actually an investment in my creative potential?" The room burst out laughing. Yet there is truth in his words. The more we live with a sense of play, the more we learn to joyfully and creatively ride the roller coaster of life.

CREATE THREE SPACES

While many minds build castles in the sky, some do what it takes to transform their dreams into castles that others can enjoy too.

One of the most extraordinary castle (and roller coaster) builders of recent times was Walt Disney, whose playful imagination has touched countless children—young and old—since he first created a little mouse character less than a century ago.

Disney's intention was simple: to bring joy to hearts of all ages. As he once said, "I do not make films primarily for children. I make them for the child in all of us, whether we be six or sixty. Call the child innocence. The worst of us is not without innocence, although buried deeply it might be. In my work I try to reach and speak to that innocence, showing it the fun and joy of living; showing it that laughter is healthy; showing it that the human species, although happily ridiculous at times, is still reaching for the stars."[40]

As Disney later expanded his work from cartoon films to theme parks, he envisioned such parks as playgrounds where people of all ages could have such joyful experiences.

It is said that Disney had a method that helped him unleash and harness his and his team's creative potential. It consisted of three distinct ways of thinking, often referred to as Dreamer, Realist, and Critic.[41] The concept has since been translated into many different frameworks to nurture creative ideas. In essence, it defines each way of thinking as a distinct physical space.[42] As is likely not surprising by now, these spaces align with the three mindstates, as we explore next.

DREAMER (3D)

We can think of the dreamer space as a creative artist's studio. The imagination is encouraged to run wild inspired by free-flowing ideas and visions. It is a boundless state of creative potential where anything is possible. We generate and explore ideas with curiosity and wonder, without giving 1D and 2D airtime. This helps us sidestep their tendencies toward fear, doubt, critique, or judgment. In a dreamer space, no one is an expert, and every voice gets equal say. There are no stupid or dumb questions, just simple ones such as: *What if? Why? Why not?*

We can imagine a 3D space as being bright and spacious with high ceilings, plenty of natural light and large windows, ideally facing nature or the skies, like an airy atelier or loft. Vast, open areas evoke a sense of possibility. We can also access this state by visiting places that inspire this feeling, such as museums, open galleries, or natural landscapes including forests, mountains, or the sea. Whether in an office or by the beach, such spaces help us feel creative, open, and free.

REALIST (2D)

We can think of the realist space as a scientist's laboratory or an engineer's workshop. Once the 3D mind has generated ideas, we bring them into a terrain where 2D has free rein. We introduce reason and logic to probe the feasibility of implementing our ideas. We may also develop sketches or prototypes.

Like a diligent researcher, we ask practical questions: *Can we make this happen? How will it work?* We also evaluate our ideas' use in the real world: *How will we test it out? Who would want it, and why?* We also consider practical logistics, asking how, when, and where we can plan out next steps. We can imagine having a curious child in the room that keeps asking, "Why?" or "How?" as we drill into different aspects of our ideas.

A 2D space, like a laboratory or workshop, often has whiteboards or hands-on materials for experimenting and prototyping, even if they are just simple supplies such as Lego bricks, cardboard, clay, or wood. This allows us to be creative in hands-on ways.

CRITIC (1D)

We can think of the critic's space as the skeptic's den. Once the 3D mind has created ideas, and the 2D mind has vetted them, the critic can make an appearance. In the context of Disney's framework, this was also referred to as the Spoiler's space. By giving 1D airtime at this stage—but no sooner—we can consider potential failure risks, downside scenarios, and contingency plans. This way, we acknowledge 1D's concerns but don't let them nag us each step of the way. We ask basic questions guided by 1D: *What can go wrong? What if it doesn't work? What are we missing? What actions can we take to test it?* We also tap into 1D's focus on action to move ahead.

A critic's space can be a small, tight huddle area, often without windows or other distractions. It keeps us focused on the critic's questions but is not so comfortable we want to linger in it the way we might in a 3D or 2D space. Another way to evoke the spirit of this space is by sharing prototypes of our ideas with potential users and asking them to be brutally honest, constructive critics.

❧   ❧   ❧

The concept of three distinct spaces can be applied in many creative ways to foster ideas and nurture play. Some writers have shared how they have three separate desks or spaces for different kinds of work (e.g., writing, editing, and proofreading). Some startup offices have different areas such as a bright boardroom (3D), a prototyping laboratory (2D), and an interior huddle area (1D).

Some creatives use different kinds of public spaces, such as a bench in a park, a library reading room, and a coffee shop, to evoke the same concept. Having three unique spaces gives us both freedom and structure, which liberates each mindstate to have free rein in its own playground without meddling from the other two.

TRUST IN INTUITION

During the final weekend before his presentation to the Board of Trustees, Arun sat in his home office and pondered how his hospital could play with all these concepts to unleash creativity among his peers, as well as, among its staff and patients.

As Arun went through the ideas buzzing in his head, he wondered on which to focus. *I wish I had a scorecard or metric to help me decide,* he thought. Then he recalled another insight from the last speaker in the incubator class: *Trust your intuition to guide your way.* At first these words seemed counterintuitive to Arun. *How can I trust anything without data?* he wondered.

Now Arun realized why he had that reaction. *Of course, trusting our intuition does not "make sense" to 2D; it is intuitive only to 3D.* Arun laughed out loud as he realized how his 2D mind had crafted a resistant story about intuition that blocked his capacity to hear its wisdom and insights.

❧   ❧   ❧

To learn to listen to and trust 3D's intuitive voice, we don't need to learn anything new. We simply release 1D and 2D resistance in all their forms, which allows resonance to flow.

Our 3D mind is always there to guide us. When we cannot hear it, 1D and 2D chatter have just drowned it out. As we begin to listen to our 3D mind, we access our truths with a sense of clarity and certainty that quiets 1D's fears and 2D's doubts.

The 3D mind harbors an unwavering sense of knowing that leads us to say, *I just know it. I cannot explain it, I just do.* While we struggle to explain our intuition to 2D, we know deep in our hearts how it resonates in our being. We gain trust that, even when we cannot see a path, there is always one we can walk.

As we cultivate our intuition, we discover its capacity to guide us no matter what we face. We also experience how it is the source of our epiphanies and eureka moments.

Minds through time have attributed some of their most creative acts to intuitive strokes of insight that seemed to appear out of nowhere. They led Woodland to draw the Morse code in sand to create the barcode. They led a composer like Beethoven to take the songs of birds in the woods and twirl them into symphonies. They guided a scientist like Einstein to play the violin and, in its soulful notes, unlock the mysteries of the universe.

The truth is, we each have such insights all the time. But to hear them, we must quiet all the other noise. As we learn to attain inner stillness, such as through meditation or contemplation, we naturally come to know our intuition. For, when 1D and 2D fall silent, 3D's magic begins to naturally unfold.

If we each have such epiphanies, Arun wondered, *what leads some to follow them and change the world and others to dismiss them to sustain the status quo?* Moments later, the answer appeared as three simple words that dropped into his heart: we simply trust.

To Arun's 3D mind, this was a deeply resonant insight, without need for explanation. To his 1D and 2D minds, the response evoked exasperation. *What do you mean? How can we just trust?*

We need concrete evidence to know what is real. We cannot just accept something. Yet, the assurance and validation those two need is the very source of the resistance that masks resonance.

To learn to trust our intuition, we accept that it exists at a level beyond what we can physically grasp or intellectually prove. Even though we cannot touch, taste, see, hear, or smell our heart's truths, we know them to be true, guided by a deeper sense that rests in the 3D state.

As we begin to listen to our intuition, we gain confidence to let it guide our way. We also learn to differentiate between 1D's instantaneous thoughts, which appear as reactions to impulsive instincts, and 3D's intuitive insights, which emerge from our deeper inner wisdom.

Though both seem to appear spontaneously, when we have a 1D "gut" instinct, it harbors fickle emotions, such as excitement or restlessness. Our 3D mind's insights, in contrast, evoke a deep sense of inner calm and peace.

Here is another way to tell the two apart. If you are constantly deliberating whether an answer you received came from your intuition, it likely did not. The deliberation itself reflects doubt, led by 2D. While this may sound vague to 2D, with practice we come to intuitively sense the difference, since 3D's answers harbor a deep sense of calm and clarity.

Reflecting on this, Arun realized he often heard his intuition's whispers but easily ignored or disregarded them. He now realized why he would feel restless whenever he agreed to do something half-heartedly. He would bounce between the truths of his heart and the rationalizations of his intellect, which could lead his mind to feel divided, fueling inner resistance.

As Arun got ready for bed, he thought to himself, *I now know what to say at the Board meeting. I trust my 3D mind to guide me.* Little did Arun realize that night how his simple resolve to abide by his truths would soon ripple through and transform hearts all around him. To see how, we turn to our last chapter together.

PLAY, PONDER, PRACTICE:

CREATE THREE SPACES

To explore the themes of this chapter, consider creating three distinct spaces for your creative work. As mentioned on page 253: "The concept of three distinct spaces can be applied in many creative ways to foster ideas and nurture play."

As you ponder potential spaces, these questions can help guide you:

1. 3D Space: In what kinds of spaces do I feel open, creative and free? What kinds of spaces make me feel alive? What helps unleash my creativity?

2. 2D Space: In what kinds of spaces do I like to tinker and experiment to try out my ideas? What helps me gain focus to map out my thoughts?

3. 1D Space: What helps me decide how to move forward with an idea? (The essence of this space can also potentially be embodied by trusted critics who offer authentic, constructive feedback).

CHAPTER 15

How We Succeed

Ever in search of new frontiers, humanity marches from one generation to the next, teetering on the edge of the impossible. In our quest for progress, we encounter an eternal struggle—between the urge to push the bounds of our knowledge and the longing to sustain what we cherish.

Through the centuries, we have learned to tinker with our genes and write laws on the physics of the universe. Yet both nature and the stars remind us of how little we know—and control—about life on earth. While we have carefully organized our world into nations and species, the sun and moon don't see our borders, and birds and viruses don't wait for visas.

Thus, as we contemplate our own blip of existence in the arc of a timeless universe, we are left with a few basic questions: *What is a good life? How do we live it?* And *how do we define success?*

While we toss the word "success" around throughout our lives, we rarely pause to define it for ourselves, as individuals, communities, or nations. We strive for it by setting goals, working hard, and celebrating achievements. We seek its secrets through the stories of those we deem successful. And we search for paths that may lead to it. Take us—we just patiently, painstakingly plowed through these pages in search of its essence. And here we are.

When we are young, success is easily defined. Classes, games, and competitions provide grades, scores, and ranks. Their aim is straightforward: to win or get to the top. Yet just a few succeed, because for some to win others must, by definition, lose or get less.

As we advance through educational and professional fields, similar zero-sum tracks lead to admissions, degrees, awards, and promotions. We follow playbooks, some written by society, others by our own minds. We add milestones: building a career, gaining financial independence, finding a partner, producing progeny, and, ultimately, leaving a legacy behind.

The quest to outlive ourselves led ancient pharaohs to be buried in pyramids with all their worldly riches; and it drives modern billionaires to etch their names on buildings. In our own way, in a world where death remains an undying certainty, we each strive for meaning beyond our own life.

Through it all, we are left with an unsatisfactory definition of success. Even those who diligently reach its milestones come to see that each destination simply reveals new roads to follow, each with new challenges and trade-offs. Even after checking all the boxes of success, many are left to wonder when they last checked in with their hearts to ask what those boxes truly meant to them.

Hence, the feeling of success can remain elusive. The once exciting becomes tedious, the once desirable boring. Priorities change. Dreams change. People change. The world changes. We realize gain and loss walk hand in hand and that everything has trade-offs: Pride breeds conceit. Power taints. Fame isolates. Money gets expensive. It's lonely at the top. And rat races are just that.

All along, the greater truth about success that obituaries rarely mention, the media doesn't spotlight, alumni reunions don't celebrate, and the "successful" least of all openly admit, is that there is no arrival terminal for success. There is no moment when you get "there" or have it made.

Sure, markers may appear along the way. But they are just that, signposts along a path on which we must keep walking, nudged ahead by time. Thus, in the ultimate irony of human existence, the lifelong road to success is a path to nowhere.

RETHINKING SUCCESS

The deeper essence behind what we seek in striving for success is not a place to reach but an inward passage whose destination is always within us because we are already there. True success is staying true to the truths of our heart. Not true to the impulses that chase ever-new excitement or shiny new things, or to the needs that search for outer approval or validation.

True success is a state of inner harmony, joy, and peace that honors our interconnectedness. It is knowing and living by our sense of meaning, purpose, and values in service to uplifting our shared humanity. All else we collect or attain is simply a means to those ends. As we reach the end of our time together, let's revisit the three states of mind one last time to briefly consider success through their lens.

1D SUCCESS

In the 1D state, attaining success focuses on meeting our own needs. Of course, satisfying 1D's impulses for hunger and safety is critical for us to sustain. Yet, once our basic needs have been met, when 1D runs our mind, its desires can become a bottomless barrel that leaves us ever starving for more. As 1D continuously chases the next source of excitement or satisfaction, we can come to believe that it—however we define "it"—is the last thing that stands between us and lasting happiness.

2D SUCCESS

In the 2D state, striving for success focuses on visible achievements that validate us in the world. While celebrating excellence recognizes the incredible bounds of human potential, when 2D yokes our sense of self to external accolades, it leads us to live at the mercy of our ego's ways.

Since 2D is a master rationalizer, to recognize how our ego drives our life, we need to bring deep humility and brutal honesty to identify and face the innermost intentions that drive us. Else, we may remain ever on the lookout for the next box to check or a new peak to climb in order to feel good about ourselves or look good in others' eyes. Along the way, we often come to neglect our heart's deeper truths.

3D SUCCESS

True success, as 3D knows, is a way of being. We abide by timeless, shared truths—kindness, compassion, and love—in our words, acts, and thoughts. We embody humanity in the truest sense of the word, knowing we are all connected, and ultimately one. As we attain such success, we grow contentment and harmony in our own hearts and foster peace, joy, and love in the world. Like a candle that lights countless others without losing its flame, the more we give from the heart the more we all gain.

Such success simplifies life. It transcends the needs of our ever-fickle emotions and never-satisfied ego. We meet life with clarity, calm, and ease. We serve selflessly, with joy and caring. In making decisions, we ask: *How will my actions affect others? What happens if everyone behaved this way? Would I want to be at the receiving end of my actions?* Whether we spend our lives nurturing a fellow being, or serving a cause, an organization, or a community, we act knowing why it matters to us and in the world.

❊   ❊   ❊

The day before Arun's presentation to his hospital's Board of Trustees, he went on a hike with his dog through the wooded hills near his home. Arun reflected on how to start transforming healthcare from the inside out. He thought about how he and his peers treated and valued each life in the hospital, whether of a caregiver, patient, or custodian. *How do we walk the talk on our vision, mission, and values? When we fall short, how do we respond? How do we define success?*

Arun began to see the difference between when he and his peers yielded to their emotions or ego, and when they stayed true to their sense of meaning and mission. As Arun reflected on the peers he respected most, it struck him they were also the most passionate, knowledgeable, authentic, and content caregivers he knew.

They loved their daily work, strove for excellence, and brought their whole selves to every encounter, whether with a patient or cafeteria staffer, sharing the spirit of healing from within. In their time with patients, they were fully present with a caring presence that, in and of itself, had a healing effect.

Arun realized that transformation did not start with leaders on committees but with *committed* beings who led from the heart. They focused on everyone's welfare and served with humility and humanity. Just thinking about them filled Arun with a warm feeling of resonance. As he made his way home, Arun wondered why it had taken him so long to arrive at such a simple truth.

WALK IN TRUTH

Some of the hardest truths we face in life are ones we were once blind to within. They are stories that feel so real to us we not only believe them to be true but let them run our lives. Unblinding ourselves from our deepest fiction tales is an act of immense courage and grace. It asks us to face our whole selves—the good, bad, and ugly—and to confront the whole truth about what we may hold near and dear.

Facing such truths can be scary or uncomfortable. It threatens to disrupt our comfort zone, our sense of self, and the stories we may have lived by for so long that we believe they define us. As we shine light into dark corners long hidden from sight, we may even risk our belonging in our tribes, especially among those who remain in the dark, blind to the fictions of their own tales.

No wonder then, that those who defy convention, speak truth to power, or live with radical courage are often branded the "crazy" ones. Yet they are the ones who see beyond the absurdity of staying in the dark, as the Prince we met in the Prologue came to see.

The 2D mind may argue that light and dark or truth and falsehood are subjective or relative or two sides of a coin, as the Chief Courtier tried to tell the Prince. Yet our heart knows deeper truths, as the Sage reminded him.

When the truth is true, it does not have two sides. This makes it mightier than any earthly force and gives us inner strength to face the truth about our stories. When we stay silent before untruths, or neglect deeper truths, whether in our hearts, families, communities, or nations, we may prolong our comfort zone or the status quo for a while. Yet we exist divided within as resistance saps our strength. When we walk in truth, instead, we unite in boundless resonance.

In this way, courageous voices that stand up for the truth affirm our shared humanity for all of us. They do not fight for the truth for themselves but to uplift us together. As they walk in truth, they inspire us to listen to and follow our own heart.

Often, like Gandhi and King, such leaders hold no formal titles of power. Yet they harness a force that can shake the foundations of nations to build more just and equal ones.

Both men were guided by the simple truth that every life is deserving of equal freedom, dignity, and respect. They recognized that embracing our diverse multitudes is the only lasting path to peace. Even when they stood alone, they harnessed the momentum of humanity, for they knew that the truth burns bright in every heart that sits with its own.

This is the source of all true power in the world and much mightier than the safeguards and walls we build to try to protect ourselves in (and from) the world.

Guided by this truth, we realize that, while we can choose what we think and how we feel, there is one matter about which we have no choice: once we have seen the light of truth, we cannot return to living in the dark.

We realize how our longing for belonging is not just with others but also with our heart's truths, which guide us toward unconditional inner peace, joy, and love. Then we can confidently walk each step in the world with an inner light that guides us and attain a sense of inner freedom that no outer force can take from us.

Even when standing up for truth commands sacrifice, we march ahead, like Gandhi and King, knowing that the cost of sitting in silence is greater. The former we may pay for directly. The latter may be paid for by generations for our lack of courage in facing and fighting for the truth.

Modern science has debunked many myths we once accepted as true. Yet we continue to perpetuate many archaic stories built on fictions or myths that are also ripe for history books. We can see through the untruth of such stories with the simple fact that they divide rather than unite us.

Minds that fight to uphold such stories rely on resistance, at times with violence, as battlefields through time remind us. Yet no such tales have ever sustained or gained power over all humans, as vanquished conquerors through time each learned in their own way. Even our oldest and most popular religions are practiced by just fractions of our species, that too through many factions.[43]

When we reflect on our existence this way, we come to realize that all our 1D or 2D stories have limited power. While those who seem to gain some power through them may fight to sustain them, and may even succeed for a while, their struggles themselves foretell their endings.

Our heart knows that, beyond all our stories, we are more alike than 1D or 2D can know. Guided by 3D, we can face why we believe what we believe, why a given is a given, and who made it so. By facing the truth about our stories, we are left with simple, universal truths that unite us in harmony.

When we refuse to face our stories, we may spend a lifetime believing we live on a flat planet and never venture out, afraid of falling off the edge.

Walking in truth this way is not just the work of trailblazers, change agents, or leaders. To build a better future, we must each strive to embody it in every step. When we see 1D or 2D stories gather strength, we can each do our part to speak truth to power, help disempower falsehood, and clear the path for 3D stories to take their place.

LEAD THE WAY

The next morning, as Arun entered the boardroom to present his ideas to the Board of Trustees, he felt relaxed and at ease. Since he often got tense before big presentations, Arun was surprised by his own inner serenity. He knew, deep in his heart, no matter what came of the meeting, he had renewed clarity on how to lead his work and life.

When Arun started talking, passion radiated from his being. His confidence and joy were palpable. When interrupted with questions, he spoke with conviction on how to best serve patients.

As Arun wrapped up, the oldest Trustee on the board raised his hand. He had donated millions to the hospital out of gratitude for the care it provided his dying daughter decades ago. Arun was impressed he still attended these meetings. *He must be at least 90 years old*, Arun mused.

"In all my years of coming to these meetings, this is the first time in a long time I have felt the true spirit of healing fill this room," the Trustee said. "I have given much of my wealth to this hospital to honor my child. The care its physicians and nurses gave her in her final days was priceless. I felt that energy again today." The room fell silent as he asked, "Arun, if you could distill your message to just one word that we can each take with us and honor as we leave here, what would that be?"

Arun paused. He realized the word was right on his final slide. The previous night, Arun had found and included a quote by Avedis Donabedian, a physician and poet who was also known as the father of quality in healthcare.

Arun clicked ahead to his final slide and read the words out loud: "The secret of quality is love. You have to love your patient, you have to love your profession, you have to love your God. If you have love, you can then work backward to monitor and improve the system."[44]

"Love," Arun said. "All you need is love." To everyone's surprise, the Trustee began to quietly hum the lyrics to the eponymous Beatles song. Within minutes, many in the room were humming along. Soon, everyone burst into song. Laughter and tears filled the wood-paneled suite. Even the stately oil portraits on the walls seemed to gently smile.

As the meeting ended, the Trustee asked Arun and the hospital's CEO to join him for dinner later that week. He finally had a plan for his largest donation yet.

When Arun walked home that evening, he had a bounce in his step as he reflected on the power and beauty of love. This was not the romantic, cheesy kind of love portrayed in Hollywood movies or Bollywood songs. This was true love, as reflected in the most universal sense of the word, which extended selfless kindness, connection, and caring toward all fellow beings, no matter who they were.

Arun realized that what the healthcare system needed most, and the world needed just as much, was love shared in simple ways—through a friendly smile, a kind act, a calm word, or a genuine sense of concern. The effects of such compassion rippled from caring for one patient to serving whole communities. *No one wants to get sick or spend time in a hospital,* Arun thought. *Patients and caregivers would feel—and heal—so much better if healthcare cared deeply about their well-being.*

The system would start by taking care of its healers first, to help them deliver the best care. When caregivers felt cared for and content, they would be empowered to bring their best selves to their work. Such a system would be guided by 3D leaders who enabled 3D communication and fostered a 3D culture where everyone could be innovative and creative in solving challenges.

As Arun prepared dinner that evening, his mind continued brimming with ideas. *Medicine offers technical skills (2D) to help patients survive (1D),* he thought. *By bringing more holistic thinking and wisdom (3D) to our work, we can foster resilience and resonance across the whole system.*

When Arun's father trained in medicine a half century ago, rote memorization was a critical skill. Now, artificially intelligent machines could make some diagnoses better than humans, trained by pattern recognition across millions of patient records, far beyond what any one physician's mind could process. *While machines can compute and diagnose, they cannot care and heal,* Arun thought. *Those are human acts. Humans need humans to feel whole. For this, we need no validating studies—we know it in our hearts.*

Later that week, when the Trustee and CEO met with Arun over dinner, they were struck by the simplicity of his solutions.

Many cost little and were simple to teach and share. Most involved a shift in what was valued, placing the well-being of patients at the center of every decision.

"We must do what is best for patients, even when that lowers profits," Arun said. "Otherwise, we risk fixing healthcare the same way we often treat patients: with short-term, expensive solutions that fall short of healing the whole in enduring ways. The system, like our patients, needs to heal from within. We must do what is right, even when it is not the easiest path. How can we tell patients to focus on their well-being when we don't do it ourselves?"

Even though the Trustee had offered to donate vast sums to the hospital, he was humbled to realize that healing healthcare did not need all his wealth. Arun quietly smiled. He recalled the story of how the Sage we met in the Prologue turned down the King and Queen's gift, saying that what we value most has no measurable price. When Arun shared that story with the Trustee, both wiped tears from their eyes.

As they walked outside to part ways, once the Trustee left, the CEO turned to Arun and said, "What you said in there sounded nice, but are you really serious? Your ideas are great but, if I may say so, seem too good to be true. You really think 'love' can solve all our problems? Let's be realistic. Most people don't think like you. I am afraid our competitors will laugh us out of the room—and take our clients with them."

Taken aback, Arun took a deep breath. He realized the CEO's mind was still anchored in the status quo. After a short pause, Arun spoke, "No, I don't just *think* love can solve all our problems. I know this to be true in my heart. To change how we are, we need to shift how we face everyone we meet, whether they are our patients or competitors. As for leaders at other hospitals, they are our partners and patients too. We are all part of the same community. Honestly, what's the alternative? It's the world we have today. It's about time we change. Old ways of thinking won't get us there."

The CEO was still filled with doubt. "I hear you, but tell me, what is the value proposition of love? Can we publish research to prove its utility? Can we do a marketing campaign to promote it? How would we operationalize it with mission-critical metrics that leverage our strategic imperative to incentivize results and optimize impact?"

Arun tried not to roll his eyes at the corporate lingo the CEO loved to use. *Maybe he needs to think more outside the box*, Arun mused to himself, drawing on another one of the CEO's favorite clichés. Then Arun calmly asked him, "If you got sick, to which hospital would you rather go—the kind I envision or what our competitors offer?" The question was clearly rhetorical. Arun continued, "If that's what all patients want—I know mine do—why are we letting fear and doubt drive our destiny? To truly heal patients, we need a healthy system. Love is free. It will not lower our margins, so why hold back?"

Arun could tell the CEO's mind was spinning but still skeptical. "Let's sleep on it," he curtly responded as they parted ways.

Later that night—at 3:21 a.m. to be precise, as the time got etched into Arun's mind—he awoke to a terse text from the CEO: "I love love. Love is it. Go for it."

This was the first time Arun had seen the word "love" in a text from his boss, that too thrice in a row. *Love truly is a magical force,* Arun thought as he rolled back to sleep with a smile.

LIVE IN LOVE

In the months that followed, Arun was amazed by the momentum of his simple ideas. Caregivers became more present with patients to deeply listen and make holistic decisions on how to best help them. They consciously strove to educate patients on their health (2D), guided by kindness and compassion (3D). They also guarded against using language that could rile fear or stress or unintentionally evoke the nocebo effect (1D).

Health coaches, fitness instructors, and nutritionists were integrated into care teams that looked after both patients and hospital staff. Mental health resources, from mindfulness teachers to therapists, were integrated into the hospital experience to offer patients and caregivers support through acute crises and trauma as well as through the day-to-day challenges of life.

Frank conversations about the "weather in our mind" became part of everyday talk, free of judgment or stigma. Such changes increased well-being and reduced burnout. Everyone's spirits were lifted as they felt cared for and loved.

Most surprising to Arun, the hospital's CEO and financial leaders shifted their mindsets on profits. They proactively cut unnecessary costs and encouraged more sustainable ways of caring for patients.

When Arun had first presented his ideas to teams across the hospital, he had faced some pushback. Some were confused by the lack of clear guidelines and metrics to accompany the suggested changes. Yet, as doubters witnessed the transformation that early, enthusiastic adopters experienced, their resistance soon changed into resonance.

Everyone was surprised to see how such transformation needed fewer incentives and metrics to implement. Most felt intrinsically motivated by the positive changes they experienced first-hand. Being caring and compassionate did not take more effort or time. It just took simple reminders until it became a natural, default way of being and changed the culture. The metrics that did sustain became more meaningful and saw higher compliance.

At the end of long days, when Arun would return to his office to wrap up his work, he often turned to these words framed on his wall: "The mediocre teacher tells. The good teacher explains. The superior teacher demonstrates. The great teacher inspires."[45] Arun realized that telling people what to do was 1D, explaining and demonstrating why they should do it was 2D, and inspiring them by example was 3D.

Many caregivers were pleasantly surprised how being led by their 3D minds made them feel more content and less stressed. Many said they gained more of what they saw as their most scarce commodities—time and energy.

Sometimes medical students would stop Arun in the halls to tell him how they felt less alone and more connected. This always warmed his heart as Arun recalled his own medical school experience.

As 3D-ness infused the hospital, caregivers gained mind space to be more creative and collaborative in solving challenges in holistic and sustainable ways. Patients experienced better outcomes and fewer hospitalizations, and felt more supported in making lifestyle changes. Many peers shared with Arun how their personal relationships improved too as they lived with more balance and led from the heart in all dimensions of their lives.

To the CEO's surprise, the hospital's profits actually grew as cost savings exceeded lost revenues. This allowed for more investments in initiatives to build a sense of community, such as programs centered on being in nature, caring for animals, creating art, and experiencing music to foster healing. Arun smiled each time he saw a laughing yoga session in the hospital's new courtyard garden and heard laughter ripple through the halls.

❖   ❖   ❖

Arun often wondered what had changed the CEO's mind to inspire his 3:21 a.m. text. Arun had casually asked him at a recent staff meeting, but just then the CEO was whisked away by his assistant, Mary, who ushered him to his next meeting.

A few days later, as Arun walked out of the hospital one evening, Mary came running after him.

Oh no, I hope there's no emergency, Arun thought.

Mary handed him an envelope and said, "This has your answer. I'm so sorry, I've been meaning to give it to you for a while."

Arun opened the envelope to find a copy of an article from the *New York Times* archives. It was about visits the American poet Walt Whitman had made to hospitals to lift the spirits of wounded and dying soldiers who fought in the American Civil War.

Mary continued, "The morning after your dinner, he said to me, 'Arun's onto something. Get this: Whitman helped heal my great-great-grandfather at Armory Square Hospital in Washington, DC. The tale is legendary in our family and was written about in newspapers of the time. Please see if you can find the article.'"

Mary said, "Arun, I finally tracked it down. I think you will like it. Have a wonderful evening." Then she hurried back inside.

As Arun stepped into the glow of twilight, he saw these words written by Whitman underlined: "To many of the wounded and sick... there is something in personal love... that does, in its way, more good than all the medicine in the world... I steadily found... that I could help and turn the balance in favor of cure, by the means here alluded to, in a curiously large proportion of cases... Many will think this merely sentimentalism, but I know it is the most solid of facts. I believe that even the moving around among the men, or through the ward, of a... generous-souled person, man or woman, full of humanity and love, sending out invisible, constant currents thereof, does immense good to the sick and wounded."[46]

As Arun walked home, he recalled one of his favorite lines from the famed poet's work: "Behold, I do not give lectures or a little charity, when I give, I give myself."[47]

Taking in the last glimpses of the evening sunset, Arun reflected on the simple beauty and power of love. He could now grasp, in the depths of his heart, the unshakable inner serenity that such love brought to his work. *The secret of quality is love,* he thought. *And the secret of love is service. All else is in service to it.*

❋   ❋   ❋

As we live from the heart, we experience a deep sense of inter-connectedness with everything around us. We realize—not as an idea in our head but as the reality of our existence—though we appear different, we all share the same stardust. Stories that divide us simply forget this.

Guided by deeper wisdom, we gain clarity on everything we face, including the greatest challenges of our times, such as pandemics, climate change, and inequality. While these may seem like daunting outer crises to tackle, they all have the same inner origins. The conflicts that surround us—and their complexity that confounds us—are simply reflections of the states of our minds.

To solve and transcend our many challenges, we remember and live by a simple truth: while millions of minds can harbor billions of stories about darkness, we all share the same story about light. Although 1D and 2D may consider this naive or idealistic, 3D reminds us that it is actually how we have sustained to this day. We trust strangers—those who fly us across oceans, ride trains across lands, rush us to the hospital, and treat us there. Despite what the news may suggest, humanity is, was, and always will be rooted in goodness, kindness, and love. We uplift each other with compassion because that is what being human means.

When darkness appears, we re-affirm the light within all our hearts, often by lighting candles that show the world our inner flame. As light enters a mind, a heart, and a people, stories of darkness lighten, lose their shadows, and eventually disappear.

FIND THE EDGE

As Arun lay in bed later that night, he recalled the stories of the Prince and the Sage, of Uno, Duo, and Trio's adventures, of Tara's triathlon, of Jim and Jill at Happy Hill, and his own labor of love. He began to see a thread through all of them.

As we connect to our own heart's peace, joy, and love, we gain the power to share them with the world in spoken or in silent ways. This is how world peace begins with inner peace. To attain this we need little of material value from the world. We just stay true to our truest selves. This is the essence of the deepest truth that minds through time have left behind as enduring legacies to outlast kingdoms turned to dust.

Indeed, it was the future crumbling of his kingdom that had brought despair into the mind of the Prince we met in the Prologue. *If nothing lasts, what is the point? Nothing really matters,* he thought, following this logical statement to its natural conclusion. The Sage helped the Prince see how the mind is a terrain of both illusions galore and magical wonder. He guided the Prince to a higher truth: "Don't believe any of the stories of your mind—no matter how real or logical they seem. They are ever shifting, like the clouds that dance across the skies. Instead, come to know truths through your heart, which shines in you like the ever-present sun."

Guided by the Sage's wisdom, the Prince realized the material world could not serve him contentment on a platter. Surrounded by round-the-clock service, he had come to know this first-hand.

As the Prince released all the stories that had imprisoned him in his mind, his inner state transformed. He realized that the world does not create our reality; our own mind does. His role as a king rested not in the conquest of kingdoms but of his own mind.

When he became a king, rather than amassing more personal wealth or power, the Prince committed himself to sharing the essence of such deeper, enduring wealth and power across his kingdom and through the ages.

Royal treasures or bank accounts, even if the world's largest, have limits. Inner riches, in contrast, are limitless. We can each have more love without anyone having less. And, the more we share our love, the more our shared wealth grows.

While many focus on outer markers of success, those with the richest inner lives often leave nothing of value behind. They live on in hearts instead, outliving museums and monuments. They lead simple lives, which gives them the freedom and peace of mind in search of which we often chase and amass all else. To realize, and live by this, is the truest meaning of success I have come to know.

As we zoom out of our own life, we realize how we are each just a momentary assembling and dissembling of molecules in an eternally reassembling universe. We each dissolve from one to another, in an eternal dance of galaxies. With each breath, we simply affirm how we are all one—neither created nor destroyed, just transformed.

While this may lead 1D and 2D to arrive at an existential conclusion on life's futility, such a view, as 3D knows, is defined simply by what they can see. As we experience a deeper connection in our hearts, we recognize a much greater truth.

We realize that, while 1D and 2D like to define a story by its ending, the stories of our lives have neither beginnings nor endings, just pages we turn. We write them not with what we gain in the world but with who we become within. We sense how our greatest joy flows through each breath, and our greatest love lives in our own heart. Ultimately, we realize that the power to transform our lives and heal our world is not far from where we are. It is right here, in each of us.

The Secret of the Sage

O ften, after we close the final pages of a book, we contemplate its ideas for a while. But then, as days turn to weeks and weeks to months, we return to the old, habitual patterns of our lives. With these final words, I urge you to not let that happen to you. Not this time.

We live in a turbulent world where chaos and turmoil can seem ever a heartbeat away. Yet, no matter what is going on outside, you always have a place within where you can go. One where the light always shines, no matter how dark it gets outside.

This space is in your heart, which beats in a steady rhythm, from your first breath to your last, in harmony with all other hearts, to the eternal drumbeat of the universe. Through our greatest joys and deepest sorrows, our heart sustains its pulse, rarely skipping a beat, never giving up on beating, even when we may feel like giving up on it.

Within you, in each moment, is the capacity to feel bound or free, even if you forget this or don't believe it at times. Even when you feel as if you have lost the connection to your heart, trust it is always there. We all experience this at some point.

Seek a place where you can hear it beat again. Whether while walking on a trail through the woods, humming with the birds at dawn, gazing at the stars at night, standing by the ocean's edge, folding into wave after wave, or sitting still in solitude, from breath to quiet breath, take in its calm until you come to know this, in the depths of your being, to be true: The universe is within you—it is you. With each breath, life, with all its majesty, moves through you. If you cannot feel it, breathe deeper. Breathe slower. Perch on the edge of your breath. Trust that the same vast force that powers all life sustains yours too.

Relax into the truth that all is ever-changing in a boundless universe whose mysterious rhythms guide us with wisdom far beyond our grasp. Remind yourself: I am limitless—I am life without limits. In the face of this, all else dissolves. Just our humanity remains, in harmony with everything.

So now, we finally get to the secret the Sage shared with the King and Queen in their chamber: The restless Prince, the rational Chief Courtier, and the wise Sage are not three kinds of beings. Neither do we have three states of mind.

We appear to create each as we dance with dark and light. Darkness seems real absent light. Yet there is just light and no light. When we live in light, we leave darkness nowhere to hide. We experience truths far beyond what our mind can grasp. We sense how our mind itself is just a construct of our thoughts, a realization that is the ultimate destination of all journeys into it.

The portal to such knowing is the 3D state. Guided by its wisdom we see how our deepest truths cannot be revealed to us by our mind. We simply experience them in our heart. We each cross this portal at our own time on our own terms, as the three states unite and lead us to joyfully dance beyond our mind's edge, with total trust in our heart.

As we part ways, this is my wish for you: May you always know the light. May you always know that, even when it feels like a foe, or acts like a fool, your mind is always your best friend. Learn to cherish its company. You will likely spend more time with it than anyone else.

May you be kind and gentle with your mind—and with all minds that cross your path. The light of love plays hide and seek with every heart. May you always shine your light into the world to help those in the dark find their own.

May you live your days with success, the kind you already have and always will, no matter what else you gain or lose in this world. And may you always remember that, with this truth, you behold the whole universe in your heart.

APPENDIX A

Affirmations

An affirmation is like a mantra, a word that traces its origins back thousands of years to the Sanskrit terms *man*, which means mind and *tra*, which means instrument or tool. Thus, a mantra is literally a mind tool. As we repeat a mantra in our mind, it transforms our default thinking tendencies, as expressed by this modern refrain: neurons that fire together wire together.

To play with this concept, the next time you notice a 1D thought pattern that doesn't serve you, create a mantra to help reduce its grip on your mind. Then, whenever you notice the thought pattern appear in your mind, simply begin repeating the mantra to yourself (silently or aloud, depending on where you are).

Such affirmations or mantras are usually simple, short, and easy to remember such as: *the tiger has no power over me.* Here are a few more examples:

1. Inhale serenity, exhale stress
2. Suspend mind reading
3. Release judgment
4. Trust your heart
5. Walk in truth
6. Let go of ego
7. Thank more
8. Live in love
9. Forgive all
10. Just be

Training 1D 2D 3D

Table 5 on the next page provides a high-level summary of the practices described in Chapters 3, 4, and 5 on how to train the 1D, 2D, and 3D minds at the level of our doing, thinking, and being. You can think of the principles in each of the nine boxes as sources of inspiration to help you discover and cultivate your own practices to train your mind.

Beyond this, you may also find it helpful to take some time to reflect on your own three states of mind and their tendencies. If you took the Mind Quiz mentioned on page 48, its result can guide your reflection alongside the below questions, which can be helpful to keep in mind as you journey on:

1. What is my relationship with my 1D mind? Do I tap into it when it can serve me (i.e., to take action)? How does it hold me back? What practices can I weave into my days to help me get out of 1D?

2. What is my relationship with my 2D mind? Do I use it when it can serve me (i.e., to think with reason)? How does it hold me back? What practices can I weave into my mind to help me release 2D?

3. What is my relationship with my 3D mind? Do I trust it to guide me when it can serve me (i.e., to listen to intuition)? What practices can help me get into 3D? How can I make them an integral part of my life?

TABLE 5: PRACTICES TO TRAIN 1D 2D 3D			
	1D MIND	**2D MIND**	**3D MIND**
DOING	Practice deep breathing, deep relaxation, or physical exercise to reverse the stress response.	Engage in an activity to give your "mind" a break (e.g., to release circular thinking, go for a walk in fresh air).	Cultivate and engage in 3D practices to transcend 1D and 2D's tendencies when they become traps.
THINKING	Practice visualization, affirmations, and gratitude to release negative 1D tendencies.	Cultivate deep, non-judgmental curiosity to reduce siloed and binary thinking.	Reflect and contemplate in solitude to learn to listen to and trust 3D's insights and wisdom.
BEING	Practice self-compassion to quiet intense emotions. Engage in mindfulness and meditation to enter the 3D state.	Bring humility to reduce and release the ego's control. Engage in mindfulness and meditation to enter the 3D state.	Lead with 3D as the intention of all your practices such that it eventually comes to guide all your doing and thinking.
EXPLORE	Visit your museum of emotions to release exhibits that hold you back.	Identify and shatter silos that constrain or confine you within their walls.	Clarify your sense of meaning, purpose, and values to help guide you.

Values Compass

As described in *Chapter 9: How We Decide Who We Become*, this exercise helps you identify and clarify your own guiding values. You may find it helpful to re-read the section on "The Value of Values" in that chapter to guide you as you complete this exercise.

1. Look at **Table 6: Some Values and Guiding Principles** further below to identify nine values that matter most to you. Use the Chapter 9 section on "The Value of Values" to help guide you. Also, feel free to add your own values to the list. Here, we define values not as what you value (e.g., health, family), but a way of being that deeply matters to you no matter what you have or who you are. Such values guide our sense of meaning and purpose and shape how we live and work. Many who completed this exercise have shared how they initially ended up with a list of 20 to 30 values but, in whittling them down, gained clarity on the values that were most foundational and fundamental to their lives.

2. Next, write your nine values on the compass below in this sequence:

    (a.) Identify ONE value that matters most to you and write it in the center of the compass. This is what you would draw on to stay centered if all that you valued were lost. It reflects your deepest source of meaning, guides your darkest days, and is core to who you are.

(b.) Then choose the next four values that are most important to you. Write them on the four directions of the compass (N, S, E, W). The specific placement of values in different directions is up to you.
(c.) Finally, write your last four values on the other four directions of the compass (NE, SE, SW, NW).

3. Once you complete your compass, contemplate how it reflects how you live and how you aspire to be. Here are some questions to help guide this:

    (a.) How are you honoring your values in your life today? Where do you sense resonance and where do you sense resistance?
    (b.) What can help you live in greater alignment with your values?
    (c.) How can you avoid potential misalignment with your values to reduce resistance and grow resonance?

Through the years, many who have completed this exercise have shared how they wove it into their lives. Some discussed their Values Compass with colleagues at work or with close family and friends. Many said that completing this exercise with another person, such as a startup co-founder, partner, or family member, helped them gain clarity on their shared alignment around their values.

Some said they hung their Compass on the wall by their desk to keep it at the top of their mind. Others said the exercise made them more conscious of how they were living by their values or what changes they wanted to make in their lives to increase alignment with them. For many, the exercise simply made them more aware and appreciative of why their values mattered to them.

Lastly, it can be valuable to revisit this exercise from time to time since some of our values shift as we grow and evolve through the chapters of our lives.

TABLE 6: SOME VALUES AND GUIDING PRINCIPLES

Action-Focus	Discovery	Industriousness	Rigor
Adaptability	Drive	Ingenuity	Risk Taking
Adventure	Duty	Integrity	Sacrifice
Agility	Elegance	Joy	Self-Motivation
Alignment	Empathy	Judiciousness	Self-Reliance
Altruism	Empowerment	Justice	Self-Respect
Attentiveness	Endurance	Kindness	Selflessness
Audacity	Enjoyment	Learning	Serenity
Authenticity	Enthusiasm	Liberty	Service
Autonomy	Equality	Love	Sharing
Balance	Equity	Loyalty	Simplicity
Beauty	Excellence	Maturity	Sincerity
Belonging	Exploration	Mercy	Solidarity
Benevolence	Fairness	Meticulousness	Spontaneity
Boldness	Faith	Non-Conformity	Stability
Bravery	Fearlessness	Novelty	Stewardship
Calm	Ferociousness	Openness	Strength
Can-Do	Fidelity	Optimism	Sustainability
Attitude	Flexibility	Originality	Team spirit
Candor	Fortitude	Passion	Teamwork
Caring	Frankness	Patience	Temperance
Challenge	Freedom	Peace	Thoroughness
Charity	Fun	Perceptiveness	Thoughtfulness
Citizenship	Generosity	Perseverance	Thrift
Clarity	Goodness	Persistence	Timeliness
Commitment	Grace	Playfulness	Togetherness
Compassion	Gratitude	Positivity	Tolerance
Composure	Growth	Preparedness	Toughness
Confidence	Happiness	Presence	Tradition
Connection	Hard work	Productivity	Tranquility
Consistency	Harmony	Professionalism	Transcendence
Contentment	Honesty	Pragmatism	Transparency
Contribution	Honor	Reciprocity	Trust
Courage	Hope	Reflection	Truth
Creativity	Holistic	Reliability	Understanding
Curiosity	Humility	Resilience	Uniqueness
Dependability	Humor	Resolve	Unity
Determination	Imagination	Resourcefulness	Valor
Dignity	Inclusiveness	Respect	Warmth
Diligence	Independence	Responsibility	Wonder
Discipline	Individuality	Reverence	_____
			add your own

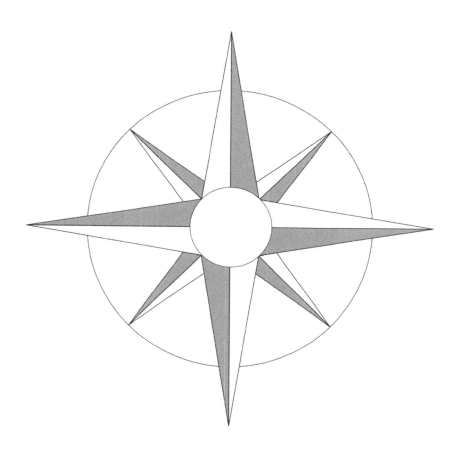

APPENDIX D

Conversation Canvas

As described in *Chapter 10: How We Talk to Each Other*, this exercise is designed to help you gain insights on how you communicate.[48] **Table 7** further below provides an example that is helpful to review after reading through the below and before completing the exercise.

1. **Identify a Conversation:** To start, think back to a recent conversation where you encountered challenges in communicating with another person. Write down a brief summary: What was it about? Who was it with? What was at stake? Why did it matter?

2. **Create a Four-Column Canvas:** Using the format and headers in Table 7 below, create a four-column canvas on a sheet of paper or in a digital file (e.g., Excel or Word). Make sure you give yourself enough space and feel free to use multiple sheets of paper, if needed.

3. **Revisit the Outer Dialogue:** Replay the conversation you had with the other person and, in Column I, write out the dialogue as best as you can recall it.

4. **Reconstruct your Inner Monologue:** Next, in Column II, write out the inner monologue that was going on in your mind as you were having this conversation. This includes thoughts, feelings, or emotions that you experienced but might not have shared with the other person.

5. **Clear Your Mind:** After completing the first two columns, it can be helpful to take a break or step away from what you have written for a short while.

6. **The Mindstates in Conversation:** After you clear your mind, re-read what you wrote in Columns I and II. As you revisit the outer dialogue and your inner monologue, mark each statement with the state of mind it reflects (i.e., 1D, 2D, 3D, or combinations thereof) based on your best judgment of what you recall.

7. **Reflect with your Voice of Wisdom:** Then, in the third column, guided by your 3D mind, reflect on what you have written in Columns I and II. You can use the questions in Column III of Table 7 to help guide your reflection.

8. **Distill Key Insights:** Finally, distill the key insights from your reflection in Column III and write them down in Column IV as pearls of wisdom to help guide you in future conversations and interactions.

Many who completed this exercise have shared how it gave them valuable insights into the subtle nuances of how their three states of mind guide them in communication. Several have also shared how the insights from the Canvas helped transform their way of being in communicating with others.

TABLE 7: CONVERSATION CANVAS

I. Outer Dialogue The words exchanged with the other person (OP)	II. Inner Monologue Your thoughts, feelings, or emotions not conveyed to OP	III. Voice of Wisdom Reflections on outer dialogue and inner monologue	IV. Key Insights Distilled wisdom from the reflections to keep in mind
Me: I want to check in on the report you were supposed to give me before leaving the office yesterday. - **OP:** I am sorry. I was sidetracked by another last-minute project deadline. - **Me:** I need the report for an important meeting with my boss today. - **OP:** I get it. I will give it to you soon. It's a busy day. - **Me:** Okay, let me know. - Continue writing out the dialogue as best as you can recall it in as much space as you need.	[I can't believe OP missed a deadline again. This has been too frequent. It's frustrating and unacceptable.] - [Why was the other deadline a priority? Why does OP always make excuses?] - [I am frustrated OP doesn't see the urgency of this. Does OP even care?] - [I feel like OP still doesn't get it. I am so sick of this behavior.] - [I am so not okay with this.] - Continue writing out your inner reactions as best as you can recall them in as much space as you need.	1. What was my **1D mind**'s role in the dialogue and my own monologue? How did that help or hinder? What role did my emotions, limiting beliefs, or memories of prior experiences play? 2. What was my **2D mind**'s role in the dialogue and my own monologue? How did that help or hinder? What role did my ego, judgments, assumptions, or biases play? 3. What was my **3D mind**'s role in the dialogue and my own monologue? How well did I truly listen? What insights or wisdom does this reflection reveal?	**Suspend mind reading:** don't try to guess or analyze what another person may be thinking. **Release judgment:** avoid creating your own stories about why others behave as they do; rather, try to understand their story, which is driving their behavior, with an open mind. **Listen to learn:** patiently focus on grasping the meaning behind others' words rather than on formulating your own arguments or defenses. **Share from the heart:** convey 1D emotions kindly, in a 3D way, to honestly express yourself and deepen mutual understanding.

APPENDIX E

Examples of 3D Leadership

Below are some examples of 3D leadership that readers and audiences have shared through the years. As we start looking for 3D leadership, we realize it is all around us. Most of these people are not famous or well-known, yet they had a profound influence on others' lives.

The last two are people you likely do know. They were not even adults when their ways of being inspired millions in distant lands. Beyond these examples, the stories that weave through these pages should give you a good sense for the essence of 3D leadership.

- An inspiring teacher who instilled a lifelong love of learning or unlocked hidden potential in a child

- A caring mentor who offered wise advice to motivate a career change or a new life path

- A kind boss who served to empower and bring out the best in others around them

- A work colleague who went above and beyond the call of duty to help out in a time of need without seeking any credit

- A friend who showed up in a crisis and helped create a support system without being asked

- A community leader who served as an anchor to unite people with healing words during challenging times

- A relative who served as an inspiring role model and shaped lifelong passions

- A physician, caregiver, or healer who patiently listened and deeply cared to understand and help heal the whole patient

- Countless frontline workers such as healthcare providers, drivers, grocers, supply chain workers, custodians, soldiers, police officers, crisis counselors, and many others who risked their lives during a global pandemic to save and serve others

- A small business leader who gave up his own income and profits to save the jobs of employees in a downturn

- A corporate CEO who only did business with companies that consciously upheld sustainable practices

- A hospital parking attendant who cheerfully greeted all visitors and radiated a positive energy that brought a smile to the faces of patients arriving at the hospital

- Countless stories of Good Samaritans who performed kind or generous acts while walking down the street or going about their lives, simply out of the goodness of their hearts, without expecting anything in return

- Neighbors who opened their homes and hearts to those facing crises such as violence and wars or environmental disasters such as fires and floods

- A teenager who stood up for girls' rights despite nearly losing her life, with her story inspiring millions around the world (Malala)

- A teenager who catalyzed a global movement for climate change by starting a simple strike outside her school in Sweden (Greta)

Gratitudes

The journey of writing this was arduous, long, and hard. At each turn, it challenged me to sit with the depths of my being and distill what emerged. The writing process itself was my practice. Ultimately, I realized that writing felt hard when I wrote with my mind, and the words simply flowed when I wrote from the heart.

At each step along the way, wise teachers, guides, and friends appeared to nudge this work along in ways they did not even realize. When I started writing the acknowledgments for this section, they took up many more pages. So I've decided to save them for personal notes and to share broader gratitudes here. From the depths of my heart, I would like to thank my:

Students through the years, from high school classrooms to graduate school courses. Your open, curious minds, your simple yet profound questions, and your unwavering commitment to learning, embodied the spirit of this work in ways that inspired and humbled me. Through hardships and challenges, each of you endured to learn and grow. They say the greatest gift of teaching is what it teaches us. I could not have asked for a more incredible set of teachers. I will always carry each of you in my heart.

Dear readers and audience members. You invited me to your gatherings and events, and into your organizations and book clubs. Your curiosity in meeting this work, and your generosity in sharing it, sustained and motivated me in more ways than I can express. My favorite conversations were ones we often had after a talk or event ended (or over a coffee later). Sometimes, I did not even catch your names or have a way to find you. But your beautiful stories lived on with me, and their truths infuse every page here.

Cherished friends. I feel so blessed for each of you and that the universe led our paths to cross. Whether we met as children decades ago, through professional paths in more recent years, or during chapters in between, and whether we speak often or every once in a random while, the true gift of friendship is having our heart reflected back to us through another soul. I would not be me without each of you and thank the universe every day for receiving the abundant wealth of love through so many amazing beings.

Beta readers. My dear students, readers, and friends who read a draft of this book with diligent care, thank you, from the bottom of my heart, for making time amidst the darkest days of a pandemic. Your generous support, brutal honesty, and incisive insights have shaped this work—and my being—in ways that transcend words. I feel immensely blessed and grateful for the sense of caring you brought to your reading of a rough draft. Each of you will, I am sure, recognize parts where your thoughts and reflections weave through these pages. This is our collective work.

Wise teachers and guides. There are vast armies of soldiers of peace and compassion who toil quietly to heal humanity and uplift their fellow beings. They serve without seeking the spotlight. Whether as teachers, mentors, coaches, therapists, or old souls who transcend the bounds of space and time, they find pockets of dark and shine their light onto them. I feel eternally blessed to have met many of you as fellow travelers on this journey. You are alchemists of the human heart and are doing the world's most valuable work in the purest way possible. Humanity sustains on your shoulders and so have I.

Wonderful writing teachers, editors, and illustrators. You approached this work with diligence and care to contribute insights that supported and deepened it in invaluable ways. I am deeply grateful for your passion for your work, which I sensed in every comment, edit, or artistic creation. Thank you for being you, and for being there when this book and I needed you.

Professional organizations and peers. Whether as fellow members of boards, organizations, or the greater community, so many of you opened your doors and hearts to this work and generously shared and uplifted it. In our high-tech times, you re-affirmed the timeless power of old-fashioned word of mouth.

Those on whose shoulders I wrote. If there is one truth that the pandemic reaffirmed for all of us, it is the power and beauty of our interconnectedness. None of us has survived it alone and each of us relies on the kindness, generosity, and courage of countless frontline heroes who risk their lives daily to feed, heal, and protect us. You are living manifestations of these words and all words fall short in expressing gratitude for how you hold and uphold our shared humanity in each act, no matter what role you play or where you are in the world. May you always remember this.

Beloved family scattered around the world. Your love, even from afar, even when we lose touch sometimes, and even from those we have lost, which I still sense, sustains me. Each one of you lives in my heart and always will.

Mom and Dad. They say we do not choose to whom we are born. I am forever grateful the universe blessed me with you. To the first words uttered by my mind you responded with endless patience and unwavering love. That conversation continues to this day as we explore wise teachings on being human together. I could not have asked for better teachers, mentors, and friends, let alone parents, to guide my journey. And to my dear sister, and little niece, our bonds run just as deep. Such love lives beyond words.

Finally, I am grateful for you. The greatest gift of writing is how it transforms both the writer and the reader. Though we may never meet in person, through the banter of our minds and hearts on these pages, we engage in a magical dance that leaves us both transformed. Thank you for being here, for being you, and for dancing with these words.

Warmly,
Amita

P.S. If you would like to get in touch, please send an email to: amitas@vitamita.com. I would love to hear from you.

Notes

Part I, Prologue

1   Milton, John. *Paradise Lost; A Poem in Twelve Books* (London: S. Simmons, 1674) Book I.

Part I, Chapter 2: A Quest for Answers

2   While this observation is pretty much conventional wisdom in the venture capital industry, in recent years, it has been studied in detail by business school professors and economists at Stanford, Harvard, the University of British Columbia, and the University of Chicago, as described in this publication: Paul A. Gompers, Will Gornall, Steven N. Kaplan, Ilya A. Strebulaev, "How do venture capitalists make decisions?" *Journal of Financial Economics,* Volume 135, Issue 1, 2020, 169-190.

3   This metaphor was also described in the author's first book: *Enduring Edge*: Amita Shukla, *Enduring Edge: Transforming How We Think, Create and Change* (Bethesda, Maryland: Vitamita House, 2014) p. 15.

4   Werner Heisenberg, *Physics and Philosophy: The Revolution in Modern Science* (New York: HarperCollins, 1958) p. 32.

5   Steigerwald, Bill. (1998, November 9). Lofty Ideals: Sir Edmund Hillary Is Still Up. *Pittsburgh Post-Gazette* (PA), p. D-1.

Part II, Introduction

6   In case you are curious, some of the frameworks most commonly mentioned by readers and audiences are below. I did not delve deep into most until after writing *Enduring Edge* so as to not bias my mind with the dogmas of specific disciplines. When I did dig into each of these frameworks, several parallels were apparent, as is to be expected. Interestingly, several of these models have been challenged, or even debunked, by experts in their own fields, though some continue to sustain mainstream popularity. The details of this are beyond the scope of this note but easily accessible through online searches. The frameworks most often mentioned by readers include:

Hindu philosophy's tamas, rajas, and sattva; Aristotle's pathos, logos, ethos; Christianity's Holy Trinity; Abraham Maslow's hierarchy of needs; the triune model of the brain; left versus right brain thinking; Sigmund Freud's id, ego, and superego; Carl Jung's conscious, personal unconscious, and collective unconscious; Daniel Kahneman's System 1 and System 2 thinking; and Carol Dweck's fixed and growth mindsets.

7   Many medical centers now offer guided imagery to patients as part of their pre-surgical preparations and post-surgical recovery. This link from Stanford University's health system provides a representative overview: https://stanfordhealthcare.org/for-patients-visitors/guided-imagery.html

Part II, Chapter 3: 1D Mind

8   Eagleson, C., Hayes, S., Mathews, A., Perman, G., & Hirsch, C. R. (2016). The power of positive thinking: Pathological worry is reduced by thought replacement in Generalized Anxiety Disorder. *Behaviour research and therapy, 78*, 13–18.

Part II, Chapter 4: 2D Mind

9   Arthur I. Miller. A Genius Finds Inspiration in the Music of Another. *New York Times*. Jan. 31, 2006.

Part III, Opening Story: Wendy's Triathlon

10   "Columbia Triathlon - May 16, 2020," TriFind.com, https://www.trifind.com/re_219064/ColumbiaTriathlon.html

11   Paz, P., Makram, J., Mallah, H., Mantilla, B., Ball, S., & Nugent, K. (2020). Swimming-induced pulmonary edema. *Proceedings (Baylor University Medical Center), 33*(3), 409–412.

Part III, Chapter 7: How We Become Who We Are

12   The scientific literature on epigenetics has grown significantly in recent years and many mainstream publications have written about its discoveries for lay audiences. Thus, online searches are a good way to find more detailed articles on this subject.

A good basic starting point is this Centers for Disease Control and Prevention (CDC) website, which also provides links to additional resources: https://www.cdc.gov/genomics/disease/epigenetics.htm

13   A fascinating example of this is the science of telomeres for which Elizabeth H. Blackburn, Carol W. Greider and Jack W. Szostak received the 2009 Nobel Prize in Physiology or Medicine.

In a recently published book, Blackburn translates the science into simple, practical guidance:

Elizabeth H Blackburn; Elissa Epel, *The Telomere Effect: A Revolutionary Approach to Living Younger, Healthier, Longer* (New York: Grand Central Publishing, 2017).

14 The placebo and nocebo effects have been extensively covered by mainstream publications in recent years. Online searches are a good way to learn more about the latest findings on these phenomena, including observations related to the conditions mentioned in this text.

15 These three references provide observations on the placebo effect in knee and back surgeries:

Moseley, J. B., O'Malley, K., Petersen, N. J., Menke, T. J., Brody, B. A., Kuykendall, D. H., Hollingsworth, J. C., Ashton, C. M., & Wray, N. P. (2002). A controlled trial of arthroscopic surgery for osteoarthritis of the knee. *The New England Journal of Medicine, 347*(2), 81–88.

Buchbinder, R., Osborne, R. H., Ebeling, P. R., Wark, J. D., Mitchell, P., Wriedt, C., Graves, S., Staples, M. P., & Murphy, B. (2009). A randomized trial of vertebroplasty for painful osteoporotic vertebral fractures. *The New England Journal of Medicine, 361*(6), 557–568.

Kallmes, D. F., Comstock, B. A., Heagerty, P. J., Turner, J. A., Wilson, D. J., Diamond, T. H., Edwards, R., Gray, L. A., Stout, L., Owen, S., Hollingworth, W., Ghdoke, B., Annesley-Williams, D. J., Ralston, S. H., & Jarvik, J. G. (2009). A randomized trial of vertebroplasty for osteoporotic spinal fractures. *The New England Journal of Medicine, 361*(6), 569–579.

16 Planès S., Villier C., Mallaret M. (2016). The nocebo effect of drugs. *Pharmacology Research and Perspectives.* 4(2): e00208.

17 The power of evoking the placebo response has been shown by Harvard Medical School professor Ted Kaptchuk in the below study (which was also mentioned in *Enduring Edge* on p. 31):

Kaptchuk, T. J., Friedlander, E., Kelley, J. M., Sanchez, M. N., Kokkotou, E., Singer, J. P., Kowalczykowski, M., Miller, F. G., Kirsch, I., & Lembo, A. J. (2010). Placebos without deception: a randomized controlled trial in irritable bowel syndrome. *PLoS ONE, 5*(12), e15591.

Beyond this paper, Kaptchuk's research offers a rich repository of research and insights on the subject.

18 Christopher Clarey. Olympians Use Imagery as Mental Training. *New York Times.* February 22, 2014.

19 Mizuguchi, N., & Kanosue, K. (2017). Changes in brain activity during action observation and motor imagery: Their relationship with motor learning. *Progress in Brain Research, 234,* 189–204.

20 In recent years many mainstream publications have written extensively about the benefits of meditation and mindfulness practices for lay audiences.

Thus, online searches are a good way to find articles on the subject. Here some resources to get you started:

Center for Healthy Minds University of Wisconsin-Madison, https://centerhealthyminds.org/

Mind & Life Institute, https://www.mindandlife.org/

UCLA Mindful Awareness Research Center, https://www.uclahealth.org/marc/research

21   Kral, T., Schuyler, B. S., Mumford, J. A., Rosenkranz, M. A., Lutz, A., & Davidson, R. J. (2018). Impact of short- and long-term mindfulness meditation training on amygdala reactivity to emotional stimuli. *NeuroImage, 181,* 301–313.

22   Brewer, J. A., Worhunsky, P. D., Gray, J. R., Tang, Y. Y., Weber, J., & Kober, H. (2011). Meditation experience is associated with differences in default mode network activity and connectivity. *Proceedings of the National Academy of Sciences of the United States of America, 108*(50), 20254–20259.

23   The CDC link below provides additional information on Adverse Childhood Experiences (ACEs). The original ACE study is also discussed in *Enduring Edge* in "Chapter 4: The One-Dimensional Mind".

Centers for Disease Control and Prevention, Adverse Childhood Experiences Resources, https://www.cdc.gov/violenceprevention/aces/resources.html

24   This story was originally told in an essay titled "The Star Thrower" that was written by Loren Eiseley, a well-known anthropologist, naturalist, and science writer of his time. The story has since been retold in countless forms with Eiseley (who was the passerby) and the Star Thrower replaced with many different types of characters. The version presented in this text represents the one I have most often heard.

The writings of Eiseley, including the essay mentioned above, are deeply philosophical and worth further exploration if you are so inclined.

Loren C. Eiseley, "The Star Thrower" in *The Unexpected Universe.* (New York: Harcourt, Brace & World, 1969), 67-91.

Part III, Chapter 9: How We Decide Who We Become

25   The quote in the text comes from a real-life story. It turns out the quote is a paraphrase of one by Ralph Waldo Emerson that says, "Money often costs too much" in an essay on "The conduct of life" in this work:

Emerson, R., Parker, B., Slater, J., Wilson, D., & Packer, B. (2003). *The conduct of life* (Emerson, Ralph Waldo, 1803-1882. Works. 1971; v. 6). Cambridge, Mass.: Belknap Press of Harvard University Press. 58

Part IV, Chapter 11: How We Become Leaders

26 Mohandas K. Gandhi, *The Collected Works of Mahatma Gandhi*, Volume 12, April 1913 to December 1914, Chapter 106: General Knowledge About Health XXXII, The Publications Division, Ministry of Information and Broadcasting, Government of India, August 1964, 158.

27 Shukla, Amita. *Vital Words for Our Times from Dr. Martin Luther King Jr.* January 16, 2017, http://vitamita.com/greatminds-mlk/

28 Sutton, A. (2020). Living the good life: A meta-analysis of authenticity, well-being and engagement. *Personality and Individual Differences, 153*, Article 109645.

Part IV, Chapter 12: How We Nurture Culture

29 Sutcliffe, K. M., Vogus, T. J., & Dane, E. (March 2016). Mindfulness in Organizations: A Cross-Level Review. *Annual Review of Organizational Psychology and Organizational Behavior*, Vol. 3, Issue 1, 55-81.

Part V, Chapter 13: How We Innovate

30 If you would like to learn more about the application of these methods in healthcare, this paper provides a good perspective:

Bhattacharyya, O., Blumenthal, D., Stoddard, R., Mansell, L., Mossman, K., & Schneider, E. C. (2019). Redesigning care: adapting new improvement methods to achieve person-centered care. *BMJ quality & safety, 28*(3), 242–248.

31 Centers for Medicare & Medicaid Services, National Health Expenditure Data for 2019, https://www.cms.gov/Research-Statistics-Data-and-Systems/Statistics-Trends-and-Reports/NationalHealthExpendData/NationalHealthAccountsHistorical

32 Terlizzi EP, Zablotsky B. Mental health treatment among adults: United States, 2019. NCHS Data Brief, no 380. Hyattsville, MD: National Center for Health Statistics. 2020.

33 American Psychological Association. "Briefing Series on the Role of Psychology in Health Care," https://www.apa.org/health/briefs/primary-care.pdf

34 Gawande, Atul. *Being Mortal: Medicine and What Matters in the End*. (New York: Metropolitan Books, Henry Holt and Company, 2014).

35 *Bapu's Letters to Mira* [1924-1948]. (Ahmedabad, India: Navajivan Publishing House), 387.

36 Gandhi, M.K. Indian Home Rule. 5th Edition. (Madras, India: Ganesh & Co., 1922) 91.

Part V, Chapter 14: How We Create

37 Ed Leibowitz, "Bar Codes: reading between the lines," *SPAN Magazine* (U.S. Embassy, New Delhi, India) July/August 1999

38 Ibid

39 This quote is broadly attributed to Michelangelo across countless resources. Yet an original source could not be found, and some quote checkers have questioned the authenticity of the attribution. Nonetheless, its words encapsulate the spirit of the ideas discussed here so it remains in this text.

40 Dave Smith (compiled by), *The Quotable Walt Disney* (Glendale, CA: Disney Editions, 1995)

41 Robert B. Dilts, *Strategies of Genius* (Capitola, CA: Meta Publications, 1995), 161-217.

42 Ibid

43 Pew-Templeton Global Religious Futures Project data on world religions: http://globalreligiousfutures.org/explorer#/?subtopic=15&chartType=pie&-year=2010&data_type=number&religious_affiliation=all&destina-tion=to&countries=Worldwide&age_group=all&gender=all&pdfMode=false

Part V, Chapter 15: How We Succeed

44 The quote comes from a longer statement by Avedis Donabedian, a physician, poet, and the father of quality in healthcare: "It is the ethical dimension of individuals that is essential to a system's success. Ultimately, the secret of quality is love. You have to love your patient, you have to love your profession, you have to love your God. If you have love, you can then work backward to monitor and improve the system."

Best, M., & Neuhauser, D. (2004). Avedis Donabedian: father of quality assurance and poet. *Quality & Safety in Health Care, 13*(6), 472–473.

45 Ward, W. Arthur. (1968). *Thoughts of a Christian Optimist: The Words of William Arthur Ward.* [1st ed.] Anderson, S.C.: Droke House; distributed by Grosset and Dunlap, New York, 16.

46 Walt Whitman. Our Wounded and Sick Soldiers: Visits Among Army Hospitals at Washington, on the Field, and here in New-York. *New York Times.* Dec. 11, 1864.

47 Walt Whitman, *Leaves of Grass* (Philadelphia: David McKay, 1891-92): 66.

48 This practice was inspired by and builds on an exercise developed by former Harvard Business School professor Chris Argyris:

Argyris, C. (Autumn 1982). The Executive Mind and Double-Loop Learning. *Organizational Dynamics*, Vol. 11, Issue 2, 5-22.

(All links were last accessed on January 27, 2022.)

Made in the USA
Middletown, DE
31 December 2023

46587069R00181